Thurso
CAITHNESS
SUTHERLAND
North
Sea

Lewis

Harris

North
Uist
Dornoch

Portree
Applecross
Dingwall
Banff

South Uist
Beauly   Elgin
Skye   Inverness   MORAY

BANFF
Loch Ness
Rhum   ABERDEEN
INVERNESS
Eigg   Aberdeen

Fort William   KINCARDINE
Loch Rannoch   Blair Atholl   Stonehaven
ANGUS
Loch Tay   Forfar   Montrose
Mull   PERTH   Dunkeld
Iona   Oban   Dundee   Arbroath
Firth of Lorne   ARGYLL   Perth   Firth of Tay
Inveraray   St Andrews
Colonsay   Loch   CLACKMANNAN KINROSS
Lomond   Stirling   FIFE
Oronsay   DUNBARTON STIRLING
Dunfermline Firth of Forth
Islay   Rothesay   Glasgow   Dunbar
RENFREW   Edinburgh LOTHIAN
WLOTHIAN MIDLOTHIAN
Kintyre   BUTE   BERWICK Berwick
Arran   Firth of Clyde   LANARK
Ayr   PEEBLES Selkirk
AYR   SELKIRK
Hawick   ROXBURGH
DUMFRIES
WIGTOWN   KIRCUDBRIGHT Dumfries

Carlisle   England

Irish Sea

SCOTTISH
CLANS And
TARTANS

SCOTTISH
CLANS *And*
TARTANS

NEIL GRANT

THE LYONS PRESS

Guilford, Connecticut

An imprint of The Globe Pequot Press

First published in Great Britain in 2000 by Hamlyn
This edition published in 2002
An imprint of Octopus Publishing Group Limited.

First Lyons Press edition, 2000

The Lyons Press is an imprint of The Globe Pequot Press

ISBN 1-58574-667-3

Produced by Toppan Printing Co Ltd
Printed in China

NOTE ON TARTANS AND CLAN ASSOCIATIONS
Some of the tartans in this book are ancient designs and
others are modern, both of which are currently available.
The publisher would like to thank the Clan Tartan
Centre, 70–74 Bangor Road, Leith, Edinburgh
EH6 5JU for supplying samples.
   The clan or family associations worldwide are
included, where applicable. Thanks to the Scottish
Tartans Authority, 51 Atholl Road, Pitlochry, Perthshire,
PH16 5BU for supplying the addresses.

CONTENTS

SCOTTISH
CLANS *And*
TARTANS

INTRODUCTION

The monument at Glenfinnan at Loch Shiel, where Prince Charles Edward raised his standard in 1745.

THE SCOTS

The Scotii came from the kingdom of Dalriada in County Antrim, Ireland around 2,000 years ago and settled in Argyll, Scotland, establishing an offshoot kingdom about AD 500. The dominant people in Scotland north of the Forth at that time were another Celtic race, the Picts, and at first it looked likely that the Scots of Dalriada would be swamped by their more numerous neighbours, but after St Columba had converted them to Christianity in the late 6th century, the Scots began to expand. The arrival of the Norsemen in the west in the 8th century pushed them east into Pictish territory, and in 843, Kenneth MacAlpin, King of Scots, gained the Pictish Crown also.

Although regarded as the first king of Scotland, then known as Alba, the kingdom of Kenneth MacAlpin, with its capital at Dunkeld, ended at the Forth-Clyde valleys in the south and at about the Moray Firth in the north. The Western Isles and part of the mainland remained Norwegian. It took nearly 300 years for his successors to extend the kingdom to, roughly, its present borders.

The reign of Malcolm III (1058–93) can be taken to signify a new era. Malcolm was English-educated and he married, as his second wife, a part-English part-Hungarian princess, Margaret. She was one of many prominent English refugees from the Norman Conquest and English influence was strong. One symptom of it was Malcolm's decision to move his capital to Edinburgh, in Lothian, conquered from the English as recently as 1018.

Of still greater importance for Scotland generally was the influx of Anglo-Norman barons, especially under David I (1124–53), who, like Malcolm, had spent his early years at the English court and was the premier English baron as well as king of Scots. When he returned to take up the Crown, he was accompanied by many prominent Anglo-Normans, whom he endowed with Scottish estates. From them sprang many future dynasties, including Bruce, Fraser, Grant, Sinclair and, eventually, Stewart.

THE HIGHLANDS

Malcolm III was the last king of Scots to bear a Gaelic nickname (Ceann mór, or Canmore, meaning 'Great Head'), and his reign also marks the growing divide between the Gaelic-speaking Highlands

CONTENTS

SCOTTISH CLANS *And* TARTANS

INTRODUCTION

ABOVE *The monument at Glenfinnan at Loch Shiel, where Prince Charles Edward raised his standard in 1745.*

THE SCOTS

The Scotii came from the kingdom of Dalriada in County Antrim, Ireland around 2,000 years ago and settled in Argyll, Scotland, establishing an offshoot kingdom about AD 500. The dominant people in Scotland north of the Forth at that time were another Celtic race, the Picts, and at first it looked likely that the Scots of Dalriada would be swamped by their more numerous neighbours, but after St Columba had converted them to Christianity in the late 6th century, the Scots began to expand. The arrival of the Norsemen in the west in the 8th century pushed them east into Pictish territory, and in 843, Kenneth MacAlpin, King of Scots, gained the Pictish Crown also.

Although regarded as the first king of Scotland, then known as Alba, the kingdom of Kenneth MacAlpin, with its capital at Dunkeld, ended at the Forth-Clyde valleys in the south and at about the Moray Firth in the north. The Western Isles and part of the mainland remained Norwegian. It took nearly 300 years for his successors to extend the kingdom to, roughly, its present borders.

The reign of Malcolm III (1058–93) can be taken to signify a new era. Malcolm was English-educated and he married, as his second wife, a part-English part-Hungarian princess, Margaret. She was one of many prominent English refugees from the Norman Conquest and English influence was strong. One symptom of it was Malcolm's decision to move his capital to Edinburgh, in Lothian, conquered from the English as recently as 1018.

Of still greater importance for Scotland generally was the influx of Anglo-Norman barons, especially under David I (1124–53), who, like Malcolm, had spent his early years at the English court and was the premier English baron as well as king of Scots. When he returned to take up the Crown, he was accompanied by many prominent Anglo-Normans, whom he endowed with Scottish estates. From them sprang many future dynasties, including Bruce, Fraser, Grant, Sinclair and, eventually, Stewart.

THE HIGHLANDS

Malcolm III was the last king of Scots to bear a Gaelic nickname (Ceann mór, or Canmore, meaning 'Great Head'), and his reign also marks the growing divide between the Gaelic-speaking Highlands and the largely English-speaking Lowlands. Increasingly divided by language and custom, the Highlands, heavily forested in parts, seemed remote and inaccessible. Queen Margaret made great efforts to reorganize the Church along Roman lines, but these reforms had little effect in the Highlands, where the more easy-going customs of the Celtic Church lingered for centuries.

Feudalism on the Anglo-Norman pattern was soon established in the Lowlands. In the Highlands, its introduction was complicated by the clan system.

It seems obvious that some characteristics of what must be called the clan system (though it was not very systematic) were older than any concept of feudal law. However, it would be wrong to say that the clan system predated the feudal system, or vice versa, and wrong too to suppose that feudalism was inimical to the clans. Feudalism and the clan system, its origins in tribalism notwithstanding, were established at about the same time and, without feudal bonds the clans would not have survived.

In a feudal society, a man held his land from the landlord, who might be the king, in exchange for service, especially military service. Among the clans of the Highlands, land was held by the chief on behalf of the clan, whose members were, in theory anyway, related to him by blood. Moreover, the chiefdom depended to some extent on general consent, though in practice it soon became hereditary. The clan was held together by land no less than by blood. The concept of personal service, bonds of 'man-rent', rather than service for land, was especially suitable to the clan system, and augmented the almost absolute authority of the chief.

Conflict over land was common, and was aggravated by the lack of legal title. There was a longstanding belief that people had the right to occupy the land on which they lived, but this was not a clearly defined legal principle, and it was more than possible for a clan to lose its land and subsequently its identity to superior force. Many did. Feudalism, however, established land rights. Major clan chiefs, including many of the founders of clans, became vassals of the king, and their landholdings were confirmed by royal charter. Eventually, this strengthened the status of the clans, as well as the authority of the chiefs.

THE CLANS

In origin and in composition, clans were less homogeneous than is popularly supposed. Some were of Pictish origin, some Norse, and some sprang from the early settlers in Dalriada. The great Clan Donald, a name which in its orginal Gaelic version means 'ruler of the world', was descended from Somerled, a formidable 12th-century chieftain who, notwithstanding his Norse name, traced his own ancestry to Irish High Kings. He gained a large dominion in Argyll and the Western Isles, and the various branches of Clan Donald sprang from his sons. In the east and north, many clan chiefs were descended from feudal Anglo-Norman landlords, whose men adopted the chief's name when surnames came into use in the Highlands towards the end of the Middle Ages.

The names and supposed origins of many clans derived from some semi-mythical hero in a much earlier period than the historical founder, such as Somerled, who acquired the land that gave them their existence. (As in Ireland, the old Celtic genealogies cannot always be taken on trust, though where they can be checked against other evidence they very often turn out to be more reliable than might have been expected.) The

Campbells are called Clan Diarmaid, after an ancient hero forever lost in antique Celtic mists, but the Campbell chief (the duke of Argyll) is called Mac Cailein Mór, 'Son of Great Colin', after Sir Colin Campbell, knighted by King Alexander III in 1280, a substantial historical figure whose own ancestors can be traced back, with reasonable confidence, for another six generations.

Lands were generally built up gradually, over time, by marriage, royal grant and other means, as well as conquest. But, whatever the legal title, in the last resort land had to be held by force. Clan chiefs were therefore eager to acquire men as well as land.

The military aspect of the clan system, combined with devotion to the clan homeland, reinforced the powerful spirit of clanship. Because the men of the clan believed that they and the chief were all kin, a much stronger bond existed between chief and clansman than between landlord and feudal tenant. Of course there were social distinctions, but there was also mutual respect and a lack of lordly superiority or servile humility. English visitors in the 18th century were surprised to observe that a great clan chief would talk with his herdsmen on terms of equality.

Clans were numerous and varied. While some prospered and expanded, others declined and disappeared. Large clans developed many branches, septs and dependants, including other, lesser clans that settled on their land. Members did not necessarily even share the same name, and if they did it might have been recently adopted for convenience and, in the event of a change of allegiance, might be changed again. The extent to which they could be regarded as true clans also varied. Some, like the Gordons, were essentially the tenantry of a powerful family, held together by feudal loyalties rather than kinship.

The clan system was essentially a Highland development, but it was also characteristic of the Borders. In both regions, clan loyalties were cemented by constant conflicts, over land, cattle or other objectives, and by the ferocious, long-lasting blood feuds that they provoked. In greater conflicts, such as civil wars, different clans fought on different sides and were motivated by clan hatreds as much as political or religious animosities. During the Jacobite revolt of 1715, MacLean of Duart addressed his men at Sheriffmuir: 'Gentlemen, this is a day we have long wished to see. Yonder stands Mac Cailein Mór (Campbell) for King George. Here stands MacLean for King James. God bless MacLean and King James! Gentlemen, charge!'

THE LORD OF THE ISLES

Gaelic culture reached its peak under the MacDonald lords of the Isles, successors to the ancient Norse- and Irish-linked kingdom of the Isles, who briefly wielded power to rival the king of Scots. From Finlaggan on Islay, they controlled a large if indeterminate region. Although the great chieftains were the Lord's feudal vassals, this was essentially a Gaelic state in which ties of kinship were dominant. There was efficient administration of justice through local judges and the lord's council, therefore comparatively little of the tribal conflict scarred the history of the clans.

The power of the lord of the Isles in the early 15th century was demonstrated by Donald, 2nd Lord (and a nephew of the king of Scots). He launched a spectacular assault on the government of the Regent Albany, who had unjustly deprived him of the earldom of Ross. Gathering the western clans, Donald swept across Scotland, meeting the Regent's army in a famous battle at Harlaw, near Aberdeen, in 1411.

Casualties were heavy, and neither side could claim a victory, though Donald was forced to withdraw to his own territory.

Ross was subsequently acquired peacefully, but King James I (reigned 1406–37) and his successors were determined to assert regal authority in the west. It was a long and bitter contest in which, arguably, the lords of the Isles brought final ruin on themselves, by internal divisions and unprofitable alliances with the English. In 1493 the lordship of the Isles was officially annexed to the Scottish Crown. John, fourth and last lord of the Isles, died in a Dundee boarding house a few years later.

THE STEWARTS

Royal authority in much of the Highlands remained nominal. James IV (reigned 1488–1513), who wore Highland dress and spoke Gaelic – the last king of Scots who did – made an effort to reconcile the clans, with some success: there were many clan chiefs among the dead in the terrible slaughter of Flodden (1513). That victory encouraged the English to renew their attempts to take over Scotland, weakened by the loss of so many of the ruling class and – an all-too-common problem – the minority of the monarch. In the Highlands, this was a time of wars in the Clan Chattan confederation, of ferocious feuds and barbarous atrocities.

The Reformation, which made the Lowlands Protestant, had little immediate effect in the Highlands. After the disastrous interlude of Mary Queen of Scots, another royal minority resulted in more Scottish civil wars and Highland feuds. As an adult, James VI coped fairly well with dissident nobles and zealous Presbyterians, but he was relieved to inherit the English Crown (1603) and move to London.

One of his last acts before leaving Scotland was to proscribe Clan MacGregor, following a massacre of the Colquhouns. This savage reprisal, making the MacGregors outlaws, was a sign of the growing tendency to regard the Highland clans as savage barbarians, best exterminated.

A happier result of the union of the Crowns was the ending of the Border wars. The great raiders – the Armstrongs, Elliotts, Johnstones, Kerrs and others – who had conducted their raids and blood feuds for centuries, turned to more productive pursuits.

One way of pacifying the Highlands was to move Lowlanders into the region. For instance, in the reign of James VI, a commercial company in Fife was granted powers in the Isle of Lewis as if it were a New World colony. However, the 'natives' (the MacLeods), promptly threw them out.

More subtle means were employed in the Statutes of Iona (1609). Officially designed to improve Highland welfare, they aimed at the destruction of the Highland way of life by undermining the Gaelic language and culture. They were widely ignored, but one beneficial outcome was to encourage whisky distilling, the result of banning spirits.

BELOW *Robert the Bruce, King of the Scots (1306–1329), Bannockburn.*

ABOVE *Craigievar castle, built in the 17th century by William Forbes, a merchant and brother of a bishop who traded with Baltic ports and was known as Danziq Willie.*

The efforts of Charles I to impose Anglicanism on the Scottish Church provoked the National Covenant (1638) and the Bishops' Wars, which preceded the civil war in England in which the Presbyterian Covenanters fought on Parliament's side. In the Highlands there was little support for the Covenant, one of whose leaders was the hated Campbell chief, the Earl of Argyll.

The most spectacular campaign of the civil wars was fought in the Highlands. The Earl of Montrose, himself a former Covenanter, changed sides, partly because he was suspicious of the ambitions of 'King' Campbell. His small force of irregulars, in particular a thousand or so Irish MacDonalds under a brilliant guerrilla leader, Alasdair MacColla, briefly gained control of most of the country until, with MacColla absent, Montrose was defeated by the Scottish army returning from England after the final defeat of the Royalists (1645). A long-term effect of Montrose's activities was to exacerbate animosities between Highlanders and Lowlanders, who became all the more determined to eliminate the threat of Highland raids.

The Scots were shocked by the execution of Charles I (1649), and several Highland clans joined the national rebellion on behalf of his son. It was crushed by Cromwell's highly professional New Model army, and Charles II escaped abroad. General Monck restored order in the Highlands with Cromwellian efficiency.

THE JACOBITES

In 1688 the English threw out James II (VII of Scots) to ensure a Protestant monarchy. James had plenty of support in both kingdoms, but squandered it by dithering, and his attempted comeback via Ireland was crushed by William of Orange at the Battle of the Boyne. The Scots who rebelled on his behalf won a famous victory at Killiecrankie (1689) under the dashing Graham of Claverhouse, Viscount Dundee, but he was killed and the rebellion fizzled out.

The new government promised a free pardon to all Highland chiefs who took an oath of loyalty to the Crown. A minor chief, MacIain MacDonald of Glencoe, through no fault of his own, missed the deadline. The result was the Massacre of Glencoe. As Highland massacres went, it was not the bloodiest, but, approved by the government and carried out by Campbell troops, it aroused widespread revulsion and intensified the alienation of the Highlands.

During the next half century there were many Jacobite revolts on behalf of James III (the Old Pretender). A significant outbreak followed the Act of Union with England (1707), which was highly unpopular in the Lowlands (and largely ignored in the Highlands). More significant was 'the Fifteen' (1715), when the Earl of Mar raised the clans and captured Perth, but then hesitated, giving the government precious time to assemble sufficient forces to deliver a fatal check at Sheriffmuir.

The Highland clans were, of course, not united. (Had they been, history might have turned out differently.) The commander of the government forces was, after all, the Earl of Argyll, chief of Clan Campbell. The Frasers held Inverness for King George and Whig (pro-government) clans – Mackay, Ross, Munro and others – commanded the north and north-east. Inter-clan hostilities were an inextricable ingredient of the national conflict.

CULLODEN

The Highland chiefs who rallied to Charles Edward, 'Bonnie Prince Charlie', in the 'Forty-Five' (1745) were motivated by loyalty and honour, but many did so with foreboding. In the event, the rebellion came remarkably close to success. The Prince and his predominantly Highland host gained control of Scotland and advanced south into England as far as Derby before discretion, perhaps fatally, overcame valour.

The dreadful end came at Culloden (1746), where the exhausted and outnumbered clansmen were decimated by the troops of the Duke of Cumberland, many of whom, of course, were also Highlanders. 'Butcher' Cumberland took few prisoners, and in the aftermath of the battle a campaign of terror was waged against the clans – and not exclusively Jacobite clans – in a determined attempt to destroy their way of life. Even the wearing of Highland dress was made illegal.

The clan system had been in decline long before Culloden, but the subsequent repression, followed by the Highland Clearances, when Highlanders were dispossessed for the sake of sheep pastures and sporting estates, put an end

to it. The new landlords, many of them Lowlanders or Englishmen, introduced other improvements, designed primarily to increase the profits of the estate though, in a few places at least, they brought social benefits. Communications were improved and some new towns built although, on the whole, the Industrial Revolution was little evident in the Highlands.

When Samuel Johnson toured the Hebrides with James Boswell in 1773 it was still possible to see a Highland chief and his clansfolk living in the old way, or at least in what Dr Johnson assumed was the old way. But time had passed on. Johnson himself, though not much enlightened by his glimpse of an alien culture, was not immune to the myths already gathering in the glens. For the Highlands, long regarded by southerners as the pit of barbarism, were, now that they had been rendered harmless, taking on a very different aspect. They were becoming romantic.

TARTANS

Tartan has been worn in the Highlands for centuries. In early modern times it took the form of the belted plaid, a versatile article in the shape of a rectangle about 5m (5½yd) long, which could serve as cloak and sleeping bag. It was less practicable on horseback, and gentlemen therefore adopted tartan tights, known as trews. The kilt is generally regarded as an 18th-century development, though it was probably worn earlier. Tartan was not worn in the Lowlands until the Act of Union, when it was adopted as a mark of national protest.

Tartan is ancient, but clan tartans are not. There is little evidence that clan tartans existed before the Forty-Five. Some clans may well have worn the same tartan, for instance in places where there was not much choice, and chiefs sometimes equipped their men with identical plaids for a particular expedition. The local companies that were raised in the Highlands as a kind of police force after the Fifteen were issued with a dark tartan that gave them their name, Black Watch, later passed to the regiment that replaced them.

The act forbidding the wearing of Highland dress after the Forty-Five enhanced its appeal. Tartan became a nostalgic symbol of the past perpetuated by the Highland regiments, formed from the shattered clans, and by emigrant clan groups in Nova Scotia and other colonies. When the act was repealed, in 1782, tartan, no longer everyday wear, had become a potent symbol.

The romanticising of the Highlands, in which the novels of Walter Scott played so great a part, made tartan fashionable. Many people were now eager to claim Highland ancestry, and clan tartans proliferated. Manufacturers produced new patterns named after districts, events or persons (there was a 'Wellington' and a 'Waterloo'). The famous visit of George IV to Scotland in 1822 marked the peak of the revival. King George wore Highland dress, possibly the Royal Stewart tartan, the origin of which is unknown.

The commercialization of tartan has continued. Strictly, a clan tartan should not be worn except by those whose families have a historic claim to it, but most Highlanders take a relaxed view of the matter. Anyone can wear the general tartans or the new tartans which are still being designed. Since clan-specific tartans were unknown when the clans flourished, a rigid attitude would be misplaced. In recent years the wearing of tartan has increased, and many who wore it for political reasons have discovered that it is a practicable and comfortable form of dress.

BELOW *An engraving of the Battle of Flodden in 1513.*

THE MEDIEVAL KINGDOM 1124–1568

1124–53 DAVID I

1152–65 MALCOLM IV
('the Maiden')
1164 Somerled sacks Glasgow

1165–1214 WILLIAM I
('the Lion')
Beginning of the 'Auld Alliance' with France
Risings in Moray and the Borders crushed
Unsuccessful efforts to assert authority in
the west

1214–49 ALEXANDER II
1217 Claim to Northumbria abandoned,
bringing peace with England
Expeditions to the west, north and Borders

1249–86 ALEXANDER III
1263 Battle of Largs ends Norse rule in
Western Isles

1286–90 MARGARET
('the Maid of Norway')
Her death aged 7 leaves throne vacant and
open to English influence
Edward I of England selects John Balliol as
King of Scots

1292–96 JOHN (BALLIOL)
1296 Rebels against English overlord; defeated
and deposed
1296 Chief Scottish lords swear fealty to
Edward at Berwick
1297 Revolt of William Wallace
1305 Wallace captured and executed

1306–29 ROBERT I
(the Bruce)
1306 Bruce has himself crowned; defeated by
English at Methven
1307 Death of Edward I of England
1314 English routed at Bannockburn, assuring
Scottish independence

1329–71 DAVID II
1332–41 Throne contested

between David and Edward Balliol
1346 David captured by the English at
Neville's Cross; in captivity until 1357

1371–90 ROBERT II
(formerly Regent for David II; first of
Stewart dynasty)

1390–1406 ROBERT III
1402 Contest for regency won by the
Duke of Albany

1406–37 JAMES I
1406–24 James a captive of the English;
Albany holds power
1411 Lord of the Isles sacks Aberdeen;
checked at battle of Harlaw

1437–60 JAMES II
1453 The Black Douglases crushed

1460–88 JAMES III
Sovereignty over Northern Isles gained by
marriage

1488–1513 JAMES IV
1493 Lordship of the Isles extinguished
1494 Goodwill royal visit to the west,
followed by repressive policies
1513 Disastrous defeat by the English
at Flodden

1513–42 JAMES V
Factional power struggle: pro-English and
Protestant v pro-French and Catholic
1542 English victory at SolwayMoss

1542–67 MARY
(Queen of Scots)
The Lowlands becoming Protestant
1547 English victory at Pinkie (Cleugh); Mary
betrothed to French Dauphin
1561 Mary, widowed, returns to take
up Crown
1567 Opposed by Protestants, Mary forced
to abdicate
1568 Mary's supporters defeated at Langside

ABERCROMBY

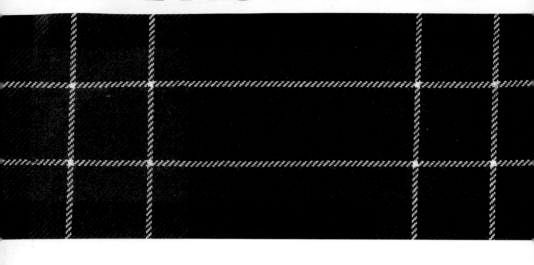

NAME AND PLACE

Abercromby lies less than ten miles south of St Andrews, one of the attractive old fishing ports now popular with rich commuters from Edinburgh, on the coast of Fife. It was a barony in the Middle Ages and in 1296 was held by William de Abercromby.

ORIGINS

This name appears in a list of inquest jurors in the same year as William de Haberchrumbi, and the many 16th-century variants of the name include Abarcrumby, Abbyrcrummy and Eabercrombie. But William is the earliest of the Abercrombys of that ilk so far discovered.

THE FAMILY

The Abercrombys remained Roman Catholics at the Reformation. One of them, John Abercromby, who was a Benedictine monk, was executed for attacking the doctrines of Knox, and another, Robert Abercromby, was a Jesuit priest who was imprisoned but escaped and, despite the offer of a huge reward for his capture, succeeded in getting out of the country. He died in exile in 1613.

Although Sir Alexander of Birkenbog (a later branch) was a Covenanter, suffering as a result of having Montrose's troops quartered on his estate during the civil war, the faith was maintained in the next generation. Patrick Abercromby (d. c. 1716), who was briefly physician to King James VII/II in 1685, was a Roman Catholic. So was his brother Francis, who was created Lord Glasford by James VII. Another contemporary, David Abercromby, was a Jesuit who had been educated at Douai. He returned to Scotland as a catholic missionary only to convert to Protestantism himself in 1682, which caused a sensation at the time. The circumstances suggest it was a genuine spiritual conversion rather than a political one.

BELOW *Dunfermline Abbey, founded by Queen Margaret, wife of Malcolm III, in what was then the capital of the Kingdom of Fife, in the 11th century.*

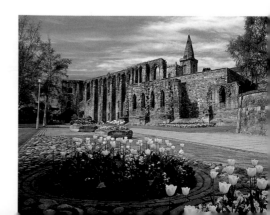

There exists a story that Patrick Abercromby, who was born in Forfar, wrote a book about the family, but it was apparently never published and the manuscript has not been found. However, to judge by the same author's weighty *Martial Achievements of the Scots Nation* (1711–16), it might not have been reliable historically.

In modern times Abercrombys have served with distinction in the army and in politics. The most outstanding was Sir Ralph Abercromby (1734–1801), a fine professional soldier of strikingly liberal opinions and courage in stating them. His avowed sympathy for the American colonists accounts for his retirement in 1783, but when the French wars began again ten years later he returned to the colours. After a string of successes he was given command of the forces in Ireland, at that time guilty of numerous outrages against the civilian population. The army in Ireland, said Abercromby, was in a state of 'licentiousness which rendered it formidable to everyone but the enemy'. The quotation has a Wellingtonian flavour, and indeed Wellington learned much from Abercromby. He would hardly have achieved his own famous victories without the army reforms which Abercromby played a large part in effecting. Abercromby's opinions, however, resulted in his being forced to resign his Irish command. He was mortally wounded at Alexandria in 1801 during a victorious operation against the French in Egypt.

One of his sons also became a general; the eldest, George, became Lord Abercromby of Tullibody and a third, James, was Speaker of the House of Commons and later Lord Dunfermline.

The original line from William de Abercromby died out in the 17th century; the senior current branch is the Abercrombys of Birkenbog, Banffshire.

ABOVE *Sir Ralph Abercromby (1734–1801), whose talents as a soldier partly overcame the drawback of his enlightened opinions – unwelcome in a military man. In particular, his sympathy for the American colonists in the American War of Independence and his disgust at the abuses by English and Scottish soldiers in Ireland made him unpopular with his masters.*

FAMILY ASSOCIATION
305 Eighth Street S, Cordele,
GA 31015, USA

ANDERSON

NAME AND PLACE

Anderson is a common name, especially in the Lowlands. The name fiz Andreu is recorded in Peebles and Dumfries in the 13th century; the usual Highland form is MacAndrew. The Gaelic form, often rendered Gillanders, means St Andrew's gillie (servant).

ORIGINS

Although it is sometimes said that all Andersons and MacAndrews have a common Highland origin, the many current Andersons are probably more diverse. In the 17th century Donald MacGillandrish was said to be the progenitor of Clan Andrish, from Ross-shire, and the MacAndrews are described as a sept of Clan Chattan, the old confederation of clans in the central Highlands dominated by the Mackintosh.

THE CLAN

In the 16th century arms were granted to an 'Anderson of that ilk', but neither the family nor the place (implied by the word ilk) has ever been discovered. However, it was possible for such a grant to be made by the Lord Lyon King of Arms on the grounds that an Anderson chieftain 'represented' the clan or 'community' of Andersons. The most notable branches of the clan in modern times have been the

Andersons of Dowhill, traced to the early 16th century, the Andersons of Wester Ardbreck in Banffshire and the Andersons of Candacraig in Strathdon.

One early hero of the MacAndrews was *Iain Beag MacAindrea* (Gaelic for

BELOW *Inside one of the domestic shelters named after Sir John Anderson (later Lord Waverley), home secretary in 1939–40. Churchill recommended him as prime minister in the event of the deaths of himself and Anthony Eden.*

Little John MacAndrew), who was famous for his bowmanship. In 1670 a party of 12 cattle lifters from Lochaber, having carried out a successful raid, were pursued by the deprived tenants led by William Mackintosh of Kellachie and his attendant *Ian Beag*. Surprised in the bothy where they had taken shelter, every one of the robbers was killed, *Iain Beag* accounting for their leader, MacDonell of Achluachrach, and, some said, most of the others too. Thereafter *Iain Beag* led a harassed existence avoiding the vengeance of the dead men's kin, but he eventually died peacefully in his bed. Despite this feud, there is a tradition of association between the MacAndrews and the MacDonells.

A number of Andersons since have been noted for their intellectual and technological accomplishments, a recent example being the statesman John Anderson, Lord Waverley (1882–1958), who commissioned the household bomb shelter named after him and was a member of the Churchill cabinet during the Second World War. 'Davie-do-a'-things', David Anderson of Finshaugh, was famous for his versatile talents in the early 17th century, his most notable exploit being the removal of an obtrusive rock from the harbour at Aberdeen. His cousin Alexander, also a resident of Aberdeen, was an excellent theorist, publishing volumes of geometry and algebra in Paris during the second decade of the 17th century.

James Anderson (1662–1728) was a noted Scottish historian of his day and author, during the controversy preceding the Act of Union, of *An Historical Essay showing that the Crown and Kingdom of Scotland is Imperial and Independent* (1705). Another James Anderson, from Mid Lothian, not known to be related, was a contributor to the first edition of the *Encyclopaedia Britannica* (1773), writing an article on 'Monsoon' which predicted discoveries made by Captain

ABOVE *The harbour mouth at Aberdeen, where 'Davie-do-a'-things' Anderson of Finshaugh won local renown for his work in the 17th century, removing a large rock that was obstructing passage into the harbour.*

Cook on his voyage to observe the transit of Venus. A prolific author, he published a periodical called *The Bee* in Edinburgh, the 18 volumes of which are said to have been written largely by himself.

There are many Andersons in the Unites States and one, Adam, was one of the original trustees of the colony of Georgia, whose fort, St Andrews, and the famous civil war prison of Andersonville, serve as reminders of the considerable Scottish contribution to the early history of that state.

CLAN ASSOCIATION

Wyseby House, Kirtlebridge,
Lockerbie, DG11 3AN, Scotland

1947 Kensington High Street, Lilburn,
GA 30247, USA

P O Box 1108, Fort Bragg,
CA 95437-1108, USA

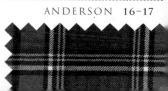

ARMSTRONG

NAME AND PLACE

The Armstrongs were one of the most powerful families who kept the Borders in constant turmoil right up into the 17th century. According to legend the Armstrongs derive from a man named Fairbairn who was the king's armour-bearer. The king's horse was killed during a battle and Fairbairn hoisted the king on to his own horse and out of danger. This fortuitous act gained him the name Arm-Strong, and, through royal gratitude presumably, estates in the Borders.

ORIGINS

However, the Armstrongs were more likely of English origin, as there were Armstrongs in Cumbria and other parts of the north of England well before they are first heard of across the border.

THE CLAN

Gilbert Armstrong was steward of the household to King David II in the 1360s, but the first reference to the Armstrongs in Liddesdale, their chief centre, occurs as late as 1376. The residence of their chief was at Mangerton: an Alexander Armgstrand was Laird of Mangerton in 1378. A lesser chieftain was established at Whitehaugh in the early 16th century.

At that time the Armstrongs were so numerous they extended into beautiful Eskdale and even into Annandale. A contemporary report says they could put 3,000 mounted men into the field which, even if somewhat exaggerated, explains why they were practically invincible in the Borders. They were eventually overcome, as so often happened, by a piece of skulduggery as reprehensible as any of their own.

Their leader at this time was the brother of the Laird of Mangerton, Johnnie Armstrong, known as Gilnockie. He built the Hollows Tower in Eskdale, still standing today, which in 1528 was sacked by Lord Dacre, the English warden of the borders. The Armstrongs' prompt response was to burn Netherby in Cumbria. They were also involved in a fierce blood feud with the Johnstons, and in 1530 King James V, on a progress through the Borders, decided to put an end to the anarchy of Liddesdale. Johnnie Armstrong of Gilnockie was persuaded (or chose) to meet the king and arrived accompanied by a 'tail' of 40-odd men, unarmed as protocol demanded. 'What wants yon knave that a king should have?' growled the king, observing the company, and he gave orders for them to be seized and hanged. Gilnockie's tardy attempts to arrange a compromise having been rejected, he memorably remarked, 'I am but a fool to seek grace

at a graceless face, but had I known you would have taken me this day I would have lived in the Borders despite King Harry [of England] and you both', a fair enough supposition.

The death of Johnnie Armstrong of Gilnockie is commemorated in a well-known ballad of the Borders, though the romantic view of him as a patriot who would have kept the English at bay must be taken with a pinch of salt. Another Armstrong hero commemorated in ballad is Kinmont Willie, ambushed by the English in Liddesdale during a truce, who escaped from prison in Carlisle with the aid of another powerful Borders family, the Scotts.

The Armstrong clan was largely dispersed early in the 17th century. Archibald Armstrong of Mangerton was executed in 1610 and the Armstrong lands passed into the possession of the Scotts. The famous court jester of King James VI was called Archie Armstrong. Gilnockie would surely not have approved of his role.

ABOVE *Carlisle Castle in Cumbria, a famous English stronghold, protected by a moat (but much altered in recent times), from where Kinmont Willie managed his spectacular escape.*

CLAN ASSOCIATION

7 Riverside Park, Canonbie, DG14 0UY, Scotland

102 Yorkshire Drive, Pittsburgh, PA 15238, USA

267 Roxton Drive, Waterloo, Ontario, N2T 1R2, Canada

105 Towers Street, Ascot, Queensland 4007, Australia

86 Braids Road, Hamilton, Auckland, New Zealand

BAIRD

NAME AND PLACE

The origin of the name, occurring frequently as de Bard or de Barde, is probably a Lanarkshire place name.

ORIGINS

A Richard Baird obtained a charter in the 13th century in Lanarkshire; he belonged to a family of Lanarkshire landholders, known a generation or two earlier.

THE FAMILY

An old and doubtful legend ascribes the fortune of the Bairds to their progenitor saving the life of King William the Lion by killing a wild boar.

Robert Baird was given the barony of Cambusnethan by King Robert I, and the family later spread to Banffshire and Auchmeddan in Aberdeenshire. 'There shall be an eagle in the craig while there is a Baird in Auchmeddan', goes the old saying. Their stature was enhanced by marriage into the great Keith family. The Bairds provided a long line of hereditary sheriffs in Aberdeenshire.

A branch of this family, the Bairds of Newbyth, produced several distinguished men, including a 17th-century judge. His grandson Sir David Baird (1757–1829) succeeded to Sir John Moore's command after the latter's death at Corunna, where Baird himself lost an arm. Other branches of the family were established at Saughtonhall and Balmaduthy.

More recent Bairds of note include John Baird of Kirkintilloch, who built elevated railways in New York City in the 19th century; John Logie Baird (1888–1946), the inventor of television; and John Lawrence Baird, Lord Stonehaven (1874–1941), a governor-general of Australia in the 1920s.

CLAN ASSOCIATION

14 Balmoral Place, Aberdeen, AB1 6HR, Scotland

2708 Hooker Street, Denver, CO 80236-2508, USA

BELOW *John Logie Baird, the Glasgow-trained electrical engineer who began working on television after retiring from his job with an electric-power company.*

BARCLAY

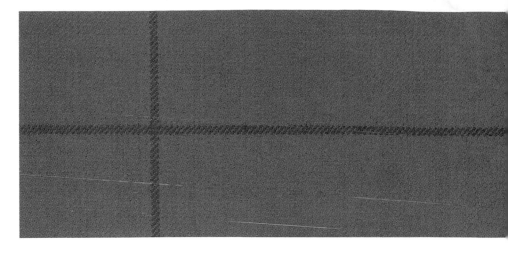

NAME AND PLACE

The name Barclay is of Anglo-Norman origin and probably comes from Berkeley in Gloucestershire, or possibly Berkeley in Somerset.

ORIGINS

The name occurs in Scotland in the 12th century when a Walter de Berchelai of Gartly was chamberlain of Scotland. He is regarded as the first chief of the Barclays.

THE CLAN

The name was fairly common in Fife and Aberdeenshire in the Middle Ages, and Barclays were hereditary sheriffs of Banffshire for several generations.

The Barclays of Mathers can be traced to an immigrant Englishman in the 12th century, whose descendant Alexander acquired the estate when he married a Keith in 1351. In 1456 the chiefship passed to the Barclays of Towie.

Colonel David Barclay of Mathers, having lost the family estates, became a leader of a band of Highland mercenaries who fought for Gustavus Adolphus in the Thirty Years War. He subsequently bought Urie in Kincardinshire and died a Quaker. His son Robert (1648–90) became, along with William Penn, a great propagandist for the Quakers, notably in his *Apology for the True Christian Divinity* (1676). From him are descended the Barclays of Buryhill. Other notable families were the Barclays of Collairnie in Fife, of Pierston and of Ardrossan.

In the 16th century a member of the Barclays of Towie settled in Russia and founded the most eminent of all the Barclay houses, the Barclays de Tolly. Michael Andreas, Prince Barclay de Tolly (1761–1818), commanded the Russian army against Napoleon in 1812–14.

Among other Barclays, Alexander (1476–1552), poet and monk, was the English translator of the German satirical classic *The Ship of Fools*. Captain Robert Barclay-Allardyce of Urie (1779–1854), a Regency sportsman, once walked 1,000 miles in 1,000 hours for a wager.

In recent times the chiefship has migrated to California and back to England. The present chief lives in Essex.

CLAN ASSOCIATION

Gatemans, Stratford St Mary, Colchester, Essex, CO7 6JH, England

7844 Lake Forest Drive, Richmond, VA 23235-5714, USA

BEATON

NAME AND PLACE

Beaton is an anglicised form of the Gaelic *mac beatha* (son of life), which also occurs as Bethune or MacBeth. The name MacBeth was fairly common in Scotland in the Middle Ages, but it is a personal name, not a patronymic like most 'Macs'. The seat of the original lordship was in Islay.

ORIGIN

According to tradition the Beatons came over from Ireland in the 13th century, following the Irish princess who married Angus, Lord of the Isles.

THE CLAN

The most famous holder of the name MacBeth was the king of Scots who reigned from 1040 to 1057, eponymous hero of Shakespeare's tragedy (and according to the historians, much maligned by the dramatist).

The Beatons were distinguished as the hereditary physicians of the lords of the Isles and other West Highland chiefs. After the fall of the lordship of the Isles (see MacDonald of the Isles), they became hereditary physicians to the MacLeans of Duart in Mull and to the Frasers, as well as to the Munros of Foulis and the earls of Sutherland. One branch in Skye was supported by both

BELOW *The Isle of Skye, where the learned Beatons were physicians, and later priests, with the Cuillin Hills in the distance. After the fall of the Lordship of the Isles members of the family became hereditary physicians to many important clans and families.*

the MacLeods of MacLeod and the MacDonalds of Sleat, despite the fierce feud between those clans.

The success of Presbyterianism was one of the causes of their decline in the 17th century, together with the deliberate oppression of Gaelic culture which resulted in the near-extinction of Gaelic as a written language by 1700.

A tombstone in Iona commemorates a Dr Beaton who died in 1658, having been family doctor of the MacLeans. John Beaton, a clergyman, retired from Mull to Ireland, where he died some time before 1715, but the contents of his remarkable manuscript library were recorded by the keeper of the Ashmolean Museum in Oxford. Manuscripts written in Irish script and dating from the 14th to the 16th centuries have survived. Some of them are now in the British Museum, and they bear eloquent testimony to the highly advanced Gaelic culture which was lost with the suppression of the lordship of the Isles. One medical treatise has corrections made as late as 1671, and there were reports of people called Beaton who possessed an extensive knowledge of wild plants living in the Outer Hebrides in the 19th century.

Like John Beaton, the 18th-century members of the family seem often to have entered the Church, and it is with the profession that the name Beaton is also notably connected.

It has been claimed that the Beatons of Skye were descended from a family in Fife, the place of origin of the famous family of Reformation ecclesiastics. The egregious Cardinal David Beaton (1494–1546) owed his rapid ascent in the hierarchy to his uncle James Beaton (d. 1539), who preceded him as Archbishop of St Andrews and Primate of Scotland. Cardinal Beaton was responsible for the burning of the reformer George Wishart, an act which, added to his general unpopularity, led to his own murder (in particularly unpleasant circumstances)

ABOVE *MacBeth was king of Scotland between 1040 and 1047. The violent character portrayed by William Shakespeare was atypical of this mainly peaceable, learned clan.*

in 1546 at St Andrews. Another James Beaton (1517–1603), a nephew of the cardinal, was the last Roman Catholic Bishop of Glasgow, driven out in 1560 and thereafter resident in France.

BLACK WATCH

NAME

The Black Watch is, of course, the name of a regiment, not a clan. After the Jacobite rising of 1715, when the English General Wade was commander-in-chief in Scotland, it was decided to create a local militia, or watch, in six independent companies of 114 men each of them under reliable local commanders. In 1739 four additional companies were raised to form a new regiment, the 43rd (from 1749 the 42nd).

ORIGINS

The regiment took the name which had been applied originally to the independent companies, the Black Watch, to distinguish its members from the red-coated regulars, and it wore the famous tartan it still wears today. The sett (though not the colours) is the same as the modern Campbell tartan, and since three of the original six commanders were Campbells (the others were a Grant, a Munro and, rather surprisingly, a Fraser – Lord Lovat), it is tempting to suppose that the Black Watch adopted the Campbell sett. However, there is no evidence for the existence of the modern Campbell tartan before 1739. A number of other tartans, such as the Grant hunting tartan, are also apparently derived from the Black Watch. The

BELOW *The monument to the Black Watch at Aberfeldy, with the Adam Bridge (1733), a survivor from General Wade's roadbuilding programme in the Highlands, in the background.*

MacNab tartan also has the sett of the
Black Watch although the change of
blues and blacks to reds and greens
makes it look altogether different.

THE REGIMENT

Many of the rank and file of the newly
created Black Watch were men of some
social standing. A well known story
relates how two of them were sent to St
James's Palace in London for inspection
by George II, who had expressed interest.
He approved their tartan, admired their
sword dancing, and gave them each a
guinea. On their way out, they tossed the
coins to a porter.

Their original dress was the belted
plaid. The 'little' kilt was worn off duty
and was not in Black Watch tartan. The
government provided musket and
bayonet and a basket-hilted broadsword
(sometimes wrongly called a claymore),
but the men were also allowed to carry
their own pistols, dirk and even target
(round shield).

Their first 'engagement' was
(paradoxically in view of their future
staunchness) a mutiny. It resulted from a
rumour that despite the government's
promise that they should serve at home,
they were to be sent to the West Indies.
Although the trouble was soon over,
three men were shot as traitors in the

ABOVE *Soldiers of the Black Watch prepare
to go on parade. The regiment's record in
war is second to none in the British army.
The tartan was adopted in 1739, when the
43rd regiment was fomed.*

Tower, 'all sons of gentlemen and
members of Clan Chattan'. They were
regarded in the Highlands as heroes,
especially as the rumours proved true:
200 men were drafted to the American or
Mediterranean garrisons. The rest of the
regiment was sent to Flanders in 1744,
fighting with great distinction and
amazing the Flemings by their dress. Its
battle honours since are second to none.
During the rebellion of 1745 the
regiment was stationed in Kent. It is a
moot point what effect its presence in
Scotland might have had on the fortunes
of the Jacobites.

Today, the official name of the
regiment is the 1st Battalion Royal
Highlanders, the Black Watch.
Its headquarters are in Perth.

BOYD

NAME AND PLACE

The name Boyd is thought to derive from Gaelic for Bute, and the original family to have taken their name from the island.

ORIGINS

They probably arrived in Scotland as vassals of the De Morevilles, a powerful Anglo-Norman family with vast estates in the Lowlands. The earliest record of them is in the burgh of Irving in 1205.

THE CLAN

The name soon became fairly common, especially in Ayrshire. Duncan Boyd was executed in 1306 as a partisan of Bruce, and Boyds were at court under the early Stewarts. In the 15th century they came very near the throne.

Robert Boyd, created Lord Boyd in 1454, became regent for King James III in 1465 and arranged the marriage of the king to a Norwegian princess. But his ambitions were viewed with suspicion and when he grew old enough James III forced him to flee to England; his brother was executed for treason.

His son Thomas, who had married the king's sister Mary and acquired the titles Earl of Arran and Lord Kilmarnock, also fled. A contemporary reported that he was 'the most courteous, gentlest, wisest, kindest, most bounteous knight,' and his widow was not pleased at being forced to marry the elderly Lord Hamilton, whose family supplanted the Boyds in nearness to the throne. The Hamiltons gained a royal wife and the earldom of Arran.

The line continued through the second son of Lord Boyd the Regent, and they remained supporters of the Stewarts. The tenth Lord Boyd was made Earl of Kilmarnock in 1661 by Charles II, but his great-grandson lost the title (and his life) for his part in the Forty-five when he commanded a troop of cavalry.

One of the fourth Earl's sons became, through inheritance in the female line, Earl of Erroll, and adopted the name of Hay, the former holders of that title. In 1941, on the death of the twenty-second Earl of Errol, his daughter became Countess of Erroll and Chief of Clan Hay, while his brother changed his name back to Boyd and became Lord Kilmarnock and Chief of Clan Boyd.

CLAN ASSOCIATION

46 High Street, Milton, Cambridge
CB4 6DF, England

419 North Superior Avenue, Baraga,
MI 49908, USA

BRODIE

The Brodies come from Moray, and their castle near Forres still stands, along with the ditch or *broth* which, some believe, gave them their name.

ORIGINS

The Brodies are one of the few clans whose origins can be ascribed without serious doubts to Pictish times. The burning of Brodie Castle in 1645 by Lord Lewis Gordon destroyed the family archives, although in 1972 a pontifical belonging to a Brodie turned up that has been dated to about 1000 (it is now in the British Museum). We know from a charter of King Robert I in 1311 that Michael de Brodie inherited Brodie from his father, and the family was certainly established much earlier. It has been said that they may have been descended from Pictish kings called Brude, although the scarcity of early evidence, partly accounted for by the disaster of 1645, may suggest that they were not of any great importance.

THE CLAN

There appears to have been a thane of Brodie in the mid-13th century (the first chief) and it is said that Brodie was confirmed in his possessions in Moray by King Malcolm IV a century earlier.

A number of the Brodies of Brodie featured in both local and national affairs in the late Middle Ages, but the first to achieve eminence was Alexander Brodie, the eleventh chief. He was one of the commissioners sent from Scotland to the Hague in 1649 to negotiate terms for the return of Charles II. Another Alexander, the fifteenth chief, as Lord Lyon King of Arms in the 18th century, had the dubious duty of attending the Duke of Cumberland during the campaign which ended at Culloden in 1746.

In general, the family never aspired to the public station suited to their heritage, status and connections. Perhaps that is why there is still a Brodie of Brodie in Brodie Castle who retains the ancient lands of his ancestors.

Cadet branches of the clan include Brodie of Lethen and Brodie of Idvies. Other Brodies may be descended from O'Brolochains, who often anglicised their name as Brodie.

CLAN ASSOCIATION

Brodie Castle, Forres,
IV36 0TE, Scotland

2601 S Braeswood No. 701, Houston,
TX 77024, USA

BRUCE

NAME AND PLACE

The first Robert de Brus, or Bruis, was a
Norman lord who came to England with
William the Conqueror. His son, Robert
le Meschin (cadet), was at the English
court and received from King David I the
grant of Annandale in about 1125.

ORIGINS

The 11th-century de Bruis family seat
was the Château d'Adam, which is near
Cherbourg in Normandy.

THE FAMILY

There is a story that at the battle of the
Standard (1138) this Bruce fought for the
English, his son for the Scots, and the son
was taken prisoner by his own father.

The fifth Lord of Annandale married a
descendant of King David I and his son
became regent and guardian of King
Alexander II in 1255. On the death of the
Maid of Norway he had a claim to the
crown, but his overlord the English King
Edward I gave his judgement in favour of
John Balliol. The decision was accepted
by Bruce, essentially still a great Anglo-
Norman noble rather than a Scot. He
and his son, remained reasonably loyal
vassals of Edward I during the growing

imposition of English control in Scotland
and the guerilla war of William Wallace.

The eighth Robert Bruce, Lord of
Annandale, is the greatest of national
heroes. Taking up the cause of Scottish
independence, he was crowned at Scone
after a *coup d'état*. He strengthened the
Crown and ensured an independent
Scottish monarchy by his victory over
the English at Bannockburn (1314),
near Stirling. He died at Cardross,
Dumbartonshire, in 1329 aged 55.

The dynasty was short-lived as Bruce's
son, David II, died childless. In 1359 he
granted the barony of Clackmannan to
another Robert Bruce. In the late 18th
century the Earl of Elgin, a descendant of
the Bruces of Clackmannan, became head
of the family. Among its most famous
members was James Bruce (1730–94),
the explorer of Abyssinia (Ethiopia),
some of whose possessions, including his
folding blunderbuss, are held at Lord
Elgin's seat, Broomhall in Fife.

FAMILY ASSOCIATION

Broomhall, Dunfermline, KY11 3DU,
Scotland

P O Box 408, Austell, GA 30001-0408,
USA

19 Chestnut Street, Bristol, NH 03222,
USA

BUCHAN

NAME AND PLACE

The name derives from Buchan in Aberdeenshire, but those Buchans were probably unconnected to the families, including the Stewarts and Comyns, who held the earldom of Buchan.

ORIGIN

Ricardus de Buchan was a clerk in the diocese of Aberdeen in the early 13th century, but other Buchans are found in Aberdeen, Edinburgh and elsewhere in the late medieval period.

THE FAMILY

Walter de Bochane or Buchan was Archdeacon of Shetland in 1391. The clerical connection often reappears: another Buchan was Bishop of Caithness earlier in the same century.

The most prominent Aberdeenshire Buchans were those of Auchmacoy, first heard of in the early 15th century. Thomas Buchan of Auchmacoy was a Jacobite general, succeeding Graham of Claverhouse after the latter's death at Killiecrankie. He did not last long and in 1692 fled to the exiled court of James VII/II. He insisted that his family were descended from the earls of Buchan.

The Buchanites were a small (46 members at full strength) and fanatical religious group in Scotland in the 1780s, named after their founder, Elspeth Buchan, who claimed to be the woman mentioned in Chapter 12 of the Book of Revelations: '... [She] brought forth a man child, who was to rule all nations with a rod of iron ...'.

Distinguished Buchans include Alexander (1829–1907), a meteorologist who set up an observatory on the summit of Ben Nevis, and John Buchan, Lord Tweedsmuir (1875–1940), author of *Greenmantle* and *The Thirty-nine Steps*, and governor-general of Canada from 1935 to 1940.

CLAN ASSOCIATION

Auchmacoy Estate Office, Ellon
AB41 8RB, Scotland

2845 Lavender Lane, Green Bay,
WI 54313, USA

6545 Arbutus Street, Vancouver
V6P 554, Canada

51 Rose Street, Armdale, Victoria 3143,
Australia

43 Newhaven Terrace, Mairangi Bay,
Auckland 10, New Zealand

BUCHANAN

NAME AND PLACE

In Gaelic *both-chanain* means the seat of
the canon, suggesting an ecclesiastical
origin. A Buchanan was called Mac-a'-
Chanonaich, son of the descendant of
the canon. However, the name really
comes from the district bordering
Loch Lomond.

ORIGIN

The Earl of Lennox bestowed lands there
on his seneschal in the 13th century, a
grant which was later confirmed by
a royal charter. The ninth Laird of
Buchanan, Sir Maurice, was the first to
assume the surname, but it is said there
were Buchanans in the French forces at
Agincourt. The war cry of the Buchanans
is *Clar Innis*, the name of an island in
Loch Lomond opposite Balmaha, where
the clan once gathered.

THE CLAN

The various branches of Clan Buchanan
include Leny, Carbell, Drumakill,
Auchmar, Auchintorlie and Spittal. This
last family, founded in the 16th century,
acquired the chiefship in 1762 when the
senior line became extinct on the death of
the twenty-second laird John Buchanan
of that ilk. By that time all the Buchanan
lands had already been sold – to the
Marquess of Montrose whose heirs have

BELOW *Buchanan Castle at Drymen, in the
heart of the Buchanan country that lies east
of Loch Lomond at its widest part. Sadly, it
is no longer home to Buchanans.*

retained them ever since. The last chief of
the house of Spittal died in 1919.

William Buchanan of Auchmar, who
died in 1747, was a noted Scottish
genealogist, the author of a work on
Scottish surnames and a genealogical
essay on the Buchanans themselves.
He recalled a time when the laird of
Buchanan could entertain 50 men, all
living within easy walking distance,
who bore his own name or that of
the Buchanan septs of MacAuslan,
MacMillan, MacColman and Spittal.
From this time, however, the Buchanans
were gradually scattered. Some settled
in Ulster, among them the ancestors of
James Buchanan (1791–1868), fifteenth
president of the Unites States.

The Buchanans have produced a more
than average number of scholars and
poets, of whom the best known was
George Buchanan (1506–82) of Killearn.
A humanist who later turned strict
Calvanist and became Moderator of the
General Assembly, he was universally
acknowledged as a great scholar and was
tutor to two generations of royalty. The
last of them was King James VI, who had
the elderly Buchanan (he was 64 when
appointed James's tutor) to thank, very
largely, both for his own erudition and
for the miseries of his childhood, the
tutor's methods being harsh even by
the rugged standard of those times.
Buchanan is also blamed for poisoning
his charge's mind against his mother,
Mary Queen of Scots, whom he helped to
the block by testifying to her authorship
of the Casket Letters and publishing an
indictment of her that contained many
deliberate falsehoods. Whatever the
felicities of his Latin style, George
Buchanan was not a very pleasant man.

Dugald Buchanan (1716–68) helps
correct the moral balance. He has been
called the Milton and Bunyan of Gaelic
Scotland and the most inspired religious
poet that Scotland has ever produced.
Kinloch Rannoch, where he was a

ABOVE *James Buchanan, president of the
United States (1857–61), was the son of a
farmer and storekeeper in Pennsylvania. His
ancestors were probably among those Scots
who settled in Ulster during the 17th-
century 'plantation'.*

teacher, became in his later years a
place of pilgrimage. There is a memorial
to him at Strathyre.

The old island gathering place in Loch
Lomond is now a bird sanctuary. It was
bequeathed to the Buchanan Society (said
to be the oldest clan society in Scotland)
in 1939.

CLAN ASSOCIATION
4599 Cedar Knoll Drive, Marietta,
GA 30066, USA

CAMERON

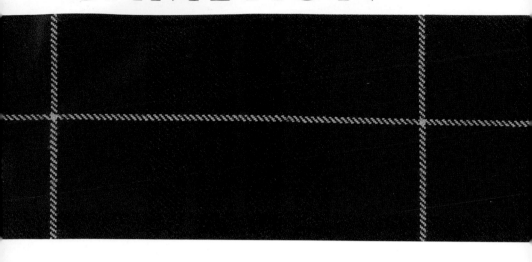

NAME AND PLACE

An old and picturesque tradition ascribes the name Cameron to the Gaelic *cam shron* (crooked nose) and traces them to the late Middle Ages, when they were established in Lochaber as subjects, allies – and sometimes opponents – of the lord of the Isles.

Sir Iain Moncreiffe of that ilk, the Highland genealogist and historian and one-time Lord Lyon King of Arms, has suggested an earlier origin and a different derivation of the name. Early versions of Cameron include Cambrun, Cambroun, Caumberen and several others sharing that intrusive 'b'. The inference is that the Camerons take their name not from some broken-nosed ancestor but from *cam brun* (crooked hill), the name of a place in the old kingdom of Fife, which has long been regarded as the principal place of origin of the Lowland Camerons, but possibly of the Highland Camerons too.

THE CLAN

The Camerons are one of the greatest of the Highland clans and one of the most ancient, for ever associated with the wild and beautiful country of Lochaber. For many generations they held on to their land, commanding the Road to the Isles, without legal title and in spite of

BELOW *The spectacular, mountainous country of Lochaber, around the northern end of Loch Linnhe, a wild region that bred a rugged people.*

continual harassment by the sword, earning a reputation for bravery and ferocity which they later displayed to equal effect in the British army.

There is a striking similarity between the coats of arms of the MacDuff earls of Fife and the Cameron chiefs, and there is other evidence that strongly suggests a connection between the famous old Clan MacDuff and the Camerons.

There were certainly Cameron chiefs in Lochaber by about 1400. The oldest branch of the clan is believed to be the MacGillonies, allegedly descended from a 7th-century king of Lorne, and their sept, the MacMartins of Letterfinlay on Loch Lochy. However, the chiefship passed to another branch, one of whom, Donald *Dubh*, married a MacMartin heiress. He is reckoned as the eleventh chief, but is the first of whom there is a documentary record. He is said to have led the clan in support of the lord of the Isles at the bloody battle of Harlaw in 1411, where the Islemen's march on Aberdeen was halted and the great MacLean chief, Red Hector of the Battles, met his end.

Donald *Dubh* left two sons, Allan, who succeeded him as twelfth chief, and Ewen, the founder of the Camerons of Strone.

ABOVE *Loch Moy, east of Strathairn, today no less remote, and perhaps more peaceful than in the past, where the Camerons held their place by tradition – and by the sword.*

CLAN ASSOCIATION
4 Winbourne Crescent, Hamilton, ML3 9BD, Scotland

14743 Hillside Ridge, San Antonio, TX 78233, USA

107 Annangrove Road, NSW 2770, Australia

CAMERON OF LOCHIEL

NAME AND PLACE

In 1528, during the time of the thirteenth Cameron chief, the lands he held were erected into the barony of Lochiel, and he was the first to call himself Cameron of Lochiel. The Cameron chiefs have borne this name ever since.

THE CLAN

The disappearance of the lord of the Isles created a power vacuum in the west, and for centuries the Camerons held the lands from Loch Oich to Glen Loy by force against incursions by the Mackintoshes in particular, and the efforts of the earls of Huntly to gain control of the western clans. In 1547 Ewen Cameron of Lochiel was beheaded by Huntly.

Throughout the successive crises of the 17th and 18th centuries the Camerons, under a line of remarkable chiefs, were loyal supports of the Stewart dynasty. Sir Ewen Cameron of Lochiel, 'the Ulysses of the Highlands', was the last Highland chief to hold out against Cromwell in the 1650s. He had been brought up under Campbell tutelage as hostage for the good behaviour of the Camerons. At times the Campbells had been a useful counterweight to the power of Clan Chattan and the Mackintoshes, as well as the MacDonalds. Lochiel was apparently not influenced by the Covenanting sympathies of Argyll, nor by his wavering political loyalties, and in 1647, at the age of 18, he took up his duties as chief.

After the execution of Charles I and the flight of Charles II Lochiel supported the rising led by the Earl of Glencairn, and when this failed he continued to harass General Monk, the English commander in Scotland, by guerilla warfare. In the end it was Monk, of course, who changed sides, and Lochiel accompanied him on his memorable march to London which led to the Restoration of Charles II (1660). After James VII/II lost his throne in 1688, Lochiel again rose to assist the king's futile campaign in Ireland. The Camerons were among the force commanded by Graham of Claverhouse at Killiecrankie.

A regiment called the Cameronians featured in this shortlived campaign. They distinguished themselves on the government side in a fierce skirmish at Dunkeld. This regiment was originally composed of followers of a Richard Cameron, son of a shopkeeper in Fife, who had been a Calvinist exile in Holland and had no connection, or sympathy, with the pro-Stewart, Catholic Camerons of Lochaber.

After this last act of defiance, 'the Great Lochiel' finally took the oath of

allegiance to William and Mary, thus
avoiding the fate planned by the Master
of Stair which overtook the MacDonalds
of Glencoe.

Lochiel lived long enough to see the
failure of the Jacobite rising of 1715,
dying at peace in 1719, one of the most
renowned warriors in Highland history.
It is said of him that he once bit out
the throat of a Cromwellian officer in
combat by Loch Arkaig. He was certainly
a giant: someone who had shaken hands
with him complained that Lochiel's grip
had made his fingertips bleed. Lochiel
was perhaps growing absent minded (he
was 87 years old at the time).

His son John, the eighteenth Lochiel,
fought in the Fifteen, for which he was
attainted and went into exile. His
grandson was Donald, 'gentle Locheil',
the man who in 1745 had to make a
fateful decision.

The nineteenth Lochiel has been called
'perhaps the finest Highland chief there
will ever have been', a tragic hero if ever
there was one. Like practically all the
Jacobite chiefs (except MacDonald of
Clan Ranald) he was appalled by the
landing of Prince Charles, unsupported,
in the Hebrides. He urged him to think
again, or at least wait until promised
French armaments arrived. The Prince
said to Lochiel's emissary (his brother,
Dr Archibald Cameron, who was to be
executed in the customary barbaric
manner eight years later), 'Lochiel,
whom my father esteemed the best
friend of our family, may stay at home,
and learn his Prince's fate from the
newspapers'. Lochiel's famous reply was,
'I'll share the fate of my Prince, and so
shall every man over whom nature or
fortune hath given me any power.'
One can only admire and deplore this
Athenian heroism. Since the other chiefs
were waiting for Lochiel's response, it
was decisive; had he held aloof, the
Prince would have got nowhere. As Sir
Iain Moncreiffe wrote, 'the hush of relief

ABOVE *Colonel Donald Cameron, the
present chief. He still lives in the castle at
Achnacarry, rebuilt early in the 19th
century after the earlier building had been
destroyed by Hanoverian troops.*

CAMERON OF LOCHIEL
34-35

when the Cameron pipes were heard approaching the Prince's gathering-place at Glenfinnan was one of the dramatic moments of history'. It was also, in retrospect, a very bad moment indeed, for it led directly to the final destruction of the clans.

At Culloden, where the Camerons were described by the future General Wolfe as the bravest of the Highlanders, Lochiel had both ankles broken by grapeshot, but was carried from the field by four of his men. He hid in the hills and eventually rejoined the Prince. They sailed on the same ship to France, where Lochiel died less than two years later.

During the Jacobite retreat towards Glasgow in 1746 Lochiel had exercised all his prestige to prevent the city being ravaged. That is why, whenever his descendant enters the city today, the bells of Glasgow ring out in his honour. The lands of Lochiel were instead ravaged by Cumberland's men. His seat, Achnacarry castle, where he had been planting an avenue of beech trees when the news of the Prince's landing was brought to him, was burnt down with most of its beautiful furniture still inside,

ABOVE The monument at Glenfinnan at the head of Loch Shiel where Prince Charles Edward raised his standard in August 1745. Lochiel's immediate response was arguably the decisive factor in the raising of the Highlands for the doomed Jacobite cause.

and the usual acts of savagery took place.

The lands of the Camerons suffered again during the Highland Clearances, when the evictions and consequent sales of land are said to have produced the money for rebuilding Achnacarry on a grandiose scale. The present Lochiel lives there now.

CAMERON OF ERRACHT

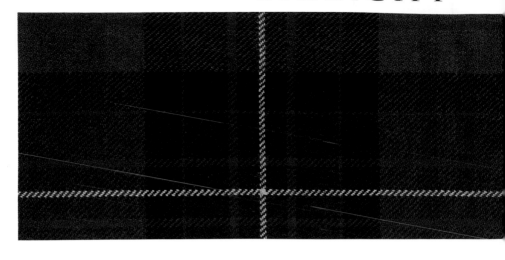

NAME AND PLACE

In the 16th century Ewen, the thirteenth chief, who first took the name 'of Lochiel', married Marjory, a Mackintosh, and their sons Ewen and John both founded branches of the clan, of which the more notable is Cameron of Erracht.

THE CLAN

After the horrors of Culloden and its aftermath, the martial pride of the Camerons was salvaged by the creation of the regiment best known as the Queen's Own Cameron Highlanders (now merged with the Seaforths as the Queen's Own Highlanders), raised by Alan Cameron of Erracht in 1793.

Relations between the Camerons of Lochiel and of Erracht were variable. There was a good deal of intermarriage but, when no other enemies threatened, a good deal of fratricidal violence.

Donald, the seventh Cameron of Erracht, was about 30 at the time of the Forty-five and was second in command to Lochiel when Prince Charles raised his standard at Glenfinnan and set off on his victorious march to Edinburgh. After Culloden Erracht went into hiding for three years. His eldest son was Sir Alan Cameron of Erracht who as a young man had killed an enemy in a duel and fled to Mull. He was for a time a clerk in the Customs at Greenock. He emigrated to America, where he joined the army and was captured during the American War of Independence, spending two years in prison in Philadelphia before returning to Lochaber. He successfully claimed the chiefship of the Camerons, briefly, but the Lyon court eventually restored the chiefship to Cameron of Lochiel.

The Cameronian Volunteers (later the Cameronian Highlanders) were raised by Cameron of Erracht in 1793, and he was able to stave off attempts to draft his men into other regiments or to make them exchange their kilts for trews. The Cameron of Erracht tartan which the regiment wore was designed, tradition says, by the Colonel's mother. It is supposedly based on an old Lochaber sett and has a close affinity with MacDonald. The yellow line, however, is distinctive.

The regiment was broken up in 1797 but the following year Sir Alan Cameron and his officers raised a second 79th regiment, with a second battalion following in 1804. Cameron of Erracht remained colonel of the regiment until his death at 68 in 1828. The male line died out on the death of his grandson, William Cameron of Erracht, in 1903.

CAMPBELL

NAME AND PLACE

The name Campbell, generally spelt Cambel until the 16th century, is thought to derive from the Gaelic *cam beul* (crooked mouth) presumably a deformity of some Campbell ancestor. It is at least equally likely, however, that it comes from a place name. The heart of Campbell territory was and is Argyll.

ORIGIN

As must usually be the case, the origins of the clan are lost in remote Celtic mists. The conjectural genealogy goes back, through the famous Somerled (died 1164) to the Norse and Irish kings. The armorial device of the Campbells is a boar's head, which commemorates the animal allegedly slain by the Ossianic hero, founder of Clan Diarmaid (to which all Campbells belong), in Kintyre.

THE CLAN

When the clan system came to an end in the 18th century the Campbells were easily the most powerful clan in the Highlands. The Campbell heritage is as old as any clan's and they had always played an important part in local and national affairs since the Middle Ages.

Success does not make for popularity, and animosity to the Campbells was strong enough to survive to the present.

BELOW *Castle Campbell (formerly Castle Gloom), in the hills above Dollar, was acquired by the Campbells in the 15th century. An impressive building on a splendid site, it is comparatively unsullied by the tramp of tourists.*

The stories of inn-keepers in the West Highlands who spit on the floor at the mention of the name may be more attempts to impress visitors than genuine antipathy. Nevertheless, an instinctive, hostile reaction remains, not entirely explained by the romanticism that has infected views of Scotland's past since the 19th century. Alasdair Alpin MacGregor, writing less than 60 years ago, recalled the 'hatred of anything connected with Clan Campbell' in his childhood home.

There are acts of treachery and atrocity in the history of the Campbells, but so there are in other clans. That the Campbells were devious and cunning is perhaps a biased way of saying that they were clever and polite. Generally, the Campbells' success was based on their support of the winning, side, almost invariably the government's. They were adherents of the Bruce and later of the Stewart dynasty. They lost their way somewhat in the difficult conditions of the 17th century, but after the Revolution of 1688 were firm supporters of the Whig, later Hanoverian, party, being the chief anti-Jacobite power not only in the Highlands but in the whole country. From the 18th century and often earlier, their outlook, or that of their leaders, was more British than Scottish, and in the words of one of their historians,

ABOVE *The Battle of Flodden (1513), one of the worst disasters in Scotland's history, which anihilated the cream of the Scottish ruling class, including several clan chiefs.*

Colin M. MacDonald, 'the prominence of the nine Campbell earls of Argyll in Scottish history and of the subsequent eleven dukes in the history of Great Britain is unsurpassed by any other single noble British family'.

The clan expanded steadily, taking advantage of their neighbours' failure and feuds, playing clans off against each other and, as government agents in the Western Highlands, moving in on the lands of defeated rebels. They always managed to secure legal title to those lands, sometimes obtaining charters from the Crown, but using force if necessary (for instance in carrying off an heiress).

CLAN ASSOCIATION

Argyll Estate Offices, Inverary Castle, Inverary PA32 8XE, Scotland

6412 Newcastle Road, Fayetteville, NC 28303-2137, USA

CAMPBELL OF ARGYLL

ORIGIN

The original, documented Campbell chief *Cailein* (Colin), died in 1294, though tradition follows his line back many generations. It is from him that the chief of the Campbells of Argyll takes his Gaelic name, 'Son of the Great Colin'.

In the days when *Cailein* lived in Lochow the chief powers in the region were the MacDougall lords of Lorne and the MacDonald lords of the Isles. Sir Colin, who was knighted by Alexander III in 1280, supported Bruce against the MacDougall lieutenants of Balliol, but the resulting feud ended with the defeat of the Campbells and the death of Sir Colin in battle in the String of Lorne.

When Bruce fled to the Western Highlands after his defeat at Methven he found staunch support in Sir Neil, the first *Mac Cailein Mór*. Bruce's eventual victory caused the MacDougalls' decline and the Campbells' rise. Sir Neil, who fought at Bannockburn with three of his brothers, married Bruce's sister. His son Colin captured Dunoon Castle in 1344, and the Campbells have remained keeper of that castle (and several others) since then, paying 'rent' of one red rose a year.

The estates in Argyll continued to expand, especially under the third Sir Colin (d. 1413), known as *Iongantach* (marvellous). His son Sir Duncan spent

some time in England as a hostage for the annual ransom payments for King James I. His grandson and successor was Colin, the first Earl of Argyll, created in 1457, whose marriage to a Stewart of Lorne brought him most of the lands of the lord of Lorne together with land in Knapdale and elsewhere. He moved his seat from Loch Awe to Inveraray on Loch Fyne, opening up access to the coast and islands and posing a clear threat to the stumbling authority of the lord of the Isles. The earl preferred peaceful acquisitions to conquest and following the collapse of the lordship of the Isles he acquired, by devious means, a substantial part of the MacDonald lands. He also played a skilful part in national affairs as chancellor and as a conspirator against James III. He doubled the Campbell lands and more than doubled the power of his house. Expansion continued under his son (killed at Flodden) and later earls, who benefited considerably from the dying spasms of the lordship of the Isles.

It was said of one of the chiefs of the Campbells of Argyll that 'he served his country well, his county better and his clan and family best of all.' These were the general priorities. The series of constitutional disturbances that began with the Reformation and ended two centuries later with the final defeat of the

Jacobites offered unrivalled opportunities for advancement but also heavy odds against always being on the right side at the right time. Not that the earls of Argyll were ruled entirely by cynical motives. There is for example no reason to doubt the sincerity of the religious conversion which resulted in Argyll's signature appearing at the top of the list on the National Covenant (1557).

Archibald, the fifth earl, nevertheless commanded Mary Queen of Scots' forces at Langside (1568) but had a seizure as the battle was about to begin, which 'contributed not a little to the defeat of Mary's forces'. He made his peace with the Protestant lords, though his brother and successor became embroiled in the quarrels over the regency of King James VI. On his death there were divisions among the Campbells over the chiefship, a rare dispute by comparison with other clans. This complicated plot, involving the murder of Campbell chieftains at the instigation of other Campbells, stretched everywhere and provoked warfare between the Campbells of Argyll and the Gordon. It was ended only after the king forced a reconciliation.

The most famous of the Campbell chiefs of Argyll was the Marquess of Argyll (1607–61), the squint-eyed adversary of Montrose during the civil war. He was not a particularly attractive character, but he has suffered unduly by comparison with his romantic, dashing opponent. Many of the accusations against him are mere propaganda, perpetrated by Argyll's enemies and embraced by later writers. His execution after the Restoration was unjust.

The marquess's eldest son, as Lord Lorne, had joined the revolt in favour of Charles II in 1653, but could not save his father. He was a wild fellow, perhaps the result of an accidental bullet wound in the head. He repaired the devastation caused by Montrose in Argyll, but was always held in some suspicion by the government. He had Covenanting sympathies, though he avoided making them dangerously obvious, and he was eventually convicted of treason on a charge connected with the Test Act which prompted Lord Halifax to remark that in England 'we should not hang a dog on the grounds on which my Lord Argyll has been sentenced'.

He escaped from Edinburgh Castle disguised as his step-daughter's page and fled to Holland. He became a rebel in earnest, invaded the Western Highlands in support of Monmouth's futile rebellion (1685), failed even to take Inveraray, and was caught and executed under the old sentence. On the day of his execution he took his midday nap, as usual.

With the accession of William and Mary the Argylls' political difficulties were over, and the tenth earl was granted a dukedom in 1701. The second duke, who as a small child fell from a third-floor window without harm on the day his grandfather was executed for treason, became a distinguished soldier, serving under Marlborough. His support of the Act of Union did not make him popular in Scotland, nor did his command of government forces during the Fifteen.

Later dukes have been men of many distinctions in Argyll, Scotland and in a wider arena. Some were also considerable historians and Gaelic scholars. The most famous is the eighth duke, whose long political career almost spanned the reign of Queen Victoria. He would probably have been prime minister had it not been for Gladstone. His son, the ninth duke, married a daughter of Queen Victoria.

The present *Mac Cailein Mór* is the twelfth Duke of Argyll, hereditary Lord Justice and Admiral of the Western Coasts. He lives in the charming blue-stone castle (the fairy turrets are Victorian) of Inveraray.

CAMPBELL OF ARGYLL

CAMPBELL OF BREADALBANE

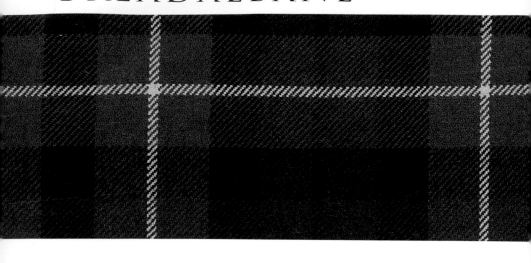

ORIGIN

Sir Duncan, known as Lord Campbell, fifth *Mac Cailein Mór*, who died in 1453, is the ancestor of the Campbells of Glenorchy, whose chieftains became earls and marquesses of Breadalbane.

THE CLAN

Though a cadet branch, the Campbells of Breadalbane became a mighty clan in their own right and at the beginning of this century it was said that the Marquess of Breadalbane could ride for a hundred miles in a straight line without leaving his own estates.

Glen Orchy, a valley lying to the east of Loch Awe, came into Campbell possession with a MacGregor heiress in the early 14th century. Sir Duncan left it to his second son, Black Colin of Glenorchy, who married an heiress of the Stewart lords of Lorne. He also built Kilchurn Castle, now a picturesque ruin at the head of Loch Awe.

The Campbells of Glenorchy still continued to extend their lands, mainly at the expense of the MacGregors, and the downfall of their rivals was made complete by the proscription of Clan MacGregor in 1603, in which the current Colin of Glenorchy had a big hand. He renovated Balloch, later called Taymouth Castle, near Aberfeldy. Black Duncan,

BELOW *The ruins of Kilchurn Castle on Loch Awe, once headquarters of Clan Campbell and built by the ancestor of the Campbells of Glenorchy, later the earls of Breadalbane.*

the seventh Campbell of Glenorchy, was also a keen builder, constructing or acquiring seven forts at various points in his ever-expanding but frequently threatened estates. He was created a baronet in 1625.

The most famous leader of the Campbells of Glenorchy was Sir John, *Iain Glas*, eleventh in line from Black Colin, born in 1635 and created Earl of Breadalbane in 1681. He is remembered for his machinations in connection with the earldom of Caithness. He obtained from the ruined Earl of Caithness his lands and jurisdictions in 1672 on payment of 4,000 pounds a year. When the earl died a few years later, he married his widow and invaded Caithness with a small army and dispossessed the earl's heir, though he was finally thwarted in his ambition by the courts. The episode was unusual in that it opposed Campbells and Gordons, who usually kept to their own spheres of influence.

The first Lord Breadalbane was described by a somewhat biased observer as 'cunning as a Fox, wise as a Serpent, and supple as an Eel'. He was for a time the most powerful man in Scotland after the senior Campbell chief, Argyll. During the plots, counterplots, revolts and recriminations caused by the collapse of the Stewart dynasty, he kept his head,

ABOVE *The Massacre of Glencoe. Historically, the Campbells have been blamed, but the real villains of the piece were members of the British government.*

turned a pretty penny or two, and occasionally played a double game. It is unfair to convict him of responsibility for the massacre of Glencoe. The Campbells of Glynlyon, who carried out that fearful act, were a sept of the Glenorchies and Breadalbane was certainly hostile to the MacDonalds, but he had no knowledge of the planned attack and subsequently condemned it in private correspondence.

He was succeeded in 1717 by his son, 'Old Rag', but the line died out with his grandson, the third earl, a diplomat and a supporter of Walpole in Parliament, in 1782. The title passed to a cousin, who was created Marquess of Breadalbane in the British peerage in 1831 and then to another cousin in 1862. The marquessate ended in 1922 with the end of another line, but the Scottish title continues. The family still holds Glenorchy and estates in other parts, though Taymouth Castle, built in the 19th century on the site of Balloch, is currently vacant.

CAMPBELL OF
BREADALBANE **42-43**

CAMPBELL OF CAWDOR

ORIGINS

In Cawdor Castle, said to be the last
privately inhabited castle (complete with
drawbridge) in Scotland, there is a
monumental fireplace, built by Sir Hugh
Campbell, Thane of Cawdor, in the late
17th century to commemorate the
marriage in 1510 from which his line
sprang. The lands were gained by what
some might call a characteristically
Campbell manoeuvre

THE CLAN

The death of John, Thane of Calder
(Cawdor) in 1494 was shortly followed
by the birth of an heiress, Muriel. The
baby's maternal grandfather, Rose of
Kilravock, who intended the heiress as a
future wife for his grandson (her cousin),
was at that time under arrest after some
Highland affray. The Justice-General was
Archibald Campbell, second Earl of
Argyll, and presumably the two came to
a mutually advantageous agreement,
which eased Argyll's task in obtaining
wardship for the Cawdor heiress from
King James IV. Argyll wanted her and her
dowry for his younger son, John. To
make sure of the plan, he sent a part
sixty strong under Campbell of Inverliver
to seize the child. A grisly legend relates
that to thwart a possible substitution the
child's mother branded her with a red-

BELOW *Clan Campbell's military prowess
remains undiminished. No fewer than three
descendents of the Cawdor branch have
won Victoria Crosses for valour.*

hot key, and/or the child's nurse bit off the top joint of one of her fingers.

The abductors were pursued by the Calders and while some made off secretly with the child the others fought to the death in defence of a hastily contrived dummy. Someone later remarked to Inverliver that it would be a pity if after all the Campbell losses in this fight the child were to die. He replied, 'Muriel can never die as long as there is a red-haired lass on the shores of Loch Fyne'. Presumably, however, the 15-year-old who became the mother of the Campbells of Cawdor was the real Muriel.

In the vault of Cawdor Castle, amid the fertile country south of the Moray Firth, there is an ancient hawthorn tree, lovingly protected now by a wire cage. In 1454 the Thane of Cawdor resolved to build a new castle, and he dreamt that he should place a chest of gold on a donkey and set it to wander. Where it stopped would be the place to build. It stopped at the hawthorn tree, and the castle was build around it.

In the early 17th century some of the Cawdor lands were sold to facilitate the wresting of Islay from the MacDonalds. Islay, though far removed, remained the property of the thanes of Cawdor until it was sold to another Campbell family, Campbell of Shawfield, in 1726.

ABOVE *The famous gardens of Cawdor Castle, which enhance one of the most charming of ancient fortresses, its present tranquility contrasting sharply with its turbulent history.*

The military record of the Campbells generally has often been remarked upon, and of the Campbells of Cawdor in particular, Sir Iain Moncreiffe calculated that the 50-odd male descendants of the Thane of Cawdor in the past hundred years who were of an age for military service in wartime won 22 British awards for bravery between them, including three Victoria Crosses.

The thane's title was elevated to an earldom in 1796, and the earls of Cawdor still live in Cawdor Castle today.

CARNEGIE

NAME AND PLACE

The Carnegies of Southesk are descended from John de Balinhard, whose forebears held lands of that name in Angus at the beginning of the 13th century. In the 14th century the Balinhard lands were sold to pay for the lands of Carrynegy (Carnegie) in the parish of Carmyllie, Angus, and the family thus acquired their modern name.

ORIGIN

The original senior line of descent from John de Balinhad died out in the 16th century, and the Carnegie chiefs of the house of Southesk derived from his younger son Duthac.

THE CLAN

The second Duthac, gained Kinnaird through marriage, but was killed at the battle of Harlaw (1411).

A later Carnegie, John of Kinnaird, died at Flodden. His son Robert was a judge and ambassador who fought the English at Pinkie Cleugh and died in 1565. His nephew David (1575–1658), eighth Carnegie of Kinnaird, was created Earl of Southesk in 1633.

The Carnegies were generally loyal adherents of the Stewart dynasty. The second Earl of Southesk, who was known as the Black Earl because of his alleged

BELOW *The steel millionaire Andrew Carnegie with dog and gun at Skibo – the weaver's son become a great laird. He believed firmly that it was the duty of a rich man, having acquired his wealth, to spend it on the welfare of others.*

familiarity with the black arts, was imprisoned during the Commonwealth, and the fifth earl, James, came out for King James in Angus during the Jacobite rising of 1715. After the defeat of the Jacobites he lost his earldom.

The Carnegie tartan appears to be based upon the tartan of MacDonell of Glengarry, and it is said that this association dates from the Fifteen, when Lords Southesk and Glengarry acted in close co-operation.

The fifth earl died without children and the succession passed to a cousin, Sir James Carnegie of Pitarro, who was descended from a younger son of the first earl and who was able to buy back the Southesk estates. Sir Alexander Carnegie of Pitarro, a scholar and Knight of the Thistle, succeeded in having the attainder reversed in 1853 and accordingly became ninth Earl of Southesk.

Another branch of the family, that descended from Lord Lour, a younger brother of the first Earl of Southesk, became earls of Ethie, later changed to Northesk, in the 17th century. The family produced two admirals, most notably William, Earl of Northesk (1758–1831), who was third in command during the battle of Trafalgar (1804) and later commander-in-chief at Portsmouth. A cadet branch of this house is Carnegie of

ABOVE Skibo Castle, looking south towards the Dornoch Firth, totally rebuilt as a comfortable residence by Andrew Carnegie in the early 20th century.

Lour. The Carnegies of Balnamoon are connected with the Southesk house.

The most famous bearer of the name was of rather humbler birth. Andrew Carnegie (1835–1919) was the son of a weaver in Dunfermline who emigrated to Pennsylvania in the 1840s. He became a leading railway magnate and the greatest steelmaster in the United States. He was a generous philanthropist and his native country benefited greatly from his good fortune. Having himself profited as a boy from a free library in Pittsburgh, he founded the Carnegie free libraries in Britain as well as other educational projects. He rebuilt Skibo Castle in Sutherland as a home for himself.

The present Earl of Southesk and Carnegie chief still lives in Kinnaird Castle, Angus.

CLAN ASSOCIATION

Kinnaird Castle, Brechin DD9 6TZ, Scotland

CHISHOLM

NAME AND PLACE

The Chisholms are first found in the
Borders, taking their name from a
barony in Roberton, near Hawick in
Roxburghshire. However, the name is
no doubt of Anglo-Norman origin, the
early spelling being 'de Cheseholm'.

ORIGIN

The Border family continued right into
modern times, the last Chisholm of that
ilk perishing in the Boer War. The move
into the Highlands occurred in the 14th
century, when Robert Chisholm of that
ilk became Constable of Urquart Castle,
near Inverness, as a result of inheritance
through his mother.

THE CLAN

There are only three people, it is said,
entitled to a definite article: the King,
the Pope and the Chisholm (alternately,
the Queen, the Devil and the Chisholm).
This isn't true of course, even among
Highland chiefs several of whom are
known as 'the …'. The chief of the
clan has, however, been known as the
Chisholm (*An Siosalach*) since the 17th
century, though the chiefship has since
migrated and the title sounds a little odd
when applied to a Suffolk farmer.

The Constable of Urquhart's key
position, commanding the northern end

BELOW *Glen Affric, in Chisholm country.
Once famous for its timber, much of the
original forest was swept away for pasture
in the late 18th and early 19th centuries,
chiefly by William Chisholm, the chief
who evicted the tenants in favour of
sheep-grazing.*

of the Great Glen, made him a powerful force in the region, especially as he had also inherited lands in Moray through another grandparent. His younger son remained Chief of the Border Chisholms, and the latter's son became the founder of the Chisholms of Cromlix, Perthshire.

Sir Robert Chisholm's eldest son – Alexander – married Mary, Lady of Erchless and Comar and thus acquired Erchless in Strathglass. Erchless became a barony in the 16th century and its picturesque fortified house was the seat of the Chisholm until the 1930s.

The Chisholms remained Catholics at the Reformation, and the Perthshire Chisholms produced three 16th-century bishops of Dunblane. However, by the time of the Jacobite risings of the 18th century the Chisholm had changed his allegiance. Despite this, the Chisholms, never a numerous clan, were 'out' in the Fifteen, fighting under the Earl of Mar at Sheriffmuir, and though the Chisholm himself did not take part, he forfeited his lands for a period. During the second great Jacobite rising 30 Chisholms were killed at Culloden, including their leader Roderick, a younger son of the chief. Two of his brothers fought on the other side and the chief himself was too old or too careful to appear. He seems to have been sympathetic to the Jacobite cause as Prince Charles briefly found shelter in Strathglass during his wanderings after the fatal battle. Three Chisholm brothers were among the Seven (actually eight) Men of Glenmoriston who sheltered and protected the prince in their cave for a week, raiding an army baggage train to get him new clothes.

The Chisholms were fortunate to avoid the worst immediate repercussions of the Forty-five, but the clan was steadily reduced by voluntary emigration and finally decimated by the Clearances. Alexander Chisholm was tempted to sell out in the 1780s but, urged by his admirable daughter Mary, eventually

ABOVE *Erchless Castle, a fortified house in which the domestic aspect now almost obscures the military, was the seat of the Chisholms for over 500 years from the mid 14th century until the early 19th century.*

issued new 18-year leases to his tenants. By the time the leases expired, however, he had been succeeded by his half-brother William, who had no such reservations. Despite the objections of Mary and her mother, the Chisholm clansmen and tenants were evicted, and a Lowland grazier moved in with his sheep. 'The abode of warriors has withered away' mourned the bard, 'the son of the Lowlander is in your place.'

CLAN ASSOCIATION
54 St Martin's Close, East Horsley, Surrey KT24 6SU, England

CLARK/BLUE CLERGY

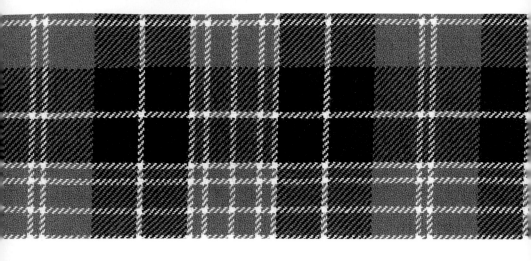

ORIGIN

A clerk originally meant a man in Holy
Orders, from the Latin which also gives
us the word clergyman. Early references
to a Clerk or Clark generally refer to a
man's occupation. Later it might mean
a learned man, a scholar, not necessarily
a clergyman, and the word continued to
be used in both senses long after it had
also become a family surname. It is a
common name in medieval Scottish
documents, but it cannot be shown to
be, without any doubt, a name rather
than a description until the 15th century
at the earliest. The Gaelic form is *Mac a'*
Chléirich.

PLACE

One district where the name seems to
have been especially common is the old
bishopric of Caithness, where there is still
a place called Clerkhill. There is an
interesting letter written by John Eldar,
Clerk, who describes himself as
'Redshanks' (ie a bare-legged
Highlander) to Henry VIII of England in
1543, in which he stoutly defends his
fellow Highlanders against the oppressive
actions of royal government. Somewhat
later two Scots called Clerk reached high
rank in the Swedish navy, and the
American explorer George Rogers Clark
(1752–1818) was of Scottish descent.

BELOW *During the conflict provoked by*
Henry VIII of England's aggressive policy
towards Scotland, powerful Border clans
had much to gain – and much to lose.

Although there was never a Highland clan of this name, it is often found among the clansmen of Clan Chattan, the loose confederation of clans in the central Highlands mainly under the leadership of the Mackintosh. The Clarks appear to have been a sept of the MacPhersons (another name which is of ecclesiastical origin), and Clarks or Clarksons were also often associated with the Camerons.

It seems quite reasonable to have a Clark tartan, therefore. It is a variation on the 'Blue Clergy' tartan worn by the clergy who, as John Prebble remarked, 'undoubtedly belonged to the Church Militant in the Highlands'. During the religious troubles of the 17th century there was one instance at least of a minister, 'dressed in the kilt and armed with a sword in one hand and a cocked pistol in the other, with his back to the church wall, defying an anti-Presbyterian congregation. The old Celtic Church had been organised very like a clan; their hereditary bishops aroused the ire of St Bernard, though the practice continued centuries later.

The Clark tartan appears to date from the post-1822 revival, although it may have existed earlier, and it is similar to an old version of the MacPherson tartan, in black and white.

COCHRANE

NAME AND PLACE

Although other sources have been suggested, the name Cochrane clearly derives from a place near Paisley, Renfrewshire.

ORIGIN

A certain Waldeve de Coueran, or Coughran, was established at Cochrane in the 13th century. A royal charter of King James II confirming the family possessions was obtained by Allan Cochrane of Cochrane, son of Robert, son of John. Cochrane Castle (now no more), or its tower, was built by William Cochrane in the late 16th century.

THE CLAN

The last Cochrane of that ilk left only a daughter, Elizabeth. Her husband, originally Alexander Blair, therefore took his wife's name along with the estates, and their son was created Earl of Dundonald in 1669. The first earl's second son was a Calvinist who went to Holland and returned with William of Orange in 1688. He was also the ancestor of the later earls, after the death of the seventh earl in the senior line without issue.

The most famous member of the Cochrane chiefs in modern times was Thomas, tenth Earl of Dundonald, generally known as Lord Cochrane (1775–1860). He inherited a streak of creative oddity apparent in some earlier members of his house. Having held commissions in both army and navy as a child, he first went to sea at 18 in a sloop commanded by his uncle, Alexander Cochrane, and made his name when, in command of the sloop *Speedy* in 1800, he captured a Spanish frigate whose crew outnumbered his own by about six to one. This was followed by other equally remarkable exploits. He provided the material for *Peter Simple,* by Captain Marryat, who had served under him. Cochrane represented the seat of Westminster in parliament, where he had a stormy career as an outspoken radical, antagonising not only the Admiralty but many others, and in 1814 he was deprived of his seat and his profession after his alleged involvement in a stock market fraud (it has been suggested that he was framed).

The republicans in Chile invited him in 1817 to command their fleet in the war of independence against Spain, which he did with dramatic success. He then performed a similar role for Brazil and for Greece against the Turks, as usual showing great ability and panache and an unrivalled capacity for irritating his superiors. He was equally radical on

the technical side, advocating the use of steam-driven warships and inventing several useful devices. His plans for laying smokescreens in battle, drawn up in 1812, remained classified for well over a century.

He was reinstated as an admiral in the Royal Navy in 1832, and was upset to be refused a battle command in the Crimean War (he was only 80!)

Among others Nelly Bly, born Elizabeth Cochrane at Cochran's Mill, Pennsylvania, the American journalist remembered for her round-the-world journey to beat Phineas Fogg's 80 days, is said to have been of Scottish descent

The Cochrane tartan was officially approved by the present Earl of Dundonald and Chief of Cochrane, removing earlier doubts as to the appropriate sett.

ABOVE *Lord Cochrane, one of Britain's most colourful naval heroes, overcame apparently fatal setbacks in his career through a combination of ability and fearlessness. After the scandal of 1814, he was struck off the navy list and thrown out of the House of Commons. Re-elected by the independent-minded voters of Westminster, he escaped from prison and reappeared in the Commons demanding to take his seat. He was removed by force.*

CLAN ASSOCIATION
Lochnell Castle, Ledaig
PA34 1QT, Scotland

P O Box 1085, Florissant,
MO 63031, USA

65 Investigator Street, Red Hill,
Canberra, ACT 2603, Australia

Levencorroch, 17 Searells Road,
Christchurch 5, New Zealand

COLQUHOUN

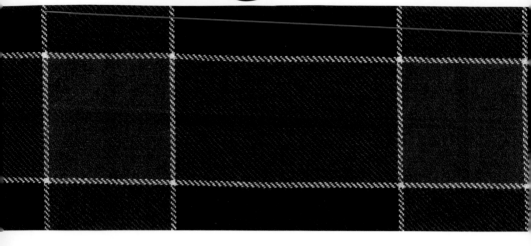

NAME AND PLACE

Colquhoun is in Dumbartonshire.

ORIGIN

During the reign of King Alexander II Humphrey de Kilpatrick received a grant of the lands of Colquhoun from the Earl of Lennox. His son Ingram was the first to take the name Colquhoun.

THE CLAN

In the 14th century a descendant of Ingram married 'the Fair Maid of Luss' (was there ever a Scots heiress who was not a 'Fair Maid'?), heiress of the house of Luss and related to the Earl of Lennox. He and his successors added the name Luss to their own.

The family profited by the downfall of their former patron, Lennox, and Iain Colquhoun of Luss became a key figure in Dumbartonshire under the early Stewarts. The eleventh Colquhoun of Luss built the castle of Rossdhu, whose lovely ruins now augment the natural beauties of Loch Lomond, and became chamberlain of Scotland.

The Colquhouns suffered at the hands of the invading Islesmen in 1439, when Iain of Luss was killed with many of his men, and there were other feuds with the Buchanans, the MacFarlanes and others. In 1592 Sir Humphrey Colquhoun of Luss had an affair with the wife of a MacFarlane chief which led to grisly retribution. Sir Humphrey was killed, though apparently by his ambitious younger brother rather than the MacFarlanes, but the latter raped Sir Humphrey's daughter and cut off his genitals, which they served up for supper to the adulterous MacFarlane lady.

Nevertheless, the Colquhouns' worst enemies were the MacGregors. Early in the 17th century the Colquhoun women enacted a remarkable kind of protest demonstration when they bought the bloodstained shirts of their menfolk killed by the MacGregors to the king at Stirling Castle (it was said, rightly or wrongly, that some of the shirts had been stained with sheep's blood). As a result the chief was granted a commission of fire and sword against the MacGregors, but the immediate result was the worst disaster yet.

In 1603 Alexander Colquhoun of Luss assembled all his men, said to have numbered 800, with the fiery cross, only to be ambushed by the MacGregors in Glenfruin, not very far from Dumbarton itself. They were utterly defeated, 200 of them killed, their cattle driven off and their goods stolen. It was this episode which led to the proscription of Clan Gregor later that year.

The Colquhoun lands were attractive. They also bridged one of the main routes running between the Highlands and the Lowlands, and even after the disaster of Glenfuin they continued to suffer depredation and violence. Indeed, the Colquhouns were no longer much of a force, and though they received cash compensation and a Nova Scotia baronetcy, they were permanently reduced. Although expected to provide 100 men in the event of an invasion, they could not be taken seriously by the government in military terms. During the Jacobite rising of 1715 their assignment was to deprive the MacGregors of boats in Loch Lomond.

In the 18th century the Colquhouns became mixed up with the Grants in a complicated way. Sir Humphrey Colquhoun, seventeenth of Luss, who died in 1715, had only one child, a daughter. She married James Grant of Pluscardine, second son of Grant of that ilk. In order to retain the autonomy of his own clan, Sir Humphrey made legal arrangements to prevent the estate passing to the Grants. On his death, accordingly, James Grant changed his name and became Sir James Colquhoun of Luss. However, the death of his elder brother without children in 1719 meant that he then succeeded to the estates of

ABOVE *Dumbarton castle, near to where in 1603 Alexander Colquhoun was ambushed and defeated by the MacGregors.*

Grant, whereupon he swapped identities again and was succeeded as Colquhoun chief by his own second son, Sir Ludovick. The same thing happened in the next generation. Sir Ludovick's elder brother died unmarried and he became Laird of Grant. His younger brother, another James, was recognised an Chief of Colquhoun in 1781. From him the present chief is indirectly descended.

That the Colquhoun estates have not been much developed or despoiled is largely due to the determined and unselfish efforts of Sir Iain Colquhoun of Luss (d. 1948), who besides being a near-legendary hero of the First World War was chairman of the National Trust for Scotland. His successor lives today in the neo-classical mansion at Rossdhu on the famous bonny, bonny banks of Loch Lomond.

CLAN ASSOCIATION

Camstraddan House, Luss, G83 8NX, Scotland

2984 Mike Drive, Marietta, GA 30064, USA

CRAWFORD

NAME AND PLACE

The ancestors of the Crawfords (or Crawfurds) can be traced back to the old barony of Crawford in Lanarkshire, in the 12th century.

ORIGINS

Sir Reginald of Crawford was Sheriff of Ayr in the reign of King William the Lion. Sir John of Crawford, who died in 1248, had a daughter who married a Lindsay ancestor of the earls of Crawford. Another daughter, Margaret, married Sir Malcolm Wallace of Ellerslie and became the mother of the great resistance leader Sir William Wallace.

THE FAMILY

Margaret's brother received a grant of Auchinames from King Robert Bruce in 1320, and the house of Auchinames continued into the present century, when the property was sold and the last representative died in Canada. Another branch, the Crawfords of Crawfordland, trace their ancestors to Sir Reginald of Crawford in the late 12th century, and a third, the Crawfords of Kilburnie, go back to the Sir John Crawford whose daughter married a Lindsay.

The Crawfords of Kilburnie, baronets since 1781, have a distinguished record in the armed services in modern times.

BELOW Lord Darnley, of whose household Thomas Crawford became a member when Darnley married Mary. His loyalty to those unsatisfactory people was limited, and he later played a spectacular part in crushing the last of Mary's supporters.

Thomas Crawford (d. 1603) was a younger son of Lawrence Crawford of Kilburnie. He was taken prisoner at the Battle of Pinkie (1547) but ransomed by his family and later went to France where he became a soldier in French service and a courtier attendant on Mary Queen of Scots. He returned to Scotland with the queen in 1561 and after her marriage to Lord Darnley became a member of the latter's household. In 1569 he denounced certain lords as the murderers of Darnley, although by that time there was little point in such a highly dangerous accusation, whether true or not. In 1571 Crawford captured Dumbarton Castle from Mary's supporters on behalf of the government with a force of only 150 men, who scaled the natural defences with ropes and ladders. He also took part in the capture of Edinburgh Castle from 'the Queen's Lords' two years later.

Lawrence Crawford (1611–45) was a fierce Presbyterian who had military experience under Gustavus Adolphus in the Thirty Years War, and fought in the English Parliamentary forces against Charles I. He came into conflict with Cromwell, no lover of Presbyterians, whom he accused of cowardice during the battle of Marston Moor, but the dispute was resolved by Crawford's death in a skirmish some months later.

ABOVE *The rock in the Clyde off Dumbarton, fortified since about the 5th century, was regarded as impregnable. In 1571 Thomas Crawford of Jordanhill took it in a brilliantly daring assault, climbing the most inaccessible rockface at night with a handful of men and taking the garrison by surprise.*

CLAN ASSOCIATION

A204 Portview, 310 Newtonards Road, Belfast BT4 1HE, Ireland

CUMMING (COMYN)

NAME AND PLACE

The origin of this name is a matter of dispute. It may be territorial: the town of Commines, near Lisle, is a candidate. More widely accepted is the suggestion that it derives from the herb cummin which, along with Comyn, was a common early spelling of the name.

ORIGIN

The family was of Anglo-Norman descent, and the first to settle in Scotland was William Comyn, an associate of King David I who, on his return to his kingdom, made Comyn Chancellor of Scotland. Comyn established his nephew Richard at Allerton, and it is from him that the clan is descended.

THE CLAN

Richard married a granddaughter of Donald *Bàn* (Donaldbane), King of Scots 1093–97, and their son married the heiress of Buchan, the first of several Comyn alliances with Celtic dynastic houses which eventually resulted in Comyns holding three of the 13 Scottish earldoms in the 13th century. From 1270 they also held the military office of constable, the guardian of the king.

Thus on the constitutional crisis caused by the death of King Alexander III in 1286 the Comyns were the most

BELOW *John (de) Balliol. He was Edward I of England's selection as king of Scotland, perhaps because Edward considered him likely to be more compliant than any of the other claimants, including the elder Bruce.*

powerful family in Scotland. With the
death of Alexander's little granddaughter
'the Maid of Norway', the Comyn chief
known as the Black Comyn was one of
the claimants to the throne, as he was a
descendant of Donald *Bàn*. The other
chief claimants, John Balliol and the elder
Robert Bruce, were, however, descended
from Donald *Bàn*'s elder brother,
Malcolm III, *Ceann Mór* (r. 1058–93)
and thus had technically superior claims.
The Black Comyn, like Bruce, eventually
acknowledged Balliol as king and
married Balliol's sister, strengthening
the future royal claims of their son John,
the Red Comyn. The results, however,
were not a crown for the Red Comyn
but the ruin of the clan.

When John Balliol was pressed into
defiance of his overlord Edward I, Bruce
was among those who as vassals of
Edward did homage to him when he
crossed the border. Balliol indignantly
seized Bruce's lands and gave them to
his nephew, the Red Comyn.

The great Scottish nobles did not give
much aid to William Wallace, but after
his death both Comyn and Bruce were
ready to move. A meeting was arranged
in Greyfriars Kirk, Dumfries, early in
1306. It ended with Bruce stabbing and
killing the Red Comyn.

For one Scottish noble to murder
another was not unusual, but this was
dangerous act and cannot have been
planned. Bruce himself, grasping the
thistle, had himself crowned at Scone.

Though Bruce faced the combined
hostility of the Church, the English and
the Comyns, he of course prevailed, and
the Comyns were gradually but ruthlessly
destroyed. The Red Comyn's only son
died at Bannockburn fighting for the
English. The hereditary office of
constable was given to the Hays of
Errol (who had some Comyn blood),
where it has since remained.

Another branch, the Cummings of
Altyre, were descended from a brother

ABOVE *Balliol College, Oxford, founded by
the John Balliol, father of John Balliol, king
of Scots, as an act of penance.*

of the Black Comyn. They became a
power in Moray by the end of the
century, conducting blistering feuds
with Clan Chattan. It is said that they
once dammed Loch Moy to raise the
level and flood the island castle of the
Mackintoshes, and they may have been
involved in the famous 'Battle of the
Clans' (1396) on the North Inch at Perth.
They were certainly warlike, and their
enemies had a saying 'So long as there
is a stick in the wood there will be
treachery in a Cumming'.

Robert, thirteenth Chief of Altyre,
married a Gordon heiress, and his
grandson, on inheriting Gordonstoun,
adopted the name Gordon-Cumming,
the name of the present chief.

CLAN ASSOCIATION
1477 Holly Oaks Lake Road W,
Jacksonville, FL 32225-4492, USA

CUNNINGHAM

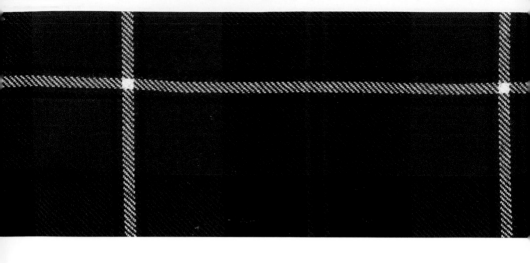

NAME AND PLACE

Cunningham is a district in Ayrshire.

ORIGIN

In the 12th century the land of Kilmaurs (later a Cunningham barony, sold in the 18th century) was granted by Hugh de Moreville, Constable of Scotland, to a vassal, Wernebald, whose presumed descendant was Harvey de Cunningham, said to have fought at the Battle of Largs against the Norwegian king.

THE CLAN

The lands were further expanded by a grant of Robert Bruce in gratitude for Cunningham support, and through the marriage of Sir William Cunningham to the heiress of Danielston of that ilk which resulted in the acquisition of Glencairn.

Sir William's grandson was created Earl of Glencairn by James III in 1488 but did not live to enjoy the honour long, dying in the same year in the battle of Sauchieburn, which also put an end to James III. His son and heir lost the earldom, but it was restored to his brother Cuthbert. The third Earl of Glencairn (sometimes listed as the fourth) was captured at Solway Moss but released in exchange for his support for the marriage of the English King Edward VI to Mary Queen of Scots, a project which foundered when he was defeated by Hamilton, Earl of Arran.

Alexander, fourth (fifth) Earl of Glencairn, was a stern Calvinist and a friend of John Knox. He is said to have been responsible for vandalising the chapel at Holyrood after the battle of Langside, where Mary Queen of Scots was defeated in 1568.

A feud between the Cunninghams of Glencairn and the Montgomery earls of Eglinton was exacerbated at this time by the Catholic Eglinton's support for Mary. The fourth Earl of Eglinton was murdered by the Cunninghams in 1586.

The eight Earl of Glencairn, though hesitant at first, became one of the most loyal Stewart supporters, leading the rising of 1653 which is named after him. With Charles II in exile abroad and Cromwell's generals in command in Scotland it had little chance of success. Glencairn was betrayed and captured but managed to keep his head on his shoulders until the Restoration (1660) when he was rewarded with the post of Lord Chancellor. His successor supported the overthrow of James VII/II.

The fourteenth earl, John, is best remembered as the friend and patron of Burns, who on the earl's death in 1791 wrote a *Lament* for him:

*The mother may forget the child
That smiles sae sweetly on her knee;
But I'll remember thee, Glencairn,
And a' that thou hast done for me.*

As he had died without having children
the earldom became dormant, though it
would seem that the claim of the present
Cunningham chief, who is descended
from Cunningham of Corsehill, second
son of the third Earl of Glencairn, could
hardly be disputed. The Cunninghams of
Craigends and Robertlane (baronets since
1630) and Auchinarvie are descended
from a younger son of the first earl; the
Cunninghams of Caprington (a barony
created by Mary Queen of Scots) from a
cousin of the first earl.

Cunningham prowess on the
battlefield was exemplified by an odd
coincidence during the Second World
War, when the three British commanders
of army, navy and air force in the
Middle East were all named Cunningham
or Coningham.

ABOVE *Holyroodhouse, the elegant
Renaissance royal palace in Edinburgh.
The Roman Catholic rites conducted there
in the reign of Mary Queen of Scots were
anathema to fierce Calvinists like the Earl
of Glencairn. After Mary's defeat he
smashed all the furniture and works of
art in the chapel.*

CLAN ASSOCIATION
5441 Mockingbird Drive
Knoxville TN 37919 USA

DAVIDSON

NAME AND PLACE

The Davidsons trace their Highland
heritage to David *Dubh* of Invernahaven.

ORIGIN

The Davidsons are believed to have
originally been a branch of the Comyns.
After the destruction of the Comyns by
Robert Bruce they were led by David
Dubh into the doubtful security of
Clan Chattan.

THE CLAN

David *Dubh* was closely related through
marriage to the sixth Mackintosh Chief
of Clan Chattan and his people were
welcomed by William, seventh of
Mackintosh. The favour shown to the
Davidsons appears to have been partly
responsible for the disastrous feuds
in which they became involved, in
particular with the MacPhersons,
another sept of Clan Chattan.

According to one old tradition the
Camerons occupied Mackintosh lands in
Lochaber for which they were dilatory
in the matter of rent. The Mackintoshes
used to make good this failure by
robbing the Camerons' cattle, and in
1370 the infuriated Camerons marched
into Clan Chattan territory. The Chief of
Mackintosh sent out the fiery cross and
the MacPhersons and Davidsons were

among those who at once responded. An argument broke out between Davidson of Invernahaven and Cluny MacPherson over who should have the honour of leading the right wing. As the Camerons were advancing, this dispute had to be cut short and Mackintosh precipitately opted for Davidson. As a result the MacPhersons withdrew, and in the ensuing battle the Davidsons were badly mauled. In the end the MacPhersons were provoked into joining in the battle (some say by a trick) and they defeated the Camerons, though too late to save the Davidsons.

A generation later the famous conflict known as the Battle of the Clans (1396) was staged in Perth, watched by King Robert III (royal policy was to let the Highlanders, whom the king was unable to control, kill as many of each other as possible). It is usually assumed that the combatants were the MacPhersons and the Davidsons. Sir Iain Moncreiffe said the Cummings were the more likely opponents, but in view of the Davidsons' former associations, this may come to the same thing. In any case, others no doubt took part, especially as the Davidsons must presumably have still been sadly depleted as a result of the battle with the Camerons. It is said that only one out of 30 Davidsons survived the

ABOVE *Tulloch Castle near Dingwall on the Cromarty Firth, Easter Ross, for several generations the seat of the chiefs of Davidson.*

combat. He escaped by jumping into the River Tay.

Later the chiefship was held for many years by the Davidsons of Tulloch. At the beginning of the 19th century Alexander Davidson of Davidson married a Miss Bayne of Tulloch, near Dingwall in Easter Ross, and bought the estates from his wife's father.

CLAN ASSOCIATION
6551 Fiji Drive, Flowery Branch, GA 30542, USA

DOUGLAS

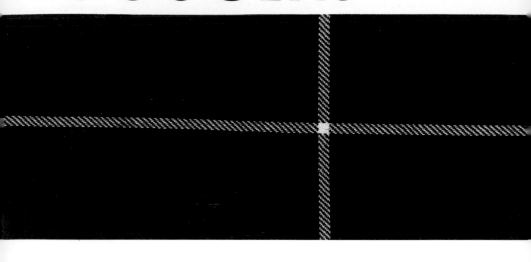

NAME AND PLACE

In Gaelic, Douglas means 'Black water'. The name derives from the dale just south of Lanark.

ORIGIN

William of Douglas held land on Douglas Water in the late 12th century. He was the grandfather of the founder of the Mortons and great-grandfather of the man who in the 14th century created the fortunes of the mighty Douglas families.

This man was 'the Good Sir James' (1286–1330), who stands with William Wallace and Bruce among the heroes of the Scottish wars of independence. He was said to have been an open man who preferred the lark's song to the mouse's squeak, yet he was a bold and cunning warrior, who captured Roxburgh by disguising his men as oxen, and he certainly showed no revulsion to squeaks when recapturing Castle Douglas (Scott's *Castle Dangerous*) from the English. At Bannockburn he commanded the left wing and thereafter led many raids into England, on one occasion almost capturing Edward I. He was the first to be called (by the English) the Black Douglas. He died fighting in Spain on his way to the Holy Land where he was taking the Bruce's heart in fulfilment of a deathbed promise.

BELOW *The red ruins of Tantallon stand high on a cliff overlooking the Firth of Forth. The surviving section of the massive curtain wall is sufficient to convey the great strength of the stronghold of the Red Douglas earls of Angus.*

Sir James's son and his brother Sir Archibald (regent for the young King David II) died fighting the English at Halidon Hill in 1333. Sir Archibald's son inherited and was created Earl of Douglas in 1358. By marriage he gained the earldom of Mar, and by the Countess of Angus he had a son, George, later first Earl of Angus. The second Earl of Douglas and Mar married a daughter of King Robert II and was killed fighting the Percys at Otterburn in 1388, a battle fought by moonlight and celebrated in both Scottish and English ballad ('Chevy Chase'). He left no legitimate heir, but his natural sons William and Archibald were the ancestors of the Douglas families of Drumlanrigg and of Craven.

The earldom of Douglas reverted to Archibald the Grim, a bastard son of 'the Good Sir James'. He married the heiress of Bothwell, thus expanding his estates further, and in the intervals between fighting the English managed to impose a degree of stability and justice in the Borders, governing from his castle of Threaves in Galloway. The Black Douglas's power was considerably greater than the Crown's under the ineffective King Robert III, and Douglas was able to marry his daughter to the heir to the throne.

His son, the fourth Earl of Douglas, has gone down in history as the Tyneman (loser). As a warrior he was sometimes victorious – his campaigns in France against the English earned him the duchy of Touraine – but in 1402 he was caught by the Percys and, the next year, fighting with the rebellious Percys at Shrewsbury, he was caught by Henry IV. He was killed in battle at Verneuil (1424).

The enemies of the Douglases were gathering strength, and soon after the death of the fifth earl in 1439 his two sons, both under seventeen, were judicially murdered in Edinburgh.

The power of the Black Douglases was diminished but not annihilated. The Douglas estates passed to the seventh earl, a younger son of the third earl who was also Earl of Avondale, and under his son and successor the family's standing was largely restored. William, the eighth earl, retained Galloway by marrying his cousin, 'the Fair Maid of Galloway', and gained favour with King James II (which enabled him to exact revenge on the chief murderer of his young kinsmen in 1440). However, this happy relationship did not last long. The king desired Douglas to withdraw from an alliance with certain other nobles that he had recently joined (such alliances were the bane of royal government) and invited him to discuss the matter, under a safe conduct, at Stirling in 1452. When Douglas refused to withdraw from the alliance, the king himself stabbed him, his courtiers finished him off, and his body was flung from the battlements.

There was little choice for the ninth earl, the last of the Black Douglases, except rebellion. After a splendid gesture of protest (he rode through Stirling with the king's safe conduct dragging in the dirt behind his horse) he was eventually forced to fly to England in 1453. The Douglas estates were forfeit and the earldom extinguished.

An extraordinary transformation then took place. The brothers of the last Black Douglas were defeated in a battle in Eskdale by the fourth earl of Angus, George Douglas. He was the leader of the Red Douglases, as they were known in distinction (allegedly due to hair colour) from their distant kinsmen. He was a great-grandson of the first Earl of Douglas and in the subsequent division of the Black Douglas's estates gained the lordship of Douglas.

To a considerable extent the Red Douglases came to occupy the space left by the extinction of the Black Douglases.

ABOVE *Scene from the myth of Aeneas.
Virgil's great work, the* Aeneid, *was first
translated into English by a younger son of
the 5th Earl of Angus.*

The fifth Earl of Angus (d. c. 1514) plotted against King James III and later became guardian of the young King James IV and Lord Chancellor of Scotland. He was known as 'Bell-the-cat', from his alleged remark when a group of nobles, dissatisfied with James III, plotted to get rid of the king's favourites. Someone mentioned the mice which hung a bell around the cat's neck as a warning. 'I will bell the cat', said Angus, and took the lead in hanging several of the king's favourites from the bridge at Lauder. He later survived Flodden (1513), where two of his sons died. A third son was Gavain Douglas (d. 1522), bishop and poet, the first man to translate a great classical poem (the *Aeneid*) into English, and the author of poetic allegories. He too was involved in the feuds of the time and died of the plague as an exile in London.

The sixth Earl of Angus married the king's widow, Queen Margaret Tudor, but had no male heir. He held supreme power in Scotland for a time in the 1520s, but was eventually forced to flee to England. His sister was burned at the stake under King James V. His daughter by Margaret Tudor married Matthew Stewart, fourth Earl of Lennox, becoming the mother of Lord Darnley and thus grandmother of James VI/I.

The earldom passed to another branch and in 1633 the Douglas title was revived when William, eleventh Earl of Angus, was created Marquess of Douglas. The third marquess was made a duke in 1703 but he died childless and his titles, including the earldom of Angus, passed to the Duke of Hamilton, while the lordship of Douglas, including the chiefship, went, after a famous lawsuit, to Lord Douglas of Douglas in the late 18th century. His 19th-century inheritors were the earls of Home.

Another branch of the Douglas family, probably descended from William of Douglas in the late 12th century, gained a small estate in East Calder in the early 14th century. As supporters of Bruce and his successors they advanced rapidly. Sir William Douglas gained the earldom of Atholl in 1342 but later exchanged it for Liddesdale. Known as 'the Flower of Chivalry' and the Knight of Liddesdale, he was killed by his distant kinsman, the first Earl of Douglas, in 1353.

His nephew, Sir James Douglas of Dalkeith, married a daughter of King James I and became Earl of Morton in 1458. The fourth Earl of Morton (died 1581) is the best known of this long line. He was implicated in the murders of both Rizzio and Darnley (respectively favourite and husband of Mary Queen of Scots) and was an unpopular regent during the minority of James VI, who had him executed at the first opportunity. Several later earls played prominent and less sinister parts in Scottish history.

CLAN ASSOCIATION

701 Montgomery Highway, Suite 209, Birmingham, AL 35216-1833, USA

DOUGLAS OF DRUMLANRIG

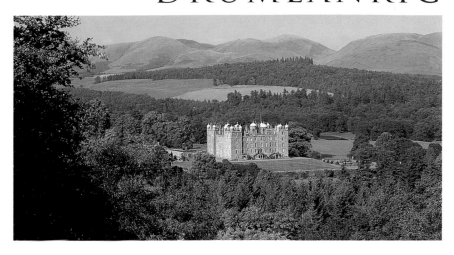

NAME AND PLACE

The family takes its name from the barony of Drumlanrig.

ORIGIN

William, the first Douglas of Drumlanrig, was an illegitimate son of the second Earl of Douglas, who bestowed the barony upon him.

THE FAMILY

The ramifications of the Douglas family, even if confined simply to the major branches, are enormous, and history seems to have conspired to ensure there was always a Douglas near the centre of events. After the Black Douglases came the Red Douglases of Angus, after them the earls of Morton and finally the Douglases of Drumlanrig.

As active supporters of the Stewart dynasty the Douglases of Drumlanrig reaped rewards in the reign of Charles I, who made Sir William Douglas of Drumlanrig a viscount and then, in 1633, Earl of Queensberry. His grandson, also William (1637–95), held high posts in Scotland and his earldom was raised to a marquessate and then to a dukedom.

His son James, the second Duke of Queensberry, followed in his fathers footsteps but, by error rather than design, became implemented in the plotting of the devious Simon Fraser, Lord Lovat. He extricated himself successfully from this embarrassment and was largely responsible, in his role as a commissioner to the Scottish parliament, for securing passage of the Act of Union (1707), by a judicious combination of diplomacy, bullying and bribes.

The third duke married the witty and fashionable Catherine Hyde but had no direct heirs and was succeeded by his cousin, the fourth Duke of Queensberry ('Old Q', 1724–1810), a well-known character and patron of horse racing, who was mocked by Burns among others. On his death the title passed to the Duke of Buccleuch. The marquessate passed to Sir Charles Douglas of Kelhead, whose descendants included the egregious eighth marquess, regulator of boxing and father of Oscar Wilde's lover Lord Alfred Douglas. From Archibald the Grim and the Knight of Liddesdale it seems a long, long way to Lord Alfred.

ABOVE *Drumlanrig Castle, Nithsdale, built at great expense in the seventeenth century for the first Duke of Queensbury.*

DRUMMOND

NAME AND PLACE

Sir Malcolm de Drymen, or Drummond, took his name from Drymen in Stirlingshire. He was a loyal adherent of Bruce, who granted him lands in Perthshire.

ORIGIN

The ancestry of the Drummonds can be traced, speculatively, much farther back, to the Celtic earls of Menteith and Lennox in the early 13th century.

THE CLAN

It is said that a major contribution to Bruce's victory at Bannockburn was an anti-cavalry device known as caltrops, four-angled prongs which always alight with one point sticking up. This was the invention of Sir Malcolm. His successor, Sir John Drummond, *An Drumanach Mór* (the Great Man of Drymen) as the chiefs of Drummond are called, having prospered in Bruce's train, married in 1345 the heiress of Stobhall. Both his sister and his daughter were married to kings of Scots, the latter becoming mother of James I.

The Drummonds have included many beautiful women; at least, several of them have attracted a royal eye, but not always with happy results. Margaret Drummond, 'the diamond of delight',

daughter of the first Lord Drummond (created 1488), was adored by the susceptible young James IV. James, however, was destined to make a more useful dynastic match to Margaret Tudor and Margaret Drummond (who may have been privately married to James) disappeared from the scene. Her two sisters also died mysteriously; natural causes were not suspected.

BELOW *A view of the formal gardens from the terrace at Drummond castle, south of Crieff. The castle was originally built by the 1st or 2nd Lord Drummond, at about the end of the 15th century. Only the tower remains.*

The fourth Lord Drummond was made Earl of Perth by James VI in 1605, after he succeeded to the throne he owed to his grandfather's politic marriage.

The Drummonds also had prickly tempers, admittedly not rare among the clans, commemorated in the prayer of their neighbours, 'From the ire of the Drummonds, Good Lord deliver us.' The first Lord Drummond was imprisoned at the age of 76 for striking the Scottish herald, and one of his sons was executed for burning a number of Murrays, who were feuding with the Drummonds at the time, in a church.

By the 17th century the Drummonds had expanded greatly, establishing the cadet branches of Carnock, Meidhope and Hawthornden. William Drummond of Hawthornden (1585–1649) was a famous poet, man of letters and sage. The first Earl of Perth was head of a considerable host which contributed powerfully to the Stewart cause in the troubles of the 17th and 18th centuries.

In 1688 the fourth Earl of Perth and his brothers the Earl of Melfort, with whom he had 'ruled Scotland' under James VII, and Lord Strathallan followed their king into exile. Perth and Melfort each received dukedoms as a reward for their loyalty. In the Jacobite rising of 1715 the second duke (fifth earl) was out, commanding the Jacobite cavalry at Sheriffmuir, and 30 years later the Drummonds were out again. At Culloden the third Duke of Perth, not a strong man since a childhood accident, commanded the left wing of the Jacobite army, made up mainly of exhausted and hungry MacDonalds embittered because their normal, honoured position was on the right. 'If you fight with your usual bravery', the duke declared, 'you will make the left wing a right wing!' He also promised that if they fought well he would himself assume the honourable name of MacDonald. Afterwards the duke escaped to France. His brother

ABOVE *Ben Jonson, the English playwright was a friend of the learned William Drummond of Hawthornden and visited him at Hawthornden in 1618–19, but considered his poems 'smelled too much of the schools'.*

Strathallan, mortally wounded in the battle took his last communion in whisky as no wine was to be had.

The Drummond estates were forfeit but were regained in the General Act of Restoration of 1784. The old Drummond lands passed through an heiress to the earls of Ancaster. Medieval Stobhall was restored by the seventeenth Earl of Perth and chief of Drummond, who is descended from the Strathallan killed at Culloden, and still lives there.

CLAN ASSOCIATION

67 Dublin Street, Edinburgh
EH3 6NS, Scotland

6 Bernard Lane, Methven,
MA 01844, USA

DUNBAR

NAME AND PLACE

The ruins of the old castle of Dunbar in Lothian still remain above the harbour.

ORIGIN

In the 11th century Cospatrick, the Celtic Earl of Northumberland, was deprived of his earldom by William the Conqueror and fled to Scotland, where he was granted lands in East Lothian, including Dunbar, by Malcolm III *Ceann Mór*, but Dunbars were to be found at an early date in many other parts of Scotland, in particular in Moray.

THE CLAN

Since Cospatrick was the son of King Duncan I's daughter, the king of Scots was his first cousin. His descendants acquired land elsewhere, in England as well as Scotland, but the seat of the earls of Dunbar remained at Dunbar Castle. The eighth earl, Patrick, was one of the numerous claimants to the Scottish crown in the 1290s, though not perhaps a very serious one. His son, the ninth earl, was for a time hostile to Bruce, and after Bannockburn he received Edward II at Dunbar and assisted his withdrawal to England. However, he came around later: he was one of the signatories of the Declaration of Arbroath (1320), the famous address to the Pope in support of

BELOW *The ruins of the old castle, the former seat of the earls of Dunbar where the Countess, 'Black Agnes', held out for months against an English siege in 1377, still stand above the harbour at Dunbar.*

Bruce and Scottish independence, and he married a daughter of Bruce's friend Thomas Randolph, Earl of Moray.

This lady was the famous 'Black Agnes' of Dunbar, 'that brawling boisterous Scottish wench' as the English balladeer called her, who in the earl's absence held the castle for several months against a besieging English army in 1337. 'Black Agnes' also became Countess of Moray in her own right, but she outlived her children and the estates of Dunbar and Moray both went ultimately to the children of her sister Isobel, who had also married a Dunbar. This era marks the beginning of the Dunbars as a Highland clan.

The earldom of Dunbar was lost in 1435 when James I, regarding it as undesirably powerful, annexed it, but in Moray the Dunbars prospered, in spite of an unremitting feud with their neighbours the Inneses. The boundary between their territories was set at the cairn of Kilbuick, between Forres and Elgin: no Innes was supposed to be seen west of that point, no Dunbar east of it. The Dunbars of Westfield held the hereditary office of sheriff of Moray until it was sold to the Stewart Earl of Moray in the 19th century.

Many other Dunbar cadet branches were founded, as distantly spread as Hempriggs in Caithness and Mochrum in Galloway. The latter family included Gavin Dunbar, who was Archbishop of Glasgow and Lord Chancellor of Scotland in the reign of James V. Another Gavin Dunbar, Bishop of Aberdeen in the 16th century, was a member of the Westfield family and uncle of yet another Gavin, tutor to the young James V.

The most famous bearer of the name Dunbar, William Dunbar the poet (d. c. 1515), was of obscure origin, though probably born in or near Dunbar itself. A Franciscan friar, he travelled widely in Britain and France and was a member of the embassy which negotiated

ABOVE *Gavin Dunbar (?1455–1532), Bishop of Aberdeen (1518–32), was a son of Sir Alexander Dunbar of Westfield. He did much to repair the cathedral of St Machair, but the church fell into ruin after 1560. It was restored in the 19th century, and Bishop Dunbar's damaged effigy is still to be found there.*

the marriage of King James IV to Margaret Tudor in 1501. His first major poem, *The Thrissil and the Rois*, is an allegory on the theme of that marriage. His literary reputation today stands very high, and many would say he comes close to Burns as Scotland's greatest poet.

CLAN ASSOCIATION
224 Riverview Road, Townsend,
TN 37882, USA

DUNCAN

NAME AND PLACE

Duncan is the old Gaelic name
Dunnchadh, and *Clann Donnchaidh* is
the name of the Robertsons, who claim
descent from royal 'kindred of St
Columba' and take their name from a
chief named Duncan who led them into
battle on behalf of the Bruce at
Bannockburn.

ORIGIN

At the time of the Norse invasions some
of the relics of St Columba were taken
from Iona for safety to Dunkeld, and the
hereditary abbot of Dunkeld came from
the same royal line as St Columba
himself. There was an Abbot Duncan of
Dunkeld, who was killed in battle in 956.

THE CLAN

The 10th-century Abbot Duncan was
probably the great-grandfather of King
Duncan I (r. 1034–1040). From a
younger son of Duncan I descended great
landholders in Atholl, the country of
Clann Donnchaidh (children of Duncan).

Eventually the chief and most of the
clan were to adopt the name Robertson,
but some were called Duncanson,
Duncan, MacConachie or Donachie.

By the time surnames were becoming
common in Scotland, Duncans and
Duncansons cropped up in many places
in the south-east.

The Duncans of Lundie held land in
Forfar and Perthshire. Sir William
Duncan was an 18th-century physician
who was created a baronet in 1764 for
services to George III, but died without
an heir ten years later. The family had
been Jacobite sympathisers in the Forty-
five, but Adam Duncan (1731–1804), a
younger son of Sir Alexander Duncan of
Lundie, entered the Royal Navy in 1746
and became a distinguished admiral.
Large, immensely strong, and handsome,
by sheer personality he prevented worse
trouble during the naval mutinies of
1797, when, with one arm, he held a
mutineer over the side of the ship, saying
'Look, lads, this fellow would deprive me
of my command.' For his victory over
the Dutch at Camperdown he was
created Viscount Duncan of
Camperdown in 1800.

ELLIOT

NAME AND PLACE

It is said that some Elliots took the name from Eliot in Forfarshire, though the early form was the old English Elwold. Modern branches of the family spelt the name in various ways, those of Stobs preferring Eliott initially and Eliot today.

ORIGINS

The Elliots were a Border clan with territory around Upper Liddesdale, where they conducted banditry for centuries.

THE CLAN

The principal family early on was the Elliots of Redheugh, who often held the captaincy of Hermitage Castle, south of Hawick. One of them, forefather of the Elliots of Arkleton, fell at Flodden (*The Flowers of the Forest*, was written by Jane Elliot, sister of Sir Gilbert Elliot of Minto, in the 18th century).

The Elliots of Stobs go back to Gawain Elliot of Stobs in the late 16th century, a descendant of the Elliots of Redheugh. Since the 17th century they have been the principal cadet house. Gawain was succeeded as Laird of Stobs by Gilbert, and the earls of Minto descend from one of his sons.

The most famous of this line were George Elliot, governor of Gibraltar, who led its defence in 1779, and Gilbert

Elliot, first Earl of Minto, governor-general of India in the early 19th century.

His great grandson Gilbert, the fourth earl (1845–1914) broke his neck in a race but became governor-general of Canada, then Viceroy of India in 1905.

The seat of the present earl is Minto House, in Hawick, and of the current Eliot of Stobs, clan chief, Redheugh.

CLAN ASSOCIATION

Redheugh, Newcastleton TD9 0SB, Scotland

Bradwell House, Sandbach, Cheshire CW11 9RB, England

2416 Deer Trail, Suwanee, GA 30174, USA

Elmeth Farm, RR1, Severn Bridge, Ontario, Canada

1 Wrendale Drive, Donvale, Victoria 3111, Australia

Jamarenne, New Zealand Post, Mayfield, Canterbury, New Zealand

7 Orchid Place, 43 7th Street, Lower Houghton 2196, South Africa

ERSKINE

NAME AND PLACE

The name is derived from the barony of Erskine in Renfrewshire.

ORIGIN

The first recorded landholder in that region is Henry de Erskine, in the reign of King Alexander II (r. 1214–49).

THE FAMILY

The Erskines were more of a dynasty than an clan, and their name is bound up with the long and complicated history of the earldom of Mar.

Sir Robert Erskine of that ilk (died 1385) profited from the success of Bruce and was for some time Chamberlain of Scotland. He gained the lands of Alloa, north of the Forth, and two of his sons were dynastic progenitors. From Thomas, the elder, who married Lady Elyne of Mar, came the Erskines of Dun (through a younger son), and from Malcolm came the Erskines of Kinnoul.

Robert, son of Thomas, the first Lord Erskine, claimed the earldom of Mar, which derived from an ancient Pictish title and had never been conferred by a king of Scots, but the confiscation of the Alloa estates forced him to withdraw. The title was not confirmed to the Erskines until the reign of Mary, who restored it and created a new earldom of Mar, so that the beneficiary, the sixth Lord Erskine, became both eighteenth and first Earl of Mar. The reason for this curious contrivance was presumably to secure the earldom against a possible future cancellation of Mary's restoration.

It shows in what great affection the Erskines were held by the Stewart dynasty. This affection dated from the appointment of the fifth Lord Erskine as guardian to James V after his father (and Lord Erskine's father also) had been killed at Flodden. A position of responsibility in relation to a royal infant

BELOW *Braemar was built by John Erskine, earl of Mar, as a combination hunting lodge and fortress. It subsequently fell to the Farquharsons, who hold it today, but it was reconstructed as a government fortress in the 18th century.*

can lead to future benefit or to future disaster, but in this case Lord Erskine performed so well that James V later put him in charge of the future Mary Queen of Scots and he accompanied here when she was sent to France to escape the unwanted attentions of the English. The association continued into the next generation when Mary's infant son, the future James VI, was given into the care of Lord Erskine's son the Earl of Mar, who carried the baby at the coronation in 1567. He later became regent and, after his death in 1572, his wife remained in charge of the young king. She later received James's son into her care – the fourth successive generation of Scottish royal heirs under Erskine guardianship.

The Regent Mar's grandson, Lord Treasurer of Scotland under James VI, was the builder of Braemar Castle on Deeside and from his sons are descended other important Erskine families who became in course of time earls of Rosslyn and earls of Buchan.

The sixth earl (1675-1732), still maintaining the close alliance of his family with the Stewart dynasty, was the Jacobite commander-in-chief during the rising of 1715, although he had previously been an advocate of the Union (1707) and a Scottish Secretary of State under Queen Anne. Having been deprived of office under George I he returned secretly to Scotland, where he told the Highland chiefs the Union had been a mistake, that he now favoured Scottish independence, and raised the banner of the Jacobites at Braemar. But Lord Mar, 'Bobbing John' as he was called, was not a great general and lingered at Perth while his opponents, at first outnumbered, gathered strength. His only serious sortie resulted in the battle of Sheriffmuir which, if not an actual defeat, was certainly no glorious victory. Eventually, Mar withdrew to France along with 'Old Mr Melancholy', James Edward Stewart. Later he changed sides again, accepting a pension from George I and abandoning Jacobite court.

He was made a duke in the Jacobite peerage but naturally forfeited his earldom and his attainder was not reversed for over a hundred years. His brother James Erskine, Lord Grange (1679–1754) a judge and MP, is remembered for a famous scandal involving his wife, 'a woman of disorderly intellect' whom he had abducted in 1732 and kept secretly in the Hebrides while her 'funeral' was staged in Edinburgh.

The two earldoms of Mar are today separately held.

FARQUHARSON

NAME AND PLACE

The Farquharsons, 'the dear ones', were members of the Clan Chattan confederation, although latterly they were an independent clan. The Gaelic name of the Farquharson chief is *Mac Fhionnlaigh*, after Finlay, a royal standard-bearer at the battle of Pinkie (where he was killed) in 1547.

ORIGIN

The Farquharsons were apparently descended from Farquhar, son of Shaw of Rothiemurchus, and were thus a branch of the Shaws.

THE CLAN

A harp now in the Edinburgh National Museum of Antiquities is said to have been given to Finlay *Mór*'s widow by Mary Queen of Scots (it is a rare survival of the old Celtic harps that predominated before the rise of the pipes).

The Farquharsons acquired Invercauld on upper Deeside by the marriage of Donald, father of Finlay, to the heiress Isobel Stewart. They produced a number of cadet branches (including those of Monaltrie, Inverey, Whitehouse and Finzean), several descended from Donald Farquharson, grandson of Finlay. The Farquharson lands were held from the earl of Mar, though during the 17th

BELOW *The young Prince Charles Edward, 'the Young Pretender'. The rising of 1745 divided families – in the Farquharsons' case husband and wife – though sympathies were sometimes less clear-cut than war made them seem.*

century they obtained royal charters for
some of them. In that troubled period Sir
Robert Farquarson of Invercauld, an
Aberdeen merchant, greatly improved the
family fortunes by his commercial and
political activities, and later the
Farquharsons acquired the former seat of
the earls of Mar, Braemar Castle which,
ironically, had been largely ruined by a
Farquharson less than 50 years earlier.
The Farquharsons of Inverey fought
under Montrose and at the battle of
Worcester in 1651. Bonnie Dundee had
Farquharsons among his forces in 1689,
including John Farquharson of Inverey,
'the Black Colonel' celebrated in ballad,
and the burner of Braemar. In the 1715
Jacobite rising John Farquharson of
Invercauld, with 140 men, fought in the
Clan Chattan regiment. He was taken
prisoner at Preston, but was able to
convince the government that he had
become involved in the rebellion
unwillingly as vassal of the Earl of Mar.

His daughter 'Colonel Anne' married
the Mackintosh and, though only 20,
played a leading part in raising Clan
Chattan for Prince Charles in 1745
in the absence of her husband, who
commanded a company of government
militia and was taken prisoner. There
was a legend current in the army that
she had led her husband's men in person
at the battle of Culloden. There were 300
Farquharsons fighting for the Jacobite
cause at Culloden, led by Francis
Farquharson of Monaltrie, 'Baron Ban',
but James Farquharson of Invercauld
fought on the government side.
Farquharson of Balmoral was among the
Jacobites and although Monaltrie was
later returned to its former owner,
Balmoral was forfeited permanently. It
was returned to the Gordons who later
sold it to Queen Victoria.

Braemar Castle is still the
headquarters of the Farquharsons.

ABOVE *An old highland harp which
tradition connects with Mary Queen of
Scots. At one time it belonged to the
Farquharsons, but is now in the National
Museum of Antiquities in Edinburgh.*

CLAN ASSOCIATION

Pig's Eye Cottage, 1510 Dora Lane, St
Paul, MN 55106, USA

607 Bridge Inn Road, Mernda, Victoria
3754, Australia

FERGUSSON

NAME AND PLACE

The best-known family is that of
Fergusson of Kilkerran, descendants
of Fergus, son of Fergus, who was
granted lands in Ayrshire by King
Robert Bruce in the early 14th century.

ORIGIN

It is doubtful whether all 'sons of Fergus'
are in fact descended from a single
ancestor, still less the royal Fergus who
divided his inheritance with his two
brothers in Dalriada about 500. The
name occurs in widely scattered locations
in Scotland at an early date.

THE CLAN

Although there was a clannish sympathy
between families of that name, the
Fergussons were not a clan in the full
sense of the word. In later times a
number of families regarded Fergusson
of Kilkerran as their chief. The later Sir
James Fergusson, Keeper of the Records
of Scotland and a famous scholar and
historian, was so regarded by Fergussons
everywhere. Sir Bernard Fergusson, the
guerrilla leader of the Chindits in Burma
during the Second World War, was his
brother. The baronetcy of Kilkerran dates
from 1703.

Among the other families were the
Fergussons of Dunfallandy in Atholl,

BELOW *The memorial to the poet Robert
Fergusson, in Canongate churchyard,
Edinburgh. His death at 25 was a sad blow
for Scottish literature. He had died in an
asylum and was buried in an unmarked
grave, but Robert Burns located it and
raised the momument above it.*

who acquired that estate by the old Highland device of killing the current Baron of Dunfallandy and forcibly marrying his heiress to their own heir; the Fergussons of Baldemund in Perthshire; the Kinmundy, Baddifurrow and Pitfour Fergussons of Aberdeenshire; and the Fergussons of Craigdarroch in Dumfriesshire, one of whom married the Annie Laurie of the well-known song. Fergussons said to have been connected with the Fergussons of Kilkerran held lands on Loch Fyne right up until the 19th century.

The Fergussons of Dunfallandy, who claimed descent from the princes of Galloway, were among the men of Atholl in Montrose's force during the civil war, and under the banner of Prince Charles during the Forty-five. A Captain Fergusson of HMS *Furnace* earned an evil reputation ferrying the oddly named Captain Caroline Scott around the Western Isles after Culloden in a search for the prince. He was described by a contemporary historian of the campaign as 'a fellow of very low extract, born in Aberdeenshire', and appears to have been related to the Fergussons of Pitfour. Otherwise, Fergussons have been more notable for learning and scholarship than savagery, and the name often appears among the lists of the judiciary.

Robert Fergusson (1750–74), the Scots poet, who was born in Edinburgh, was one of the leaders of the 18th-century revival of writing in the Scots vernacular. He was an important influence on Burns whom, had he lived longer, he might have rivalled. He died insane after an accidental head injury and Burns himself was responsible for erecting the monument on his grave. His contemporary Adam Ferguson (1732–1816) was Presbyterian chaplain to the Black Watch and took part, sword in hand, in their charge at the battle of Fontenoy. He lived to become professor of philosophy at Edinburgh University

ABOVE *Dr Adam Ferguson was a man of many talents. He was chaplain to the 42nd regiment at the Battle of Fontenoy, professor of first mathematics, then moral philosophy at Edinburgh as well as a member of the commission sent to negotiate with the American colonists before the outbreak of the American War of Independence.*

and a commissioner appointed to negotiate with the American colonists in 1778. His epitaph was written by his friend Sir Walter Scott.

CLAN ASSOCIATION

Kilkerran, Maybole KA19 7SE, Scotland

3061 O'Brien Drive, Talahassee, FL 32308-2752, USA

151 Pine Forest Drive, Lawrenceville, GA 30245, USA

FLETCHER

NAME AND PLACE

Fletcher is a trade name, like Smith or Gow, and derives from an Old French word for feathers. A 'fletcher' was one who fitted the feathered flights to arrows, later simply an arrow-maker.

ORIGIN

In the days when bows and arrows were common weapons all the clans had their Fletchers, and at the time when surnames were becoming common in Scotland Fletchers are found in many places. By the 17th century bows were becoming obsolete, although the Scots who fought with Gustavus Adolphus in the Thirty Years War carried them and they were occasionally used during Montrose's famous campaign.

In the 17th century, which was an era of idiosyncratic spelling, the name became understandably confused with 'Flesher', another trade name, meaning a butcher. A Fletcher today, therefore, may well be descended from a butcher rather than an arrow-maker.

THE CLAN

Around the end of the 15th century the Fletchers are to be found seeking support from the Stewarts of Appin against the MacDonalds. There were also Fletchers in Glenorchy: they claimed to be the

BELOW *William Paterson (1658–1719) is remembered for a great commercial success, the founding of the Bank of England, and a great commercial failure, in which he was associated with Andrew Fletcher – the Darien scheme. The disaster helped to persuade many Scots that union with England was commercially desirable.*

original inhabitants, predating the
Campbells, a claim expressed in the old
saying, 'Clan Fletcher raised the first
smoke to boil water in Orchy'.

The Fletchers of Glenlyon were
associated with the MacGregors, and one
of them is said to have saved the life of
Rob Roy when he was wounded in a
skirmish with government forces. The
most notable representative of this
family, however, was Archibald Fletcher,
a lawyer – 'one of the most upright men
that ever adorned the profession' – and
friend of Charles James Fox.

In the 17th and 18th centuries the
Fletchers of Innerpeffer in Angus and of
Saltoun (Salton) near Haddington in
Lothian produced a number of notable
men, of whom the most famous is the
Scottish patriot Andrew Fletcher of
Saltoun (1655–1716). In his youth
the future bishop and historian
Gilbert Burnet was minister of Saltoun
and played some part in his education.
He had a high opinion of Fletcher's
mental capacities but remarked less
favourably on his political opinions and
his somewhat volcanic temperament —
which led him to shoot a brother officer
dead, admittedly after severe
provocation, during Monmouth's
rebellion (which he supported). He was
later associated with William Paterson in
the unfortunate Darien Scheme (1690),
an attempt to establish a Scottish colony
in Panama, and became one of the most
powerful opponents of the Union of
Scotland and England. His oratory in
1703–04 almost turned the tide against
union in the Scottish parliament. His
writings, praised by the philosopher
David Hume, contain the famous remark
about a wise man who 'believed if a man
were permitted to make all the ballads,
he need not care who should make the
laws of a nation'.

His namesake and descendant, as
Lord Milton, was a judge at the time
of the Forty-five. He advocated

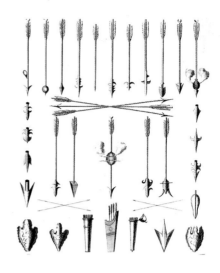

ABOVE *The Fletchers, never a substantial,
independent clan, are assumed to take their
name from the trade of arrow-maker,
although this does not seem to have been
always a specialised trade.*

colonising the Highlands with sober
Protestant southern gentry and
consigning able-bodied beggars to
permanent servitude.

FORBES

NAME AND PLACE

The name comes from the Gaelic *forba*, meaning a field or district. It was originally pronounced as two syllables (when the new pronunciation became general someone remarked that it would 'throw Lady Fettes into Fits'). Aberdeenshire is peppered with the houses and castles which belonged, or belong, to various branches of the clan.

ORIGIN

According to tradition the clan took possession of the Braes of Forbes after killing a ferocious bear which, having killed nine maidens at the well that commemorates them, had kept previous settlers at bay.

THE CLAN

Clan Forbes is traditionally connected with the Urquharts, though no one now knows how. Duncan Forbes held a charter for his lands from the king, Alexander III, in the 13th century. Sir Alexander Forbes, who married a granddaughter of King Robert III, was raised to the peerage in 1445. In the same year, however, the Gordons acquired the earldom of Huntly, a less welcome elevation for Clan Forbes. For some 300 years the Gordons were hostile and dangerous neighbours.

BELOW *King's College, Aberdeen, founded in 1494 and the oldest part of the university, one of many glories in the granite city. Patrick Forbes (1564–1635) – a descendent of the Second Lord Forbes – was first Bishop of Aberdeen and then Chancellor of the college.*

Broadly speaking the Gordon clan members adhered to the 'Right': they were Catholics, pro-Stewart and pro-Jacobite, while the Forbeses embraced the 'Left', becoming Protestants, Covenanters and Whigs. There were exceptions however, and the eighth Lord Forbes married a daughter of the Earl of Huntly. Their sons, Catholics, became friars, and the ninth Lord Forbes (died 1581) was their Protestant half-brother.

By the 17th century some decline was apparent at the centre: the tenth Lord Forbes was described as 'a naked life-renter of a small part and portion of his old estates'. But there were other prominent families, notably Forbes of Pitsligo, of Tolquhon and of Brux, with their numerous cadets, who descended from younger brothers of the first Lord Forbes. At the end of the 16th century Lord Forbes had been able to provide a thousand men for the king's service, and he could raise nearly as many in 1628 for service in the Thirty Years War.

Clan Forbes played a notable part in the Jacobite risings, with representatives on both sides. Alexander Forbes, fourth of Pitsligo (1678–1762) was 'out' in the Fifteen, and it says much for clan loyalty that he was able to hide out in the Forbes country for years after the Forty-five, despite the contrary loyalties of most of his fellow-clansmen.

The Rev. Robert Forbes of Leith made an invaluable collection of stories of the Forty-five, published as *The Lyon in Mourning*. But the greatest figure, a man in some ways the very symbol of that disastrous conflict, was Duncan Forbes of Culloden (a branch of Forbes of Tolquhon), Lord President of the Court of Session and virtually the sole representative of the government in the north. He was a man of honour, good sense and sympathy, whose brave efforts to influence the government after the battle of Culloden to adopt more humane and productive policies were

ABOVE *The name Forbes is derived from the Gaelic word* forba, *meaning a field or district.*

almost totally ignored. The loutish Duke of Cumberland referred to him as 'that old woman'.

The present Lord Forbes, the premier baron in the Scottish peerage, still retains part of the ancestral lands on Donside.

CLAN ASSOCIATION
Castle Forbes, Alford AB33 8BL, England

P O Box 1118, Alexandria, VA 22313, USA

FRASER

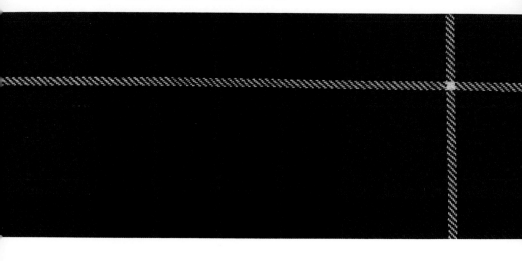

NAME AND PLACE

The flowers of strawberries (French *fraises*) appear on the Fraser coat of arms, but this is probably just a heraldic pun. The origin of the name is certainly French (early forms include de Fresel and de Frisselle) and possibly derives from Freselière in Anjou. The heartland of the Frasers of Lovat was the districts on either side of Loch Ness.

ORIGIN

The first known Simon Fraser, who was probably a descendant of the Frezels of Anjou, held lands in Keith, East Lothian, in 1160.

THE CLAN

The Frasers are genealogically somewhat complicated. By no means all Scots of that name belonged to the Highland clan, and the lands and families of the Frasers were spread over a wide area.

The original estates soon passed to another family, while the Frasers acquired Tweeddale and Oliver Castle through marriage.

A famous member of this family was the Scottish patriot, Sir Simon Fraser, who fought with Wallace and Bruce. He is justly celebrated for defeating the English in three separate engagements on one day at Rosslyn in 1302, but he was

BELOW *The late Sir Hugh Fraser, Conservative politician and businessman, younger brother of the 22nd Lord Lovat and husband of Lady Antonia Fraser, the popular historian.*

eventually captured and suffered the
barbaric type of execution which the
English had also inflicted on Wallace.
His luckier contemporary Sir Alexander
Fraser fought at Bannockburn, married
Bruce's sister and became Chamberlain of
Scotland. His grandson, also Alexander,
married a daughter of the Earl of Ross
and so acquired the lands of Philorth in
Buchan, plus the castle of Cairnburgh.
Fraserburgh was founded by his
descendants as a rival port to Aberdeen,
and the ninth Fraser of Philorth married
the heiress of Lord Saltoun, a title since
borne by the Fraser chiefs.

For a time the chiefship was in dispute
between the Frasers of Philorth and
another branch, which also sprang from
Tweeddale, the Frasers of Muchal-in-
Mar. Their seat, Castle Fraser, was built
in the early 17th century by Andrew
Fraser, who was created Lord Fraser in
the reign of Charles II. The peerage
expired with the fourth Lord Fraser, who
died in 1716 while on the run as a result
of his participation in the 1715 rebellion.

Probably the best known Frasers are
the chiefs of the Highland clan, Fraser of
Lovat, who bear the Gaelic name *Mac
Shimi* (son of Simon).

This original Simon Fraser is assumed
to have been the patriot who fought with
Wallace. The first known chief was Hugh
Fraser, Lord of Lovat near Beauly in the
Aird in 1367, and it is certain that he
was a kinsman of Fraser of Philorth. The
Frasers subsequently acquired, mainly
through marriage, considerable territories
in Inverness and Aberdeenshire.

The Frasers took a battering in the
great clan battle against the MacDonalds
in 1544, *Blar-na-Léine*, the Battle of the
Shirts. Only five Frasers and eight
MacDonalds are said to have survived
this engagement, yet within a hundred
years the Frasers were stronger than ever
before. (See MacDonald of Clan Ranald.)

Undoubtedly the most famous – or
notorious – of the Frasers of Lovat was

ABOVE *Castle Fraser, a splendid Scots
baronial pile north-west of Aberdeen built
when military considerations were
beginning to seem less important, and
largely undamaged in the disturbances of
the 17th and 18th centuries.*

Simon, eleventh Lord Lovat (1667–1747)
who, despite being the second son of a
third son, assumed the title in 1699 after
a scandalous episode in which he forcibly
married the widow of the tenth Lord
Lovat and fled to France from a charge of
rape (the lady, though forced into bed at
the point of a dirk, her protests drowned
by the playing of bagpipes, is said to have
grown fond of him later).

The usual verdict on this remarkable
man is that the was 'a born traitor and
deceiver'. He certainly earned such a
reputation, and the double game he
constantly played is not easy to follow
nearly 300 years later (and possibly
harder at the time), but there was
perhaps more to him than his popular
image suggests. Had the Jacobites been
capable of carrying out his suggested
strategy for a rising in the Highlands,
they might have fared much better.

His manifold duplicities eventually brought him to a grisly end. Though old and sick at the time of the Forty-five, he contrived as usual to play both sides, but the government classed him with undeniable accuracy as a traitor and he was hunted down, conveyed to London on a litter and after a trial lasting a week in which he conducted his own defence, beheaded – the last peer to suffer this type of execution – in front of a huge and fascinated crowd.

His last words were a quotation from Horace. Though undoubtedly a tremendous rogue, he remains one of the most fascinating characters in the history of the Highlands.

His son, having fought on the Jacobite side at his father's insistence (old Simon told Forbes of Culloden a different story), was pardoned, and later raised the Fraser Highlanders in the service of George II. Their service in North America in the Seven Years War goes some way to explain the frequent occurrence of the name in Canada (Simon Fraser University in British Columbia is named after one of them).

The line became extinct in 1803 and the chiefship eventually passed to the

ABOVE *Beaufort Castle in Ross-shire is now home to the Lovat lords. The ruins of Beauly Priory, where many of their forbears are buried, lie nearby.*

Frasers of Strichen, a family which has produced many distinguished men, including the sixteenth Lord Lovat, who raised the Lovat Scouts in the Boer War, Brigadier Lord Lovat, twenty-second *Mac Shimi*, the dashing commando leader who is said to have landed in France on D-Day wearing a white polo-neck sweater and preceded by his piper, and his brother, Hugh Fraser, the politician and businessman.

Cairnburgh remains the seat of the Fraser chiefs to this day.

CLAN ASSOCIATION

47 Councillor's Walk, Forres IV36 0HA, Scotland

P O Box 1526, Chico, CA 95927, USA

71 Charles Street E, #1101, Toronto, Ontario, M4Y 2T3, Canada

122/61 Bakers Lane, Erskine Park, NSW 2529, Australia

GALBRAITH

NAME AND PLACE

The name comes from Gaelic words meaning 'Foreigner-Briton', and the Galbraiths came from the kingdom of Strathclyde, which did not become part of Scotland until 1124. Inchgalbraith (Island of the Foreigner-Briton) in Loch Lomond was once their stronghold.

ORIGIN

The first recorded Galbraith chief appears in the 12th century. His house was of noble status, possibly connected with the old royal house of Strathclyde, for he married a daughter of the Earl of Lennox. The fortunes of these two houses remained intimately connected.

THE CLAN

The fourth chief, Sir William Galbraith, was powerful enough to make himself one of the co-regents of the kingdom in 1255. His son Sir Arthur (a favourite name among the Galbraiths), married a daughter of 'the Good Sir James' Douglas and fought for Bruce. He was possibly the originator of the Galbraiths of Culcreuch in Strathendrick, to whom the chiefship later passed.

When James I set about diminishing overmighty subjects, the Galbraiths supported the Earl of Lennox. They were reported to have been involved in the sack of Dumbarton in 1425. The twelfth chief, Thomas Galbraith of Culcreuch, was, with Lennox, opposed to the conspirators of 1488 but, after the death of James III, was captured and hanged. Similarly the fourteenth chief, Sir Andrew, was involved with Lennox in the attempt to rescue the young King James V from the Douglases in 1526.

The Galbraiths were in the thick of things throughout the 16th century, some of their activities, like those of others, dishonourable. The sixteenth chief, Sir James, administered the Lennox estates in a capable and responsible manner during the absence of the duke, Esmé Stewart, but his successor Sir Robert, was a thorough bandit whose misdeeds included the ambush and attempted murder of his brother-in-law, to whom he owed money. He was forced to surrender Culcreuch Caste and fled to Ireland, where he died. The Galbraiths thereafter faded from the scene.

CLAN ASSOCIATION

Culcreuch Castle, Fintry G63 0LW, Scotland

4704 Alesia Road, Millers, MD 21107, USA

GORDON OF HUNTLY

NAME AND PLACE

Speculation on the origins of the Gordons run rife. One of the wilder suggestions is that the name derives from Gordium, from where it was brought back by one of the Crusaders! There seems little reason to doubt that it really derives from the district in Berwickshire where the family held land in the 12th century.

ORIGINS

However, at some early time the Gordons were genealogically linked with the Swintons, neighbours and rivals in the Middle Ages, who had exactly the same coat of arms, and there is evidence of a link with a prominent 13th-century English family named Gurdon (the Swintons also held land in England), giving the Gordons a possible Anglo-Norman provenance.

Sir Adam, Lord of Gordon during the wars of independence, originally supported the Red Comyn who was killed by Bruce in 1306, and thereafter he was inclined to support the English. However, after the death of Edward I of England in 1307 less sensible commanders allowed their men to harry the Gordon lands in the Borders and thus effectively alienated a useful ally. From 1313 Gordon became a loyal supporter

BELOW *Findlater Castle, Banff. The fourth Earl of Huntly persuaded the Ogilvie to leave him his lands by pretending that the Ogilvie's son was planning to lock him away and drive him insane. Huntly married the Ogilvie's widow and gained the rest of the property, but after his own death two years later the property was returned to the Ogilvies.*

of Bruce, and he was one of those who carried the Declaration of Arbroath to the Pope in 1320.

His service to Robert Bruce brought the Gordons to the north, to Strathbogie in Aberdeenshire. Their fortunes expanded rapidly. On the extinction of the senior male line in 1402 the heiress Elizabeth Gordon married Alexander Seton of that ilk and their son became the first Early of Huntly. The earldom passed to the first earl's second son, who took the name of Gordon.

In their efforts to bring the Highlands under control the early Stewart kings of Scots were compelled to employ local agents or to set clan against clan. Their agents in the west were the Campbell earls of Argyll, and in the east the Gordon earls of Huntly. The Gordons, like the Campbells, were able to exploit their vice-regal authority to further their own interests and to create – as long as the authority of the Crown was weak – their own 'empire' in the north-east.

Their greatest success was acquiring the earldom of Sutherland in 1514 following the destruction of so many of Scotland's leaders at Flodden. Their attempt to wrest Findlater away from the Ogilvies by a plot of truly baroque proportions was ultimately unsuccessful, and they were defeated in battle at Corrichie in 1562, the fourth Earl of Huntly, the most powerful nobleman in Scotland but fat and asthmatic, suffering a fatal stroke in the field.

Under King James VI the power of the Gordons threatened to spread still further, as the Earl of Huntly, elevated in 1599 to a marquessate, was granted a royal commission to extend his operations into the Western Isles, with the object of extirpating 'the hole Clan Donald in the North'. However, there were problems over the terms on which the expedition should be undertaken, and the king, no doubt realising the stupidity of the plan, changed his mind, while the

ABOVE *Huntly Castle, home of the Gordons, today a total ruin yet still appropriately conveying more the air of a Renaissance palace (built in the late 15th century) than a stern, defensive fortress.*

Catholic Huntly's personal authority was jeopardised by his excommunication by the Kirk.

The first marquess had a colourful existence: not many men have been elevated in noble rank within a few years of fleeing abroad to escape a charge of treason. His private wars against Grants, Mackintoshes, Stewarts and others included the murder of the Bonnie Earl of Moray, commemorated in ballad.

The Gordons gained overlordship of the Mackay territory of Strathnaver, from which they prepared an (unsuccessful) assault on the earldom of Caithness, but in the 17th century the power of Huntly, 'the Cock of the North', was in decline. The second marquess, though brought up in England as a Protestant, met the humiliating fate of execution at the hands of the Covenanters in 1649.

GORDON OF HUNTLY
88–89

GORDON

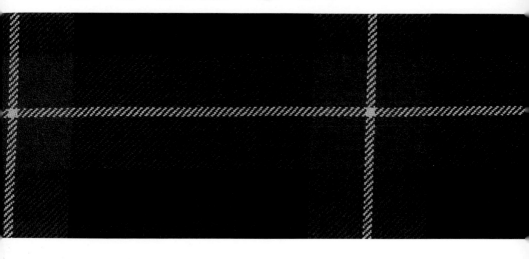

THE CLAN

It has often been said that the Gordons were never a clan, since the relationship between lord and men was strictly a feudal one. Nevertheless, the Gordons for a long period dominated much of the north-east. There were a number of families in that region called Gordon who did not belong to what became the house of Huntly, though most could probably claim Sir Adam of Gordon as an ancestor (genealogists have recorded over 150 main branches of the Gordons).

The estate of Haddo was acquired by the Gordons of Methlic in 1533. Although they were comparatively junior in genealogical terms, this family was to prove perhaps the most eminent. The Gordons of Haddo were also remarkable for longevity. One of them obtained royal charters for his lands from Kings James III, IV and V, whose reigns covered a period of over 80 years. The fifth Gordon of Haddo fought for King Charles I, was captured in 1643, imprisoned in 'Haddo's Hole' in St Giles's Cathedral in Edinburgh, and later executed.

The family's properties were restored in 1660 and in 1682 Sir George Gordon of Haddo was created Earl of Aberdeen. The beautiful Haddo House was built in the 18th century and the estate was greatly embellished by the fourth earl,

BELOW *Haddo House, north of Aberdeen, basically the work of William Adam (father of the more famous Robert), begun in the 1730s with later additions generally faithful to Adam's simple but elegant style. The interior is especially fine.*

who was prime minister at the time of the Crimean War. The seventh earl and first marquess was governor-general of Canada in the 1890s.

Many other titles are associated with various branches of the Gordons. The first Viscount Kenmure, created 1633, was Sir John Gordon, of the Gordons of Kirkcudbright, who traced their descent from the original Berwickshire family. He married a sister of the Marquess of Argyll and was a keen Covenanter, but the sixth viscount adhered to the Jacobite cause: he was captured at Preston and executed in 1716.

The dukedom of Gordon was created for the fourth Marquess of Huntly by Charles II. The title became extinct in 1836 (it was later recreated for the Duke of Richmond when he inherited the Huntly estates), but the Marquessate of Huntly passed to the Earl of Aboyne, a direct descendant of the first marquess.

This line has since held the chiefship and Aboyne Castle, though not the large estates that once went with it. Huntly Castle is today a magnificent ruin. Gordon Castle itself, the Bog o'Gight as it was once called, which was the principal seat of the marquesses of Huntly, is also largely ruined, though what remains is well preserved. Haddo House, designed by Robert Adam, is now owned by the National Trust for Scotland.

ABOVE *George Hamilton Gordon, 4th earl of Aberdeen (1784–1860) was a prominent British politician. Undogmatic if not unprincipled, in 1852 he was seen as the ideal leader of the coalition government, but his popularity as prime minister declined during the mismanaged Crimean War, and he resigned in 1855.*

CLAN ASSOCIATION
Harlaw House, Harlaw Hill, Prestonpans
EH32 9AG, Scotland

6499 Will Dupree Lane, Acworth,
GA 30102, USA

GOW

The name Gow is a corruption of the
Gaelic *gobha*, meaning a smith, or
armourer. The Gaelic name is *Mac a'*
Ghobhainn, or MacGowan. The place
name Galnagowan, found throughout
the Highlands, marks the site of a former
smithy, and some Gows and MacGowans
who moved to the south appear to have
changed their name to Smith. Another
name connected with their trade is
MacEachern, and MacEacherns were
smiths to the MacDonalds and others.

ORIGINS

Gows and MacGowans, as smiths, were
to be found among many clans, though
they are particularly associated with
Clan Chattan and the MacPhersons.
According to MacPherson historians the
ancestor of the Gows was a younger son
of a captain of Clan Chattan.

THE CLAN

Obviously the Gows were never a clan,
nor a great family, since there was never
a common ancestor of the descendants of
blacksmiths.

An old tale relates how at the famous
clan battle on the North Inch at Perth in
1396 one side found itself a man short
and therefore hired *an Gobha Crom* (a
crooked smith) who swiftly despatched

his opponent but then ceased to take any further part in the battle until he was promised additional remuneration. This character, Hal o' the Wynd, was immortalised by Scott in *The Fair Maid of Perth*, but the suggestion that he was the ancestor of the Gows is unfounded.

The most famous bearer of this name in the Highlands was the musician Niel Gow (1727–1807), 'the Prince of Scottish fiddlers'. He was born (and died) at Inver, near Dunkeld, and began to play the violin before he was 10 years old. Someone took him along to Dunkeld House, the Duke of Atholl became his patron and he was taken up by the nobility. He wrote many popular reels and strathspeys and was succeeded by his son Nathaniel (1766–1831).

Taught by his father and, later, more formally at Edinburgh, Nathaniel Gow was something of a fashionable band leader when the 'Celtic Revival' was in full swing. He played at private parties for the Prince Regent as well as at the fashionable balls at Almacks, where London society ladies delighted to dance to Scottish country music. His compositions, together with those of his father, run to half a dozen published volumes.

Niel Gow's portrait was painted several times by Raeburn (according to Sir Iain Moncreiffe of that ilk, popular engravings of these works 'were hung up in several English country-house lavatories'), and on each occasion the sitter wore tartan breeches of the same pattern. This is now the Gow tartan, and it is therefore one of the oldest tartans with an authentic history – although, of course, there is no evidence that it was worn by other Gows in the 18th century.

ABOVE *The famous fiddler Niel Gow, after a portrait by Raeburn. Dance tunes for the fiddle were composed in Strathspey in the 17th century, though the characteristic 'Scotch Snap' – a short note on the beat followed by a longer one until the next beat – came later.*

GRAHAM

NAME AND PLACE

Graham is an English name, deriving from the manor of Graegham (Grey Home), which is mentioned in the Domesday Book. The Scottish Grahams were first established in the Lowlands, and are popularly associated with Montrose in Angus.

ORIGINS

There is a legend of a Graham chieftain in Caledonia repulsing the Roman legions, but historically the first Graham was one of the Anglo-Norman barons who came to Scotland when King David I came to the throne in 1124, William de Graham, that is, of Graegham.

THE CLAN

The Grahams have a noble tradition of patriotism and military leadership, dating back to the wars of independence and including two of the greatest pro-Stewart generals. Sir Patrick, son of Sir David Graham of Dundaff (regarded as the real founder of the house of Montrose) was keeper of Stirling Castle. He died carrying the royal standard against the English in 1296. His nephew Sir John was the 'Richt Arm' of Wallace; he fell at the battle of Falkirk in 1298.

Sir Patrick was the first to hold lands in the Highlands through his marriage into the old Celtic house of the earls of Strathearn, and his son was the first to hold lands at Montrose in Angus (as a result of an exchange with the king) in 1325. In 1445 Patrick, the current Graham chief, became Lord Graham, and his grandson, the third Lord Graham, who was to die at Flodden, became Earl of Montrose in 1505.

The most distinguished military leader this house produced was unarguably James, fifth earl, and from 1644 Marquess of Montrose, the royalist leader in the civil wars. Although his achievements have been obscured by clouds of romance now hard to dispel, the bald facts of his campaign in the

BELOW *The 3rd Duke of Montrose (1755–1836), who was instrumental in restoring the legality of Highland dress.*

Highlands remain astonishing – the almost incredible speed of movement, the succession of smashing victories against superior numbers. How much of the credit was due to the Clan MacDonald war leader Alasdair MacColla is a matter for strategists to debate.

Among the remarkable facts about Montrose is that he originally supported the Covenant (his name appears at the head of those signing the National Covenant of 1638) and was a Lowlander. It is doubtful that he spoke much Gaelic.

What caused Montrose to change sides was his concern at the ambition of the Marquess of Argyll. It looked to him (and others) as though King Charles would be replaced by King Campbell. But in the field Argyll was always a step or more behind the dashing Montrose.

Montrose (without MacColla) was eventually defeated by Leslie's army of seasoned regulars. He returned to assist Charles II but was betrayed and executed in 1650. After the Restoration the various parts of his bodies were collected from the places where they had been put on vulgar display and he received a grand funeral. The head of Argyll replaced the head of Montrose on the spikes of the Tolbooth in Edinburgh.

The other great military hero of those grim times was 'Bonnie Dundee', John Graham of Claverhouse, Viscount Dundee, scourge of the Covenanters, who died at Killiecrankie fighting for King James VII/II.

The fourth Marquess of Montrose became a duke in 1707. The third duke should be remembered as the man who in 1782 secured the annulment of the act which proscribed Highland dress.

Of the many cadets of the Grahams the most notable houses were those of the earls of Menteith and Strathearn. There is a separate tartan for Graham of Menteith (top left), branches of which include Graham of Duchray and Cunningham-Graham of Ardoch. The seat of the Graham dukes of Montrose was the now ruined Buchanan Castle, built on the site of a former Buchanan stronghold by Loch Lomond and acquired by the Grahams in 1680. The former seat was Mugdock Castle, later renamed more becomingly Montdieu, in Strathblane.

CLAN ASSOCIATION

Dolphins, Clay Head Road, Baldrine, Isle of Man IM4 6DJ, England

1228 Kensington Drive, High Point, NC 27262-7316, USA

GRANT

NAME AND PLACE

The name is generally agreed to derive from the French *grand* and thus means the same as the Gaelic *mór*. The Grant homeland is Strathspey, with a branch beyond Loch Ness in Glenmoriston.

ORIGIN

Assuming the Grant chiefs had an Anglo-Norman ancestor, that does not explain the origin of the clansmen who adopted his name (a common puzzle). There is a strong tradition which holds that the Grants belonged to *Siol Ailpein*, the stock of Kenneth MacAlpin, first monarch of all Scotland. According to this belief the Grants are kin to the MacGregors, Gregor *Mór* MacGregor being their 12th-century ancestor. Significantly the Grants were good friends to the MacGregors at the time when that clan was proscribed.

THE CLAN

Tradition alone supports Sir Laurence le Grant, Sheriff of Inverness in the 1260s, being the son of Gregor and the ancestor of Grant chiefs. His son John, who was captured by the English in 1296, held land in Strathspey (later lost but repurchased), but there is a gap before Sir Ian, the first chief from whom an uninterrupted line can be traced, appears as Sheriff of Inverness in 1434.

At that time there were other Grant families around. Grants were already established in Glenmoriston and Glenurquhart, and Sir Ian's marriage secured them their lands in Strathspey, later increased by purchases. His son Sir Duncan was the first Grant of Freuchie (later Castle Grant), as the chiefs were known until the late 16th century. Freucie became a barony in the time of his grandson John, in 1494.

Clan Grant's history is less sensational than many others', but is comparatively well documented. In the troubles of the 17th and 18th centuries the Grants were generally Whiggish, though the Grants of Glenmoriston, relatively independent of the laird of Grant, remained loyal to the Stewart dynasty. One of the Seven Men of Glenmoriston who succoured Prince Charles was named Patrick Grant.

BELOW *Castle Grant, the seat of the chief variously known as Laird of Freuchie, of Grant, or simply Grant of that ilk.*

Until the 17th century the chief power
in the north-east was the 'Cock of the
North', the earl of Huntly, with whom
the lairds of Grant usually remained on
good terms. Numerous bonds of manrent
between the two families survive. This
did not save the Grants from the raids by
Camerons or MacDonalds, and by the
end of the 16th century relations between
Grants and Huntlys were cooling: the
Grants fought for Argyll against the
Gordons in the battle of Glenlivet (1594).
In the 17th century the decline of Huntly
power tended to advantage the Grants.

The seventh Laird of Grant was a
moderate Covenanter in the civil war,
which led to Montrose's occupation of
Strathspey and, after he had secured the
Grants' submission, similar trouble from
the Covenanters' army. At the battle of
Worcester in 1651, 150 Grants from
Strathspey were on the royalist side, but
the chief supported William of Orange in
1688. After the Fifteen the Laird of
Grant, who played a part in regaining
Inverness from the Jacobites, repurchased
Glenmoriston – forfeited because of
Glenmoriston's Jacobitism – for his
kinsman, clan loyalty outweighing
ideological differences.

Like other loyal Highlanders, the
Grants were poorly treated by the
government, and Ludovick Grant (the
chief's son then living in London), was
not very enthusiastic in his support for
the Hanoverians in 1745. The Grants
defending Inverness did not put up much
of a fight against the besieging Jacobites,
and many cadets, including
Glenmoriston, fought for the prince.
Colquhoun Grant of Burnside, a member
of Prince Charles's bodyguard, is the hero
of many tales of derring-do. But Sir
Ludovick was active after Culloden in
hunting down Jacobite fugitives.

In the Elgin Raid, which took place in
1820, the Grants were summoned to
their chief's aid by the fiery cross – the
last time a clan was raised in that way.

ABOVE *Blair Atholl where the Grants and
MacGregors met to discuss reunion while
the latter were proscribed.*

Grantown-on-Spey was founded by
Sir James Grant in 1766 as part of his
effort to avoid Clearances and discourage
emigration. James VI/I is said to have
offered to make the fifth Lord of Freuchie
Earl of Strathspey, an offer he declined:
'And wha'll be Laird of Grant?', and the
Grants of Grant rejected ennoblement
until 1855, when the chief became Lord
Strathspey in the British peerage. The
Scottish earldom of Seafield was acquired
through marriage some years earlier. The
titles are now divided: Sir Patrick Grant
of Grant is fifth Baron Strathspey and
thirty-second chief; the present Earl of
Seafield is his first cousin once removed.

CLAN ASSOCIATION

Creg-Ny-Baa, Skye of Curr Road,
Dulnain Bridge, Grantown on Spey,
Scotland

372 Churchtown Road, Narvon,
PA 17555, USA

1058 Wembley Road, London, Ontario
N6H 3X6, Canada

GUNN

NAME AND PLACE

It is usually said that the Gunns were of
Norse origin and that their name derives
from the Norse *gunnr*, meaning war – a
suitable enough name for a very warlike
clan. However, the researches of Sir Iain
Moncreiffe of that ilk suggest that the
name comes from Gunni, who is
known from a Norse saga of the Orkney
jarls (earls).

ORIGIN

Gunni inherited estates in Caithness and
Sutherland through his wife at about the
end of the 12th century, and his
descendant Ottar, living on the mainland
in 1280, was the assumed progenitor of
the chiefs of Gunn.

THE CLAN

In the 15th century the Gunns were
engaged in a ferocious feud with their
neighbours, the Keiths. In one romantic
story the Fair Helen, only daughter of
Lachlan Gunn, was betrothed to her
cousin when carried off by Keith of
Ackergill, whose advances she had earlier
rejected. She subsequently threw herself
from the top of the tower at Ackergill.

Clan Gunn suffered several defeats at
the hands of the Keiths and in 1464 their
chief, Crouner (Coroner) George Gunn
arranged a meeting to discuss peace.

BELOW *Neil M. Gunn, after a portrait in
the National Portrait Gallery in Edinburgh.
His 20 novels based on his childhood
experiences are among the best works of
modern Scottish fiction.*

Each side was to bring 12 horsemen, but the Keiths interpreted this as 12 horses, and mounted two men on each horse. In the ensuing fight all the Gunns were killed, including the chief and four of his sons, despite taking refuge in the chapel of St Tyr. The dead chief was robbed of his badge of office from which he was known as *Am Bràisdeach Mór*, 'He of the Big Brooch'.

Revenge was later exacted by the grandson of Crouner George, who killed Keith of Ackergill and ten of his men at Drummoy. This grandson was the first to hold the title *Mac Sheumais Chataich*, 'son of James of Caithness' (his father).

Though fierce fighters the Gunns were not a large clan and their history is largely one of retreat and retrenchment. They were harassed by the Mackays to the north-west, and were caught up in the feud between the Gordon earls of Sutherland and the Sinclair earls of Caithness during the 16th and 17th centuries. They inflicted some notable defeats on their enemies at times, particularly in a famous raid on the Sinclairs led by Alasdair Gunn of Killearnan in 1589.

In the end it was the Clearances of the early 19th century that did the most damage to the Gunns. Driven from Kildonan and their homelands in the hills on the Caithness-Sutherland border, some descended to the coast and became fishermen in little ports without harbours, where boats had to be perilously landed on the beach. From this milieu emerged the fine Scottish novelist Neil M. Gunn, whose novels based on his childhood in Dunbeath present a marvellous picture of those communities at the end of the 19th century (and include the finest description of salmon poaching ever written).

ABOVE *Memorial to the novelist Neil M. Gunn near Dingwall.*

HAMILTON

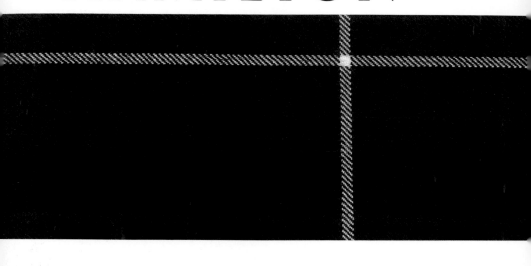

NAME AND PLACE

Hamilton probably derives from a Northumbrian place name. It occurs in the Lowlands in the late Middle Ages.

ORIGINS

The first known possessor of the name in Scotland was Sir Walter Fitz Gilbert of Hameldone, who held land in Renfrewshire in the late 13th century.

THE CLAN

Hamilton is an illustrious name in Scottish (and British) history, but it is not the name of a Highland clan, except in a very limited sense.

Although Sir Walter at first supported the English, after Bannockburn he wisely changed his allegiance and was rewarded by Bruce with confiscated Comyn lands and the barony of Cadzow, later renamed Hamilton, where the remains of the old castle still stand above the Clyde. He is said to have married a sister of the Earl of Moray, Bruce's associate, and his son David was caught along with David II by the English at Neville's Cross (1346).

The sixth Lord of Cadzow was raised to the peerage as Lord Hamilton in 1445. He married as his second wife a daughter of King James II, the young widow of the Master of Boyd who had been Earl of Arran. The island and the earldom subsequently passed to the Hamiltons, who thus acquired Highland property. They built Brodick Castle as their Highland home.

As a result of Lord Hamilton's marriage the family were closest, as heirs presumptive, to the throne and thus involved in high affairs of state. The frequent minorities of the sovereign made things all the more fraught.

That their political success in this favoured position was not greater has been put down to lack of determination, of which Queen Mary of Guise accused the second Earl of Arran, Regent of Scotland for the infant Mary Queen of Scots. His international machinations,

BELOW *Linlithgow Palace, now a ruin. Sir James Hamilton of Finnart was legitimated by his friend James V for his work on the Renaissance additions to the palace.*

however, did earn him the dukedom of Châtelherault from the king of France.

Disputes over precedence lay behind the vicious feuds of the Hamiltons with the Stewart earls of Lennox and the Douglas earls of Angus in the 16th century. The former ended only when Lennox's son Lord Darnley married Mary Queen of Scots; the latter was never completely resolved until this century when the Duke of Hamilton became Earl of Angus.

In a famous incident in the Hamilton-Douglas feud in 1520 their followers clashed in Edinburgh and the Hamiltons were driven out of the city. It is still remembered as 'Cleanse the Causeway'.

A memorable character who took part in this bloody episode was Sir James Hamilton of Finnart, a bastard son of the first Earl of Arran. Six years afterwards he was responsible for killing the Earl of Lennox, after Lennox had surrendered his sword to him. He also helped to bring about the burning of his kinsman Patrick Hamilton, the first Protestant martyr in Scotland, in 1528, but was himself executed on a probably unjust charge of treason in 1540.

Finnart was also largely responsible for introducing the ideas of French Renaissance architecture to Scotland. The façade of Falkland Palace is his work.

Another illegitimate son of the first Earl of Arran became Archbishop of St Andrews (succeeding Cardinal Beaton) and was hanged by partisans of Lennox partly in revenge for the murder of the Regent Moray by a Hamilton.

In 1599 the Earl of Arran became Marquess of Hamilton, and in 1643 the marquess became a duke. The first duke was beheaded in 1649. His brother, the second duke, was mortally wounded at Worcester in 1651. His niece and successor married a Douglas, who in 1663 was created Duke of Hamilton. The Hamilton earls and dukes of Abercorn were descended from a younger son of

ABOVE *The 1st Duke of Hamilton, after a portrait attributed to Vandyke. He was an arrogant man, stupid and deceitful and his behaviour contributed in no small measure to Charles I's demise. He was beheaded in the same year as the king.*

the second Earl of Arran, who fought for Mary Queen of Scots at Langside in 1568. The earls of Haddington are another ennobled cadet house.

Today the chiefship remains with the Duke of Hamilton, the premier peer of Scotland. Brodick Castle in Arran, much rebuilt, is the property of the National Trust for Scotland.

CLAN ASSOCIATION
Box 71881, Charleston, SC 29415-1881, USA

HAY

NAME AND PLACE

The name comes from La Haye in Normandy, meaning 'stockade' or 'hedge', and the Gaelic name of the chiefs, *Mac Garaidh Mór*, is, rather unusually, a translation of this term.

ORIGIN

The chiefs of Hay are of Anglo-Norman descent, and stem from William de la Haye, who received the barony of Erroll in 1178.

THE CLAN

The chief of Clan Hay is the Earl of Erroll who is also hereditary lord high constable and enjoys precedence over all other holders of hereditary titles in Scotland outside the royal family. The family has held that honour since the time of King Robert Bruce.

According to tradition the Hays played a leading part in a victory against Danish invaders, employing ox yokes for lack of more orthodox weapons, but the battle is not recorded in history. This colourful story, commemorated in Hay heraldic device, relates that as reward for the victory a falcon led the way to Erroll and outlined the boundaries of the barony in flight before alighting on the Falcon Stone (now at Bowness, near Port Erroll). The legend may have come from the family of the wife of the first Lord of Erroll, or that of his son, who married into the old Celtic house of the earls of Strathearn.

The third Hay of Erroll was twice co-regent of Scotland and married a Comyn. The fifth, Sir Gilbert, as a loyal adherent of Bruce was rewarded with the castle and estate of Slains, formerly Comyn property, on the Aberdeenshire coast, as well as the hereditary office of constable, the king's personal guardian.

Two of his successors fell in battle against the English, at Neville's Cross and Flodden, where 87 gentlemen of the name Hay, including the ancestor of the earls and marquesses of Tweeddale, are said to have been killed, along with Sir Thomas de la Haye, seventh Lord of Erroll and fourth High Constable, whose wife was a daughter of King Robert II. His grand-nephew William, Lord Hay, became Earl of Erroll in 1452.

By this time cadets of the house of Erroll had considerably extended Hay territories. A younger son of Sir Thomas was the ancestor of the Hays of Delgaty, from among whom came Montrose's chief of staff Sir William Hay, who was executed in 1650. Another branch held land in Lochloy.

The earls of Erroll continued to play an important part in national affairs.

The ninth earl was an ardent Catholic and leader of that cause after the death of Mary Queen of Scots. With his allies Angus and Huntly he secretly negotiated with Spain to depose Elizabeth of England and unite Britain under the Catholic James VI. The king was privately not unsympathetic to such a project, but after Argyll's government forces had been defeated by the Counter-Reformation earls in 1594 (Erroll being wounded leading the charge with his personal war cry, 'The Virgin Mary!') he was compelled to take more authoritative action, which included blowing up Slains Castle (no less effectively, it would appear, than the attempt to demolish its equally robust successor at Bowness early in this century).

As (generally) adherents of the old religious and political regime the Hays were heading for trouble in the events of the next half-century, yet they survived more or less unscathed. The thirteenth earl was a powerful opponent of the union with England (1707) and was imprisoned in 1708 for his part in an abortive Jacobite invasion. He was succeeded by his sister, the redoubtable Mary, Countess of Erroll in her own right, under whom New Slains became a receiving centre for Jacobites entering the country secretly (as a later visitor, James Boswell, remarked, Erroll's nearest neighbour was the king of Denmark). In 1745 she raised the clan for Prince Charles, whose secretary at the time of Culloden was a certain John Hay, described by John Prebble in his account of the battle as 'a weak and silly man', partly responsible for the logistical failures which sapped the fighting spirit of the Highlanders.

The earls of Erroll tended to be men of intelligence and fine physical stature. The lord high constable at the coronation of George III, a great nephew of the countess (and as son of the executed Jacobite Lord Kilmarnock, a Boyd by

ABOVE *Slains, home of the earls of Erroll from the early 17th century to the 1920s. After it was sold by the 20th Earl an attempt was made to demolish it, with only partial success, as this photograph demonstrates.*

birth) was described by Horace Walpole as 'the noblest figure I ever saw'. The nineteenth earl (died 1891), founder of Port Erroll, was a splendid Victorian patriarch, accustomed to take early-morning baths at Slains in sea water pumped daily up the cliffs by his 'fool'.

His successors live in a modern house built within the ruins of Slains.

CLAN ASSOCIATION

Rocklee, Cove, Argyll G84 0NN, Scotland

6058 Alexander Avenue, Alexandria, VA 22310-4382, USA

11 Homewood Crescent, Wellington 5, New Zealand

HENDERSON
(MACKENDRICK)

NAME AND PLACE

Traditionally, the Hendersons, Clan *Eanruig*, inhabited Glencoe long before the arrival of the MacIain MacDonalds, and their ancestor was *Eanruig Mór Mac Righ Neachtain*, 'Great Henry, son of King Nectan', a preposterous claim according to one authority.

ORIGINS

The line of chiefs supposedly descended from this legendary ancestor terminated in an heiress, daughter of Dugald MacHendry, who married a brother of the lord of the Isles. Their son Iain was the first MacIain MacDonald of Glencoe.

THE CLAN

The assimilation of Hendersons and MacDonalds seems to have proceeded smoothly – not always the case elsewhere. The Hendersons, who had a reputation for physical strength, enjoyed certain honorific duties reflecting their priority, forming the MacIain chief's bodyguard and, on his death, bearing his coffin. Hendersons were also hereditary pipers to the clan.

There were other groups of Hendersons, or Mackendricks (Gaelic *Mac Eanruig*) in other parts, apparently unconnected with the Hendersons of Glencoe. One group, possibly a sept

BELOW *St Andrews University was founded in about 1410 (the first in Scotland). Alexander Henderson was educated here, graduating in 1603.*

of the Elliots, has been located in
Upper Liddesdale in the Borders. The
Hendersons of Caithness in the far north
were a sept of Clan Gunn, descended
from Hendry, a son of Crouner George
Gunn, hereditary coroner of Caithness in
the 15th century, who is said to have
separated himself from his many brothers
as a result of some family quarrel.

The tartan illustrated is that of
Henderson of Fordell, perhaps the most
distinguished family. The first Henderson
of Fordell was James Henderson
(originally Henryson), who moved from
Dumfriesshire to Fife in the 15th century
and was Lord Advocate in 1494. From a
branch of his family descended
Alexander Henderson (1583–1646), who
is regarded as the greatest leader of the
Reformation in Scotland after Knox.

Henderson was born in Fife and went
to St Andrews University, where he
became a professor of philosophy in his
twenties. When he first went as minister
to Leuchars he was received without
enthusiasm because of his episcopalian
views, but he soon changed them and
within a few years was one of the most
respected Presbyterian leaders. He was
largely responsible for drafting the
National Covenant (1638), and he was
chosen by acclamation as moderator of
the historic assembly at Glasgow which
completely reformed the Scottish Kirk on
Presbyterian principles. He was also the
chief influence in drafting the Solemn
League and Covenant (1643) and went to
Westminster to see it pass the English
parliament. His personal relations with
Charles I, despite their vast ideological
differences, were good, and Henderson's
death in 1646 ('mourned throughout
Scotland' says a biographer, but one can
think of places where this was unlikely)
was reported to have resulted from a
broken heart.

ABOVE *Alexander Henderson, as moderator
of the General Assembly in 1643, presented
the Solemn League and Covenant, the
Anglo-Scottish alliance against the authority
of king and bishops.*

CLAN ASSOCIATION
Craigielea, Hallhill, Dunbar
EH42 1RF, Scotland

1828 Mission Road, Birmingham,
AL 35216, USA
(and in many other states)

5475 Inglis Street A306, Halifax,
NS B3H 1J6, Canada (and other
provinces)

125 Annie Street, Torwood, Queensland
4066, Australia

HOME

NAME AND PLACE

The name comes from the barony of Home in Berwickshire.

ORIGINS

The holders of the barony, later earls of Home, may be descended from the Northumbrian earls of Dunbar. Aldan de Home was a probable 12th-century ancestor.

THE CLAN

The name Home is pronounced, and often spelled, Hume. Apparently the Polwarth branch of the family generally adopted the 'u' spelling while the earls of Home preferred the 'o'. The great philosopher David Hume is said to have spelt his name thus because he was so irritated by Englishmen pronouncing it to rhyme with comb.

Aldan de Home's presumed 14th-century descendant Sir Thomas Home of that ilk gained the barony of Dunglas in East Lothian through marriage. His son Sir Alexander died with Douglas fighting in France against the English at the battle of Verneuil in 1424. His grandson (d. 1491) became Lord Home, and the first Lord Home's son and heir, in alliance with Archibald Douglas and supported by the Campbell Earl of Argyll, was leader of the conspiracy

BELOW *The 14th Earl of Home, later Sir Alec Douglas-Home, in 1955. He was probably the last British prime minister to hold a hereditary peerage, which he had to give up when he became prime minister in order to lead the government in the Commons.*

which sought to replace King James III
with his young son, leading to the king's
death after the battle of Sauchieburn in
1488. The third lord, called Alexander
like most of his predecessors and
successors, survived the slaughter of
Flodden, where many of his name died,
but was executed by the Regent Albany,
against whom he had been plotting with
the English, in 1516.

The second lord was Warden of the
March, an office frequently held by
the Homes, who were at least partly
responsible for the greater order (or
lesser disorder) in the Borders on the
east than the west.

The divisions of the Reformation also
split the Homes. The fifth Lord Home
became a Protestant but was a supporter
of Mary Queen of Scots for a time. His
estates were forfeit but they were
returned to the sixth baron – a close
adviser to King James VI/I – who was
created Earl of Home in 1605. The
second earl died childless and the title
passed to a distant relative who was
descended from John Home of Whiterigs
and Easton, younger son of the first Lord
Home. The fourteenth earl renounced his
title to become prime minister (1963–64)
as Sir Alec Douglas Home and was later
created Lord Home of the Hirsel, the
family seat in Berwickshire.

The Homes proliferated fairly rapidly
throughout the early years and a number
of other important cadets should be
mentioned here. Sir David Home of
Wedderburn near Duns, ancestor of
the Homes of Polwarth, was a younger
son of Sir Thomas in the 14th century.
His descendant Sir Patrick Home, an
adherent of William of Orange whose
court in the Hague he attended, became
Lord Polwarth and later Earl of
Marchmont. Sir David's Wedderburn
descendants included 'The Seven Spears
of Wedderburn', sons of the third Home
of Wedderburn, who in turn became
ancestors of the Homes of Blackadder,

ABOVE *The Hirsel, seat of the earls of
Home, whose ancestors were a powerful
force in the Borders, their record more
honourable than most.*

Broomhouse and other families.

David Hume (1711–76), perhaps the
greatest British thinker of the 18th
century, was son of Joseph Home of
Chirnside, Berwickshire, and the Homes
include an unusual number of writers.
Among them are the playwrights John
Home (a Lowlander who fought for
the Jacobites in 1745), the author of
Douglas, a melodrama which prompted a
patriotic Scot in the London audience to
crow, 'Whar's your Wullie Shakespeare
now?', and William Douglas Home,
brother of the prime minister. The
famous spiritualist medium of the 19th
century, Daniel Dunglas Home, was
alleged to have been the son of a natural
son of the tenth Earl of Home.

FAMILY ASSOCIATION
605 W Loch Hasmine Circle #105
Vero Beach FL 32962, USA

INNES

NAME AND PLACE

The barony of Innes, meaning 'greens', lies on the Moray Firth between the Spey and the Lossie.

ORIGIN

A charter of King Malcolm IV in 1160 granted the barony to Berowald, a Fleming, whose grandson was the first to use the name in the early 13th century.

THE CLAN

When the twenty-fifth Chief of Innes succeeded to the duchy of Roxeburgh in the early 19th century he published a history of Clan Innes to prove to those dazzled by ducality that 'he was of as good blood on his father's side as on his great-grandmother's' (through whom he inherited the Kerr dukedom). An early account of the family ascribed their good fortunes to three facts: the heirs of Innes had always been male, none had ever married a bad wife, and they had never been in debt.

The chiefs of Innes built up very large family estates, thanks partly to the ninth chief's marriage to the heiress of the thane of Aberchirder, and spawned many cadets. Amity did not always reign among them, however, nor were all the chiefs men of admirable character. The eleventh Laird of Innes, who took part in

BELOW *John Innes, Bishop of Moray from 1407–14 rebuilt Elgin Cathedral after his had been destroyed in the 14th century by the Wolf of Badenoch, the son of King Robert II (from an 18th-century engraving).*

the battle of Brechin in 1452, had a bad reputation, known as 'Ill Sir Robert' in contrast to his grandfather 'Good Sir Robert' (d. 1381). The eighteenth chief was murdered by the head of another branch, Innes of Invermarkie, in a quarrel over the succession in the 16th century. Sir Robert Innes of Balveny, who was descended from a younger son of the 'Ill Sir Robert', was a supporter of Mary Queen of Scots and was killed after being betrayed by his son and successor.

Sir Robert, twentieth chief, was a Covenanter, but supported Charles II, whom he welcomed on his arrival in Scotland in 1650. He was the builder of Innes house (his father, nineteenth chief, had been responsible for founding Garmouth, east of Elgin, in 1587). Balveny Castle on Speyside was built by Sir Robert Innes of Invermarkie, grandson of the murdered constable, whose family's support for Charles I had been disastrous for their fortunes.

Croxton Tower was built in the 16th century by a branch of this family. The Inneses of Croxton, like most of their name, were loyal Jacobites. Sir Alexander Innes of Croxton fought with Dundee at Killiecrankie and was prominent in the failed rising of 1708. His son was fatally wounded at Sheriffmuir.

ABOVE *Balvenie Castle, near Dufftown, originally a Douglas stronghold, whose remains are mostly of the Renaissance conversion. After the eclipse of the Douglases, it passed to the Stewart earls of Atholl, who paid the customary 'peppercorn' annual rent of one red rose, and later to various others, including the Inneses.*

CLAN ASSOCIATION
129 Ravenna Drive, Long Beach,
CA 90803, USA

JOHNSTON

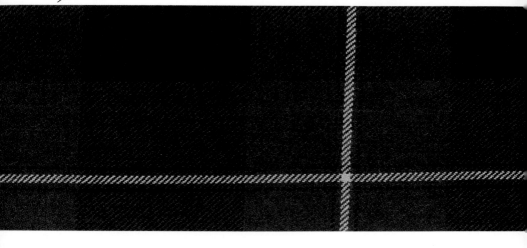

NAME AND PLACE

The name Johnston is of territorial origin, but there are many 'John's towns' or 'John's tuns' (farms or agrarian settlements) in Scotland and there is little doubt that the Johnstons were not all descended from a common ancestor. Annandale was the home of the famous Border clan.

ORIGINS

The name was in use as a surname in the late 12th century, and the presumed progenitor of the clan received a charter for lands in Annandale. The well-known beauty spot near Moffat where the River Annan rises is now called the Devil's Beef Tub, but its proprietor was formerly said to be not the devil but the Johnstons, which some of their neighbours would have regarded as much the same thing.

The Johnstons were a tough and violent clan for whom raiding was a way of life. They were also prolific, and besides Annandale itself they were to be found in the nearby valleys of Moffat Water and other tributaries. Their stronghold was at Lochwood.

Sir Gilbert de Johnstoun, son of John, is the first to appear in historical records, at the end of the 12th century. Sir John, of the fifth generation after Sir Gilbert, had one son, Adam, who was the

BELOW *The Devil's Beef Tub, a spectacular cavity in the hills north of Moffat once used to hide stolen cattle. The monument commemorates a Covenanter, 'shot by Douglas's Dragoons' in 1635.*

ancestor of several branches, including (by different wives) the Johnstons of Westerhall and of Elphinstone. Sir James Johnston became Lord Johnston in 1633 and Earl of Hartfell ten years later. His son was also made Earl of Annandale, and in the following generation the earl became a marquess. In the 18th century this line of the clan became extinct and the Johnstons of Westerhall in Dumfriesshire became the leading family of the Border clan.

The Johnstons generally supported the monarchy, and a Johnston of that ilk often held the office of warden of the Western Marches (he sometimes interpreted his duties rather loosely). They were great rivals of the Maxwells of Nithsdale, earlier holders of the office, which gave rise to one of the last great Border feuds, in which both Johnston and Maxwell chiefs fell, about the end of the 16th century. King James VI/I reconciled the two clans in 1623.

There were also some Johnstons in Strathspey, who were unconnected with the Johnstons of Annandale. They originated from the marriage of Stephen the clerk to the heiress of Sir Andrew Garioch in the 14th century, which brought them the land of Johnston. In the 18th century they fought on the Jacobite side in the major risings.

Archibald Johnston, who came from Annandale and is known as Johnston of Warriston (the title he held as a judge), was with Alexander Henderson author of the National Covenant in 1638. He was a stern, unbending Covenanter and though he supported Charles II after he had accepted the Covenant his lectures had aroused the king's bitter dislike. Moreover, he made the mistake of accepting judicial office under Cromwell in 1657. At the Restoration in 1660 he was excluded from the general pardon and was hanged in Edinburgh in 1663.

The Johnstons of Strathspey are now represented by an American family.

ABOVE *Thomas Johnston (1882-1965), journalist, politician and administrator. He was appointed Secretary of State for Scotland by Winston Churchill. He was instrumental in introducing hydro-electric power, and in furthering hospital schemes.*

CLAN ASSOCIATION
4020 Stonewall Avenue, Fairfax,
VA 22032, USA

KEITH

NAME AND PLACE

In the reign of Malcolm IV (1152–65) Harvey Keith held lands in Buchan, although his name probably derived from estates in East Lothian. Later, the homeland of the clan was Caithness.

ORIGIN

Harvey Keith was the earliest known holder of the hereditary office of marischal (since 1458 earl marischal) of Scotland, and the Keiths were an ancient Celtic family of great distinction.

THE CLAN

It was not until the time of Bruce that the Keiths became really powerful, and by the 16th century it was said that the earl marischal could travel from Berwick to John o' Groats stopping each night on his own property (on a two-week journey).

As a result of a marriage to the heiress of Ackergill the Keiths moved into Caithness in the 14th century, where they became involved in a long and bloody feud with the Gunns (see Gunn).

At Bannockburn the success of the Scots' cavalry, mounted on mere ponies compared with the great heavy horses of the English, reflected credit on the current marischal, Sir Robert Keith. His great-grandson Sir William founded the castle of Dunnotar (later rebuilt) on its

BELOW Dunnotar, on its precarious site south of Stonehaven. The ruins include the four-storey keep, begun in the 1390s, and enough remain to show that the castle could have accomodated a large number of people.

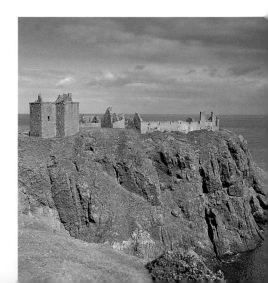

superlative site south of Stonehaven on the Kincardineshire coast.

In the 16th century at least three Scottish monarchs were entertained at Dunnotar, and during the civil wars the royal regalia were taken there for safe keeping. When the castle was besieged they were smuggled out, let down the cliffs to an old woman supposedly gathering kelp on the seashore, and buried in a nearby churchyard.

The castle expanded, along with the influence of the Keiths, in succeeding generations. For in spite of what would seem to be the excessive dangers of such an office as marischal – attendance at all battles obligatory – the Keiths flourished until the 17th century. The Earl even survived Flodden, and his standard in that battle has survived to this day.

There is some confusion over the numbering of the earls marischal. The fourth earl (d. 1623) is sometimes called the fifth. He was a firm Protestant, who had spent part of his youth in Geneva, and was one of the commissioners who arranged the marriage of James VI/I and Anne of Denmark. He founded Marischal College, Aberdeen. His grandson William, the seventh earl (d. 1661), was a leading Covenanter and opponent of Huntly, but later supported the royalists and invaded England with Hamilton in 1648.

Naturally, many of the earls marischal gained a reputation in the military field (they were not so good at sea: William, fifth earl, was also Admiral of Scotland, but 'wold never boate'). James, a younger son of the eighth earl marischal, was 'out' in the Jacobite rising of 1715 and afterwards became a distinguished mercenary, fighting in the service of Spain, Russia and most notably the Prussia of Frederick the Great, who made him a field marshal and erected a statue to him in Dresden after his death in battle in 1758. His brother George, ninth and last earl marischal, was also

ABOVE *At the Battle of Bannockburn the Keith Marischal only had ponies to mount troops on, rather than the great warhorses of the English army. However, they managed the vital role of scattering the Welsh archers, a strategy which was vital to the Scots victory.*

compelled to travel on the continent after his participation in the Fifteen. He became a close friend of Frederick the Great, his brother's commander-in-chief.

CLAN ASSOCIATION
164 South Main Street, Jasper, GA 30143, USA

KENNEDY

NAME AND PLACE

The Kennedys come from Carrick in
Ayrshire. The branch of the Kennedys
who found their way to the Highlands
about the 15th century were known as
Ceannaideach.

ORIGIN

The earliest record of the Kennedys
dates back to the reign of King William
the Lion (1165–1214).

THE CLAN

The Kennedys of Carrick were probably
connected genealogically with the old
Celtic lords of Galloway. John Kennedy
of Dunure, recognised as chief of the
Kennedys by King Robert II, married an
heiress of the old Carrick earls and was
established in Cassillis, which he had
possibly acquired as a result of an earlier
marriage. His grandson James Kennedy
of Dunure married a daughter of King
Robert III, bringing the Kennedys to a
prominent place on the national stage.
Their son Gilbert became the first Lord
Kennedy (1457) and was one of the
numerous regents during the minority of
King James III. A kinsman, Sir Hugh
Kennedy, fought with Joan of Arc against
the English.

The most famous member of the clan
in the Middle Ages was a brother of the

first Lord Kennedy, James, Bishop of St
Andrews from 1441 to1465, Chancellor
of Scotland and one of the most effective
statesmen of his time. He is regarded as
a co-founder of St Andrews University,
originated by his predecessor. A younger
son of the first Lord Kennedy was the
poet Walter Kennedy (d. c.1508), best
known for his participation in William
Dunbar's *Flyting*, a battle of wits
between the two poets.

Few of the early Kennedy chiefs died
peacefully: the third Lord Kennedy,
created Earl of Cassillis in 1510, died at
Flodden, the second earl was murdered
by Campbell of Loudon in 1527 and the
third was captured at Solway Moss and
died in mysterious circumstances in
Dieppe when returning from the wedding
of Mary Queen of Scots to the Dauphin.

His son the fourth earl, known as
'King of Carrick', was a Protestant who
nevertheless fought for Queen Mary at
Langside. Described as 'ane werry greedy
man', he is best remembered for literally
roasting the Abbot of Crossraguel at
Dunure Castle in 1570 in an attempt
to persuade him to renounce title to
the abbey's lands, which had been
appropriated while the earl's uncle was
abbot. The unfortunate man was rescued
by the Kennedys of Bargany. They were
engaged in a feud with the senior house

which ended in their virtual extinction in the time of the fifth earl (d. 1615), a lord high treasurer of Scotland.

The childless fifth earl was succeeded by his nephew John (1595–1668), 'the grave and solemn Earl', who was a strict Presbyterian and a leader of the Scottish resistance to Charles I. According to a probably false tradition the heroine of the ballad 'The Gypsie Laddie' can be identified with the sixth earl's first wife, who was Jean, daughter of the Hamilton Earl of Haddington. The gypsy hero was Johnnie Faa, Sir John Faa of Dunbar, the name borne by the gypsy king acknowledged by King James V long before but not known to history in this later identity. The countess was in love with him; he carried her off, but was caught by the earl who hanged Johnnie from the Dule Tree in front of her eyes and kept her captive the rest of her life.

The seventh earl gave his support to the Glorious Revolution of 1688. The eighth earl had no children and the title passed to the Kennedys of Culzean, descended from a younger son of the third earl. The subsequent history of the Kennedy chiefs is less romantic and more honourable. The eleventh earl was a notable admiral whose son was created Marquess of Ailsa, the title held by his descendants.

The famous home of the chiefs from the end of the 18th century was Culzean Castle, perhaps the most remarkable of the sham castles built by Robert Adam in his later years (and now owned by the National Trust for Scotland). Its rugged neo-Gothic exterior conceals rooms of exquisite delicacy, from which one may contemplate the splendours of a stormy sea from a position of the utmost graciousness and security.

The present Kennedy chief still maintains his seat at Cassillis.

ABOVE *Culzean Castle, one of the most remarkable residences in Scotland, one of the masterpieces of Robert Adam and the pride of the Kennedys (and today of the National Trust for Scotland). It replaced a medieval tower house.*

CLAN ASSOCIATION

The Estate Office, The Castle, Maybole
KA19 7BX, Scotland

520 Harrison Avenue, Cambridge,
OH 43725-1472, USA

KERR

NAME AND PLACE

The Kerrs were a Border clan centred
on Teviotdale. The name, which may be
British or Norse, was fairly common in
the Borders at an early date, variously
spelled, and possibly not all its bearers
come from the same stock.

ORIGINS

By tradition the Kerrs were of Anglo-
Norman origin and the earliest known
bearer of the name was described as a
'hunter' of Swinhope, in the reign of
King William the Lion.

THE CLAN

The governing theme of the Border Kerrs
is the long rivalry between the two chief
branches, said to have descended from
two brothers, Ralph and John, resident
near Jedburgh in the early 14th century.
The Kerrs of Ferniehurst were descended
from Ralph, the elder brother, the Kerrs
of Cessford from John. The rivalry was
even reflected in the name, the Kerrs of
Ferniehurst usually using the spelling Ker.

   One or other of these two groups,
whose homes were only a few miles
apart, usually held the title of Warden
of the Middle March – Sir Andrew of
Ferniehurst was appointed in 1502, Sir
Andrew of Cessford held it after Flodden
– and although they sometimes combined

BELOW *The remains of the tower at
Ferniehurst, south of Jedbergh. Its owners
usually spelled their name with a single 'r',
perhaps as a mark of disassociation from
their rivals and relatives at Cessford, ten
miles away.*

against the English, their frequent brawling among themselves brought violence and destruction to Teviotdale.

The rivalry took on a national political dimension in the 16th century when the Kerrs of Cessford supported the pro-English policy of the Douglases (led by the Earl of Angus and his wife Margaret, the Tudor widow of King James IV), while the Kerrs of Ferniehurst adhered to the party of King James V.

During the siege of the Castle of Ferniehurst by the English the attackers claimed that its defence was assisted by 'spirits' and even the devil himself. Fearful atrocities were committed there when the castle fell. On its recapture from the English in 1549 great efforts were made to take prisoners alive so that they could be slowly tortured to death, in revenge for the rape of Kerr womenfolk by the English.

The dispute between the two Kerr houses continued. Besides warden of the Middle March, they contended for the office of provost of Jedburgh. Sir Walter of Cessford was against Mary Queen of Scots, Sir Thomas of Ferniehurst for her. Eventually the feud died down. The union of the Scots and English crowns reduced the importance of the Border clans, and the final solution was the marriage in 1631 of Anne Kerr of Cessford to William Kerr of Ferniehurst, who had inherited the title Earl of Lothian, formerly held by the Cessford branch. Their son became the Marquess of Lothian in 1701.

The first Earl of Roxburghe (created 1616) was a descendant of Sir Andrew Kerr of Cessford, Warden of the Middle March a century earlier. The fifth earl was a strong supporter of the union with England (1707) as a result of which the grateful government made him a duke. The title was later inherited by Sir James Innes of that ilk, twenty-fifth Chief of Innes, who adopted the name Kerr.

ABOVE *Cessford. Feuds between rival branches of the same family were not rare, although in the face of danger from another source, they were usually forgotten, at least temporarily. The feud between the rival branches of the Kerrs lasted for four or five generations.*

CLAN ASSOCIATION
Lothian Estate Offices, Jedburgh
TD8 6UF, Scotland

7980 Ridgewood Road, Goodlettsville,
TN 37072, USA

LAMONT

NAME AND PLACE

In the late 12th century Ferchar was a chief in Cowal and his grandson Lauman, or Ladman, was the ancestor from whom the clan took their name. The Gaelic name of the chief was *Mac Ladhmainn Mór Chòmhaill uile* (Great Son of Lamont of all Cowall).

ORIGIN

When the Scots came from Ireland to Dalriada one district, Cowal, was named after King Comgall (d. 537) and the Lamonts who made their home in Cowal were probably all descended from the same family.

THE CLAN

Clan Lamont was a relatively small and therefore not very powerful clan with the misfortune of formidable neighbours (the Campbells), but their history is well documented. A fine history of the Lamonts by Hector McKechnie was published in 1938.

A famous relic of the Lamonts is the Lamont harp now in Edinburgh, which was made about the middle of the 15th century. It is said to have travelled to the Robertsons in Perthshire with a Lamont daughter who married a Robertson.

The original home of the chiefs was at Inveryne on Loch Fyne, but their

BELOW *Castle Toward, ancient seat of the Lamonts, whose ruins stand opposite Rothesay Bay, at the tip of the peninsula defined by Loch Striven and the Firth of Clyde, about eight miles south of Dunoon; from an engraving of about 1830.*

main stronghold from the 15th century
was Toward Castle, the ruins of which
can still be seen.

The clan was virtually destroyed in
the 17th century in a notorious episode
for which the chief was partly to blame.

The civil wars offered plenty of
opportunities to pay off old scores, but
because fortunes tended to change with
dramatic swiftness, those who took
advantage of such opportunities laid
themselves open to future retribution.

Sir James Lamont of Inveryne
sympathised with Charles I in the
religious quarrel of the 1630s, which
put him on the opposite side from his
powerful neighbour, Campbell of Argyll.
Sir James was a man of some ability, who
established a school at Toward in 1643,
one of only two in Argyll. He was
anxious to escape Campbell thraldom
and recover lands in Cowal which the
Campbells had taken. Nevertheless he
was compelled to fight on Argyll's side,
and was taken prisoner, to his relief
presumably, by Montrose at the battle
of Inverlochy, a resounding defeat for
Argyll. Montrose soon released him, with
a commission to act against rebels, which
in Lamont's case meant the Campbells.
Together with some of Montrose's Irish
MacDonalds the Lamonts ravaged the
Campbell country, undoubtedly
committing atrocities in the process.

After Montrose's defeat the Campbells
took a terrible revenge. They besieged
and destroyed Toward Castle and the
other main Lamont base at Ascog and
slaughtered the Lamonts without mercy
in spite of having granted a safe conduct.
The women and girls were killed first,
the men kept prisoner for a week, then
massacred in Dunoon churchyard, where
36 'chiefs and special gentlemen' were
hanged on the same tree before being cut
down and buried alive. Sir James himself
was kept a prisoner for five years in
Dunstaffnage Castle without being able
to change his clothes. A memorial to the

ABOVE *A peaceful scene, where once
Lamonts and Campbells fought, Loch Eck
in Cowal.*

dead was erected at Dunoon by the Clan
Lamont Society in 1906.

Subsequently the Lamont chiefs lived
at Ardlamont, but the property was sold
in the 19th century. The Lamonts of
Knockdow were an old cadet branch,
descended from a younger son of the
15th-century chief. Sir Norman Lamont,
fifteenth Laird of Knockdow, left the
estate in trust for the clan.

The chiefship has twice passed to
different branches of the clan, the current
one being resident in Australia.

CLAN ASSOCIATION
130 Halstead Court, Alpharetta,
GA 30202, USA

8 Wanjina Place, North Rocks,
NSW 2151, Australia

LESLIE

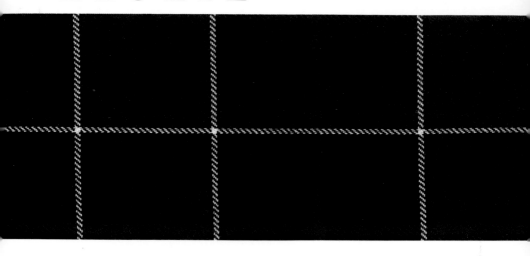

NAME AND PLACE

The lands of Leslie in Aberdeenshire were granted to a Fleming named Bartolf in the 12th century. Bartolf's son Malcolm took his name from the lands.

ORIGINS

The question of who among later Leslies were descendants of this line is impossible to answer. Sir Andrew Leslie was one of those who signed (more strictly, sealed) the Declaration of Arbroath in 1320.

THE CLAN

A descendant of Sir Andrew Leslie was created Earl of Rothes by King James II. William, third Earl of Rothes, was killed at Flodden and George, fourth earl, fought in France with King James V. His son Norman, Master of Rothes, also fought in France and was killed there in 1554. Earlier, he had made a name for himself by taking part in the assassination of Cardinal Beaton.

The Leslies are famous for producing soldiers of fortune. At one point in history there was a General Leslie on active service in three European countries (including Scotland).

Although there was no recognised chief, the Leslies individually gained their greatest fame in the 17th century.

BELOW *Leslie Castle, a fine tower house near Huntly in Aberdeenshire.*

Alexander, son of George Leslie of
Galgonie and a member of the family
of Leslie of Balquhain, fought under
Gustavus Adolphus in the Thirty Years
War and returned to Scotland in 1638 as
a field marshal to command the Scots in
the impending Bishops' War. He was an
ardent Covenanter, but in the course of
the next few years it was sometimes
difficult to say exactly where his true
loyalties lay (the same could be said of
many others in those difficult times).
Although 'Sandy' Leslie was small and
'somewhat deformed' in person, he was
an excellent commander who was able to
enforce discipline on turbulent Scottish
nobles. The king made him Earl of Leven
in 1641, and he retained his command
until he was in his seventies (he died in
1661, aged over 80), finally relinquishing
it in favour of David Leslie. He was
succeeded as Earl of Leven by his
grandson, but after the deaths of the
latter's two daughters, both Countesses
of Leven in their own right, there was a
dispute over the succession between John
Leslie, Earl (created duke in 1680) of
Rothes and the Earl of Melville. Rothes's
death in 1681 decided the matter and
Melville, a great-grandson of 'Sandy'
Leslie, became Earl of Leven and Melville.

David Leslie, who succeeded Leven as
Lord General, was a grandson of the fifth
Earl of Rothes. He ended the legend of
Montrose with a convincing victory at
Philiphaugh (1645). He was later
defeated, but not disgraced, by Cromwell
at Dunbar and Worcester. After the
Restoration he became Lord Newark.

The Leslies of Balquhain were
perhaps the most distinguished branch.
They held that barony in the early 14th
century, and were long involved in a feud
with the Forbeses, in the course of which
Balquhain Castle was destroyed and
rebuilt. The Walter Leslie who
assassinated Wallenstein in the Thirty
Years War came from this family, of
whom the most notable member was

ABOVE *Bishop John Leslie (1527–96), a
strong supporter of Mary Queen of Scots
who, finding no comfort in Scotland or
England, eventually took refuge in France
and died in a monastery.*

John Leslie, Bishop of Ross during the
Reformation, a staunch supporter of the
Roman Catholic Church and later of
Mary Queen of Scots against Knox.
While in England he was involved in the
Ridolfi plot and spent some time as a
prisoner in the Tower of London. He
used the time profitably in gathering
material for his history of Scotland,
published (in Latin) in 1578.

The chiefship of the Leslies remains
with the earls of Rothes today.

CLAN ASSOCIATION

612 North Maple Avenue, Ridgway, PA
15853-9756, USA

LINDSAY

NAME AND PLACE

Baldric de Lindesay, a Norman who held lands in England and Normandy, took his name from the district south of the Humber.

ORIGIN

Early in the 12th century Sir Walter de Lindsay was a member of the council of Prince David, Earl of Huntingdon, who became King of Scots in 1124, and his successor acquired the lands of Crawford in Clydesdale.

THE CLAN

Though originally of Lowland origin, there are Lindsays now spread all over Scotland, not to mention other countries, as well and, thanks perhaps to the high proportion of literary talent for which the name is famous, their early history is quite well known.

Sir Baldric de Lindesay married an English heiress, and the family continued to hold lands on both sides of the border.

Sir David Lindsay, who died on crusade in 1268, had served as Regent and later Chamberlain of Scotland, but his descendants were torn between two loyalties. His son Sir Alexander had been knighted by Edward I of England but nevertheless became a supporter of Wallace and Bruce, losing his English

BELOW *The remains of fortified dwellings are numerous in Scotland, and there is nothing particularly remarkable about Edzell Castle, Tayside home of the Lindsay earls of Crawford until 1715, except its startling red colour and the walled, octagonal garden, created by Sir David Lindsay in about 1604.*

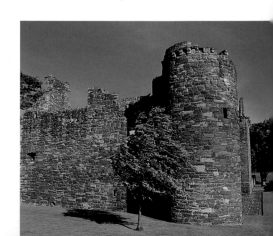

properties as a result. His son and successor, another Sir David, was taken prisoner, but survived to become one of the signatories of the Declaration of Arbroath, the Scottish declaration of independence in 1320. His great-grandson, yet another Sir David, was created Earl of Crawford by the king in 1398. He is thought to have been the organiser of the famous battle of the Clans at Perth in 1396.

The first earl was a famous champion, who fought a duel against the English champion Lord Welles at a tournament on St George's Day in front of the king of England. He unhorsed his opponent so easily that the spectators suspected he was somehow fastened to his saddle, which he disproved by leaping to the ground and back into the saddle, no mean feat in full armour.

By this time the Lindsays of Crawford had acquired lands in Angus through marriage, and made their home there. The earls of Crawford were one of the mightiest families in Scotland, overlords of a truly vast area which included Strathnairn. By the end of the Middle Ages there were about one hundred landed Lindsay families of varying note in Scotland, especially in Angus and adjacent counties, and most of them acknowledged the Earl of Crawford as their chief.

The Lindsays were involved in some spectacular feuds in Angus, notably with the Ogilvies and with Lyons of Glamis, both near neighbours.

Generally the Lindsays remained loyal to the Stewarts. The sixth earl fell at Flodden, the tenth supported Mary Queen of Scots, and the sixteenth fought for Charles I (though the Lindsays of Edzell were Covenanters). Despite their reputation as 'the lightsome Lindsays', not all the members of the chiefly family were amiable gentlemen. The fourth earl, known as 'Earl Beardie', was a ferocious character, and Alexander, heir to the eighth earl, was known as 'the Wicked Master', having failed in an attempt to murder his father. He was disinherited, but later regained the title after the death of his cousin, a Lindsay of Edzell, who had replaced him. From his younger son descended the earls of Balcarres (created 1651), who in the 19th century inherited the chiefship and the Crawford title and became earls of Crawford and Balcarres.

Sir David Lindsay (1490–1555), a courtier and Lyon King of Arms in the reign of King James III, was author of *Ane Satyre of the three Estaits*, in the Scots vernacular, a play that attacked national, religious and court vices. It was revived with great success at the Edinburgh Festival in the 1980s. The witty if unreliable historian Robert Lindsay of Pittscottie (d. c. 1565) was his contemporary. The playwright belonged to a branch of the family descended from Lord Lindsay, a younger son of a 14th-century laird of Crawford, whose successors became earls of Lindsay (1633).

CLAN ASSOCIATION

36 Broncourt Terrace, Edinburgh
EH8 7EP, Scotland

4621 Saybrook Drive, Norcross,
GA 30093-4741, USA

LIVINGSTONE

NAME AND PLACE

The name comes from what is today a somewhat blighted 'New Town' in West Lothian, and the Lowland spelling of the name generally omits the final E. The town itself probably took its name from a Saxon named Leving. The Highland Livingstones were originally named MacLeay, an anglicised version of the Gaelic *Mac an Léigh*, meaning 'the son of the physician', and they were at one time connected with the famous hereditary physicians to the lord of the Isles, the Beatons. They were also found in Kintyre and Appin, as followers of the Stewarts. They adopted the name Livingston because of similarities in sound and meaning: *Léibhe* (whence *Léigh*) = Living; *Mac* = s(t)on.

ORIGIN

Leving's grandson, 'of Livingstone', is named in a charter of King William the Lion.

Some writers refer to Sir James Livingstone of Stirling, who as a result of a royal grant settled in Lismore at the entrance of Loch Linnhe in the 17th century and gave his name to his tenants, as the source of the Highland Livingstones. However, their origin is surely much earlier than this.

BELOW *Statue to the Africa explorer David Livingstone in Glasgow.*

THE CLAN

Sir William Livingstone, a descendant of Leving's grandson, was taken prisoner fighting in northern England in 1346 with David II, from whom he got the forfeited barony of Callander, marrying the Callandar heiress into the bargain. A number of landed Livingston(e) families descended from his grandson, Sir John Livingstone of Callandar (d. 1402).

One of these grandsons was Sir James Livingstone of Callandar, who became first Lord Livingstone in the mid-15th century. His descendant Alexander, fifth lord, was one of the guardians of the young Mary Queen of Scots before the battle of Pinkie, and his son fought for the queen at Langside. The seventh lord was created Earl of Linlithgow in 1600, but the title was forfeited after the fourth earl joined the Jacobites in 1715. A branch descended from the first earl, who had become earls of Callandar, suffered the same fate.

The holy isle of Lismore had once been the home of St Moluag (d. 592), who had left behind him his bishop's staff, known as the *Bachull Mór* or *Bachull Buidhe* (yellow staff) because for a long time it was cased in copper. Of this sacred relic, which is associated with highly unChristian rites performed at Hogmanay, the MacLeays were hereditary keepers, and that office is held to be this day by the chief of the Livingstones.

The great explorer David Livingstone (his father spelt the name without the E), was descended from the Livingstons of Argyll. His grandfather had been a tenant farmer on the island of Ulva, west of Mull, but he was evicted in 1792 and went to the Glasgow area to find work. His famous grandson was born in a miserable tenement beside the mill at Blantyre.

ABOVE *David Livingstone (1813–73), after his account of his African travels, during which he crossed the continent from west to east and discovered what he called Victoria Falls, had made him a world famous figure.*

CLAN ASSOCIATION

Bachlui, Isle of Lismore, Oban
PA34 5UL, Scotland

LOGAN (MACLENNAN)

NAME AND PLACE

There may be no connection between the MacLennans of the Highlands and the Lowland Logans, although they are usually grouped together. The Logans' seat was at Drumderfit.

ORIGINS

According to ancient and demonstrably unreliable tradition the Lobans or Logans were led by a chief named Gilligorm in a feud with the Frasers in Easter Ross somewhere about 1200 (too early for 'Frasers' or 'Logans' of course). In a battle at Drumderfit, Gilligorm was killed and his widow carried off by the Frasers. She later gave birth to Gilligorm's posthumous son, called *Crotair* (humpbacked) MacGilligorm. His disability was supposedly due to the Frasers breaking his back when a baby to prevent him taking revenge on them when he grew up. He went into the Church and had a son (priests in the Celtic Church were not barred from marriage), called *Gillie Fhinnein* (disciple of St Finnan) and MacLennan is the anglicised version of this name.

THE CLAN

There was a saying, 'as old as the Lobans of Drumderfit', and they were still in residence in the early 18th century. At the

house they kept a wooden figure of the legendary Gilligorm, but it was unfortunately destroyed (along with the house) in the wake of the Jacobite rising of 1715.

There were, and are, many MacLennans in Ross. They were connected with the MacRaes and were standard bearers to the Seaforth Mackenzies (two MacLennans died in defence of the standard at the battle of Auldearn in 1645), but there are few records of them as a clan, and the chiefship was lost for many years until recently traced to Canada.

The name Logan appears in the south at an early date. The 'Good Sir James' Douglas was accompanied by two knights of that name when he set out to take Bruce's heart to the Holy Lands. They died fighting alongside him in Spain in 1329.

Sir Robert Logan of Restalrig, near Edinburgh, married a daughter of King Robert II and was Admiral of Scotland in 1406. This family held Fast Castle on the coast of Berwickshire, but they fell from favour and the last Logan of Restalrig died an outlaw. Fast Castle ('Wolf's Crag' in Scott's *The Bride of Lammermoor*) passed into the possession of the Homes.

In relation to the history of the Highlands, and of tartan in particular,

ABOVE *Logan Botanic Gardens, at Port Logan on the Rhinns of Galloway, established in the mid-19th century. A sheltered position and the warm current of the Gulf Stream permit subtropical plants to flourish.*

few names are more honoured than that of James Logan, author of *The Scottish Gael* (1831). This was the first serious effort to record the history of Highland dress. He gave details, though not illustrations, of about 50 tartans and most scholarly work on the subject starts with him, Gaelic sources notwithstanding.

CLAN ASSOCIATION

Balgate House, Kiltarlity, Beauly IV4 7HH, Scotland

31 Ascaig Crescent, Glasgow G52 1QN
1003 West Anderson, Pensacola, FL 32501, USA

MACALISTER

NAME AND PLACE

The MacAlisters of Loup take their name from Alasdair, younger son of Donald of Islay, grandson of the mighty Somerled. Their homeland was Kintyre.

ORIGINS

They were thus a branch of Clan Donald – the senior branch in fact – though some of the MacAlisters were later vassals of the Campbell earls of Argyll and survived Campbell hegemony in their homelands with more success than most.

THE CLAN

Alasdair *Mór* died in battle against his cousin, the MacDougall Lord of Lorne, in 1299 and his descendants settled mainly in Kintyre. Charles MacAlister was appointed steward of Kintyre by King James III in 1481; his headquarters were at Dunaverty Castle. By about this time branches of the MacAlisters were also settling in Arran, where they were to give bonds of manrent to the Hamiltons, and in Bute.

Charles's son was known as 'John of the Lowb', or 'Loup', from a Gaelic word meaning bend or curve and apparently referring to the shape of the coastline of MacAlister territory. Later chiefs retain this appellation and the Gaelic title *Mac Eoin Duibh* (son of Black John).

The MacAlistairs of Tarbert belonged to a cadet branch of the MacAlisters of Loup. They became hereditary constables of the royal castle of Tarbert, on behalf of the earls of Argyll, hereditary keepers. A 'tarbert' is a place where a boat can be dragged overland from one shore to another (in this case the neck of land linking Kintyre and Knapdale), and it was by this trick that King Magnus Barefoot of Norway in 1093 defined the fertile and therefore desirable peninsula or Kintyre as an island – and thus part of Norway's possessions, not Scotland's. It consequently passed into the domain of the lord of the Isles until the Campbells took over in the 17th century.

BELOW *Kintyre was the early homeland of the MacAlisters as well as other kinfolk of the Campbells of Argyll. The photograph shows the supposed footprint of St Columba landing on the Mull of Kintyre on his mission from Ireland.*

Another branch of the clan, who took the name Alexander (equivalent to Alasdair), settled at Menstrie in Clackmannanshire, as vassals of the Earl of Argyll, in the 16th century. In 1603 William Alexander of Menstrie (1567–1640), poet and courtier, was among those who accompanied King James VI to London. He was knighted by the king, an admirer of his poetry, and later created Viscount, then Earl of Stirling. He was acknowledged as chief of the clan by the MacAlisters of Tarbert, presumably impressed by these honours, but not by the MacAlisters of Loup.

Another family of Alexanders, claiming descent from the house of Menstrie, settled in Ireland in the 17th century and became earls of Caledon. Their most famous descendant was Field Marshall Lord Alexander of Tunis.

The MacAlisters of Loup, the senior house, were supporters of the royal house of Stewart. Alexander, eighth of Loup, fought at Killiecrankie with Bonnie Dundee and took part in King James VII/II's ill-fated campaign in Ireland which ended with the battle of the Boyne (1690). His brother, who succeeded after the early death of his son, married the daughter of Lamont of that ilk.

In the late 18th century their grandson made a much more fortunate marriage

ABOVE *The Battle of the Boyne (1690) ended the first effort to restore the Stuart monarchy by force. MacAlister of Loup was among a number of veterans of Claverhouse's campaign who fought in Ireland for James against the forces of William III.*

than this, to Janet Somerville, an heiress who brought him the estate of Kennox in Ayrshire. Thereafter the chiefs of Clan MacAlister, styled MacAlister of Loup and Kennox, continued to maintain their seat in Kennox.

The Tarbert family went bankrupt in 1745, losing their lands and castle, but they survived to produce a famous principal of Glasgow University, Sir Donald Macalister of Tarbert (1845–1934).

CLAN ASSOCIATION
Glenbarr Abbey, Glenbarr, Tarbert PA29 6UT, Scotland

MACALPINE

NAME AND PLACE

The name means 'son of Alpin' and the original MacAlpin was of course Kenneth MacAlpin himself, that rather mysterious figure who was the founder of the Scottish kingdom in 843. It is said that former MacAlpine chiefs had their seat at Dunstaffnage Castle in Argyll, an early capital of Kenneth MacAlpin.

ORIGIN

The main question about Kenneth MacAlpin is: How did he do it? A hundred years earlier the Picts had practically wiped out the Scots of Dalriada, and had defeated them again less than ten years before, yet Kenneth MacAlpin's victory was so conclusive that even the Pictish language soon disappeared. He was helped by having a claim to the Pictish throne through his mother, and he appears to have helped himself in a misty episode in which the seven Pictish earls of Alba were apparently murdered at a stroke during a conference at Scone where they were supposed to be discussing the question of the succession with MacAlpin. Probably the decisive factor was the attacks of the Vikings. Norse attacks drove the Scots

towards the centre, while the attacks of the Danes, with whom MacAlpin may possibly have been in league, weakened the Picts.

THE CLAN

The name MacAlpine is fairly common today, but there is little trace of a Clan MacAlpine and, although there is a modern tartan, there is no chief.

A great many clans and families can claim indirect descent from the royal house, but those particularly associated with *Sìol Ailpein* (descendants of Alpin) were the MacGregors, Grants, MacNabs, Mackinnons and MacAulays, all of whom have the pine tree as their badge. *Sìol Ailpein* was never as effective a confederation of clans as Clan Chattan, but there was a strong tradition of friendship, particularly between the MacGregors and the Grants, on the face of it unlikely allies. The name MacAlpine is associated with the MacGregors especially. Among the Grants, when a famous laird of Rothiemurchus was adopted into Clan Gregor because of the good services he had rendered them, he took the name of MacAlpine.

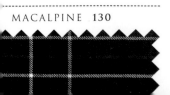

MACARTHUR

NAME AND PLACE

Argyll is the MacArthurs' homeland, and they claim as their progenitor King Arthur of the Round Table.

ORIGINS

Several old Gaelic sayings testify to the ancient origins of the MacArthurs. For instance, things are said to be 'as old as the hills, the MacArthurs and the Devil'.

THE CLAN

In the 13th century a MacArthur married the heiress of Duncan MacDuibhne or O'Duin who in a royal charter was later acknowledged as the progenitor of the Campbell lords of Lochow (Loch Awe).

The Campbells are also called *Ua Duibhne*, and as their modern surname had not yet been generally adopted in Argyll, there is some reason to suppose that the MacArthurs and the future Campbells belonged to the same stock. The hereditary pipers to the MacDonalds were named MacArthur, and so were the armourers of MacDonald of Islay.

The MacArthurs of Loch Awe supported Bruce and they were rewarded, at the expense of the MacDougalls who unwisely opposed Bruce, with considerable lands in Lorne together with the keepership of Dunstaffnage Castle.

This was the peak of their prosperity, and it did not last. When James I returned from exile in England and launched his campaign to re-establish the authority of the Crown by crushing all who threatened it, one of the sufferers was Iain MacArthur, Chief of Clan Arthur. 'A great prince among his own people and leader of a thousand men', he was executed in 1427 and his lands, or most of them, forfeited. For practical purposes this was the end of the clan.

Later MacArthurs of Scottish origin include John MacArthur (1767–1834), who arrived in New South Wales in 1790 as a soldier. He was among the first sheep farmers in Australia, and is said to have planted the first Australian vineyard.

The American General Douglas MacArthur was the grandson of an emigrant from Strathclyde.

CLAN ASSOCIATION

14 Hill Park Wood, Edinburgh EH4 7TA, Scotland

24479 Audubon Drive, Brooksville, FL 34601, USA

44 Kiora Street, Panania, NSW 2213, Australia

MACAULAY

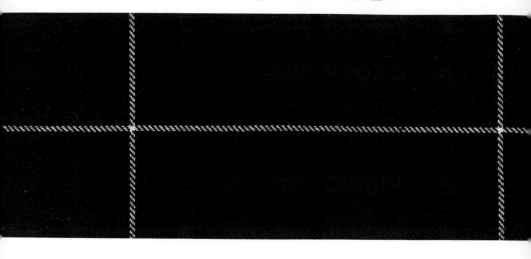

NAME AND PLACE

There were two Clans MacAulay,
who were unconnected by blood and
occupied widely separated regions, in
Dumbartonshire and the Isle of Lewis.

ORIGINS

The MacAulays of Ardencaple were in
Dumbartonshire by the 16th century. Sir
Aulay MacAulay of Ardencaple appears
in a roll of landlords in 1587, as a vassal
of the Earl of Lennox. Although
separated by rather a long period, it is
reasonable to assume he was a
descendant of *Amhlaidh Mac Amhlaidh*
(Aulay MacAulay) who lived in the
late 13th century and was possibly the
son or grandson of Aulay, a younger
son of the Earl of Lennox, whose name
appears in charters somewhat earlier.
The Lennox connection would give the
MacAulays ancestors among the royal
house of Munster.

    The derivation of the name of the
MacAulays of Lewis is different, meaning
'son of Olaf', though there is some doubt
as to the Olaf in question. He is
presumed to have been Olaf the Black,
King of Man and the Isles (including
Lewis), who died in 1237. An early
ancestor was Donald *Cam* (crooked),
who lived around 1600 and is the subject
of heroic folk tales. Sir Iain Moncrieffe of

BELOW *Ardencaple Castle. The original
house was converted to this baronial hall by
a Campbell in the 19th century.*

that ilk suggested that these MacAulays
originated on the mainland (perhaps at
Ullapool ('Olaf's Palace'), where they
were certainly quite numerous in later
times. These mainland MacAulays
regarded themselves as a sept of the
MacAulays of Lewis.

THE CLAN

The MacAulays of Ardencaple thought of
themselves as members of *Siol Ailpein*,
and so connected with the MacGregors.
MacAulay of Ardencaple gave a bond of
manrent to MacGregor of Glenstrae in
1591 in which he described his own
family as a branch of MacGregor's house
(which would throw some doubt on the
Lennox connection). This was at a time
when kinship with the MacGregors was
not something to broadcast, and
MacAulay's motive may have been his
need for friends in a feud provoked by
the murder of a MacAulay by the
Buchanans the previous year.

However, the MacAulays escaped the
fate which overtook the MacGregors in
the 17th century, despite the enmity of
the Campbells, and remained in
possession of Ardencaple until 1767,
when the bankrupt twelfth chief was
compelled to sell out to the Duke of
Argyll. The Campbells turned the castle
into a typical Victorian Scots-baronial
hall in the 19th century before selling it
to Colquhoun of Luss. It is now a ruin.

The northern MacAulays produced a
notable line of Presbyterian ministers.
Zachary Macaulay (1768–1838), a
famous opponent of slavery and one-time
governor of Sierre Leone, came from this
line. His son was Thomas Babington
Macaulay (1800–59), the historian and
essayist, who was created Lord Macaulay
in 1857 but had no descendants.
Macaulay was born in Leicestershire and
had little affection for his Highland
heritage (see his 'A Jacobite's Epitaph').

MACBEAN

NAME AND PLACE

Like so many names derived from Gaelic
(there are several possible originals),
MacBean poses a number of problems.
MacBain and MacVean are common
variations. MacBeath or MacBeth,
McVane, etc also occur. The 19th-century
scholar Alexander MacBain stated that
the clan name *Mac Bheathain* (MacBean)
would earlier have been MacBeath. It has
also been suggested that the name may
derive from *Bàn*, meaning fair-headed,
although this is perhaps unlikely.

BELOW *Detail of a portrait of a warrior of
Clan MacBean by the 19th-century
Highland artist, R. R. MacIan, in his Clans
of the Scottish Highlands.*

ORIGINS

According to tradition the MacBeans
came from Lochaber with Eva, a Clan
Chattan heiress, when she married Angus
Mackintosh of Mackintosh.

THE CLAN

A MacBean with his four sons settled in
Petty, near Inverness, in the 14th century
and came under Mackintosh protection,
engaging in a feud with the Red Comyn
and killing his steward, though whether
the steward's death was the cause or
effect of their Mackintosh alliance is
unclear. Many MacBeans are said to
have died at 'Red' Harlaw in 1411,
when Mackintosh supported Donald,
Lord of the Isles, in his claim to the
earldom of Ross.

The MacBean territory was established around the northern end of Loch Ness, the senior family in Kinchyle, and with heavy concentration in Dores, site of the modern MacBean memorial. The surname does not appear in historical records until the 17th century, although thanks to the form of patronymic name-giving (X son of W, son of V, etc.), a series of MacBean chiefs can be traced to the 15th century.

The MacBeans were powerful warriors. Aeneas MacBean of Kinchyle served with the Mackintoshes in the Jacobite rising of 1715 and his brother, the mighty Gillies, was one of the heroes of Culloden. A major in the Clan Chattan regiment, he was felled by a bayonet but rose and retreated as far as a stone wall, where he was overtaken by dragoons and infantry. Broadsword in hand, he placed his back against the wall and fought with such courage and tenacity that he won the admiration of the chivalrous Earl of Ancrum, who tried to call his men off. But Gillies had killed 14 of them and they were not inclined to be merciful. The dragoons trampled him under their horses' hooves and left him for dead, but he managed to crawl to a farm where the farmfolk covered him with straw and, when he died, buried him under a lathe stone.

Echoing this achievement, William MacBean, who enlisted in the Sutherland Highlanders and eventually rose to command the regiment, gained the Victoria Cross for an incident at Lucknow (1858) in which he single-handedly killed 11 of the enemy.

The MacBeans of Tomatin, who were in business, survived the difficulties of the late 18th century and held on to their lands in Strathdearn, but the chiefly family of Kinchyle was less fortunate. The chief himself was forced to join the army, and in his absence Kinchyle had to be sold. The chiefship continued among his

ABOVE *Loch Ness. The MacBean territories lay mainly around the northern end of the Loch, in Kinchyle and Dores.*

descendants in Canada and in 1958 passed to an American businessman, Hughston MacBean, who repurchased part of Kinchyle and founded the MacBean memorial park east of Dores.

CLAN ASSOCIATION
441 Wadsworth Boulevard, Suite 213, Denver, CO 80226, USA

MACCALLUM (MALCOLM)

NAME AND PLACE

The name MacCallum means 'son of Colm', that is (it is said) St Columba. A thousand years divides St Columba from the earliest mention of the MacCallums in documentary records, when they were settled in Lorne, Argyll.

ORIGINS

Legend tells us that their original seat was at Colgin, near Oban, where the chief lived with his three sons. They spread in the following manner. On their father's direction each son went out with a donkey loaded with panniers to settle wherever the panniers slipped from the donkeys' backs. In the case of the eldest son they fell off before he had left the parental homestead. The panniers of the two younger sons slipped off at Glentive and Kilmartin, where they accordingly founded their cadet houses. As Sir Thomas Innes remarked, 'a more definite account ... from documentary sources would be preferable' to this tale.

THE CLAN

Documentary sources may be fairly meagre, but we do know that in 1414 Sir Duncan Campbell granted lands in Craignish to Ranald MacCallum, whom he also made hereditary Constable of Craignish Castle. The MacCallums of

BELOW *Duntroon (Duntrune) Castle, overlooks the sea Loch Crinan and the sheltered entrance to Crinan harbour.*

Poltalloch can be dated from 1562, when by a charter of Duncan Campbell of Duntrune that property was bestowed on 'Donald McGillespie vich o Callum', that is, Donald son of Gillespie (Archibald), son of the descendants of Callum. Both Poltalloch and Duntrune thus became MacCallum property.

In 1647 Zachary MacCallum of Poltalloch, a man renowned for his strength, died in a famous fight. Like all his line he was an adherent of the Campbells, and at Ederline he encountered a party of MacDonalds. He killed seven of them and was fighting the redoubtable Alasdair MacColla (Sir Alexander MacDonald) when treacherously attacked from the rear by a man wielding a scythe. This enabled MacColla to kill him.

A later Zachary MacCallum, fifth MacCallum of Poltalloch (d. 1688), inherited Corbarron from his kinsman, who was the last of the line of Ranald MacCallum, Constable of Craignish.

The MacCallums of Poltalloch have held the chiefship since the time of Donald MacGillespie. In the 18th century they changed their name to Malcolm, which also occurs as an earlier variant, apparently because it was simpler. John Malcolm, fifteenth Laird of Poltalloch, was a member of parliament for Argyll in the late 19th century and was subsequently raised to the peerage as Lord Malcolm of Poltalloch. The title expired with him in 1902. The home of the present Malcolm of Poltalloch and chief of the clan is Duntrune Castle, a venerable but more amenable house than Poltalloch. (See also Malcolm.)

ABOVE *Figure of St Columba, supposed ancestor of the 'sons of Colm', from a modern stained-glass window at Iona.*

CLAN ASSOCIATION
P O Box 494, Carrboro, NC 27510, USA

MACDONALD

NAME AND PLACE

The Gaelic name of which Donald is an anglicisation is *Domhnall* (world ruler), and some clans adopted the spelling MacDonell, which is the same as MacDonald – son of Donald – and rather closer to the Gaelic form. It is worth noting that the name MacDonald (or MacDonell, or most other clan names), did not come into general use as a surname until about 1500).

ORIGINS

Clan Donald, as any MacDonald will readily tell you, is the oldest and greatest of the Highland clans. Originally it was a single clan, but some branches later became substantial independent clans. The progenitor of the MacDonalds was Donald, son of Ranald, son of Somerled (d. 1164).

THE CLAN

In spite of his Norse name (or nickname?), Somerled was a Gael on his father's side: both his father and paternal grandfather had Gaelic names. He ended Norse dominance on the mainland of Argyll and built up his own principality which included Arran and Bute. By marriage to a daughter of King Olaf of the Isles, backed up by force, he acquired the Southern Isles (Bute to Mull), leaving the Norse king (now Olaf's son) in possession of the Outer Hebrides, which were traditionally Norse.

The kings of Norway and the Scots were Somerled's nominal overlords, but he was effectively an independent ruler of considerable military and naval might. However, in challenging the King of Scots he overreached himself. The great fleet which he led up the Clyde to attack the heart of the Lowlands was defeated in 1164 and Somerled was assassinated.

His lands, according to Norse custom, were divided between his three sons. Dugall, presumably the eldest and the ancestor of Clan Dougal, received the mainland possessions plus some adjacent islands; Ranald (Reginald) received Kintyre and Islay; Angus received Bute

BELOW *The Clan Donald Centre at Armadale above the Sound of Sleat, in the region known as 'the garden of Skye'.*

(which by marriage of his granddaughter,
eventually passed to the Stewarts).
Ranald had two sons who divided their
father's inheritance between them.
Donald, founder of the MacDonalds,
held part of Kintyre and some of the
Southern Isles, including Islay, the future
heart of the lordship of the Isles.

Donald's possessions were small
compared with those held by his
descendants, but they were soon to
increase. The MacDonalds did not
benefit much from the administrative
reorganisation of 1266 which followed
the defeat of the Norwegian King
Haakon at Largs and the secession of the
Norse kingdom of the Isles to Scotland.
The main beneficiary then was the Earl of
Ross, whose territories were extended to
Skye and Lewis. However, during the
wars of independence the MacDougalls
of Mull, who as sons of Dugall were
senior to the MacDonalds of Islay, were
allies of Balliol and, after Bruce became
king, fought on the side of the English.
As a result they were forfeited and the
MacDonalds of Islay, under the
leadership of Angus *Mór* (son of Donald)
and his son Angus *Òg* received Mull, in
line with Bruce's policy of bestowing
forfeited lands on near-relations to avert
resentment. Loyalties were complex in
these years: Angus *Òg* was actually a
younger son: his elder brother Alexander
was allied by marriage with the Red
Comyns, enemies of Bruce, and he too
was forfeited to the benefit of Angus *Òg*.

Angus *Òg*'s territories thus extended
from Ardnamurchan to Islay, including a
section of Lochaber on the mainland.
This, however, was only about a fifth of
the territory of the lords of the Isles, the
first of whom was Angus *Òg*'s son and
heir John (or Iain or Eoin).

ABOVE *Loch Scridail, Mull. Mull belonged
to the MacDougals until the time of Robert
Bruce, when that clan was forfeited and the
island was passed to the MacDonalds.*

CLAN ASSOCIATION

Clan MacDonald Centre, Armadale, Isle
of Skye, IV45, Scotland

Donald Society of Glasgow, 21 Carr
Meadow, Bamber Bridge, Preston
PR5 8HR

17 Glenview Drive NE, Rome,
GA 30165-9000, USA

45A Vermont Street, Sutherland,
NSW 2232, Australia

MACDONALD OF THE ISLES

NAME AND PLACE: see MacDonald

ORIGINS: see MacDonald

In spite of his father's support for the Bruce (it was probably Angus Òg who sheltered and supplied Bruce after the battle of Methven in 1306), John of Islay did not feel bound to obedience to Bruce's successor King David II, who, however, brought him round by granting him the island of Lewis. Greater acquisitions were made through marriage. John's wife was the sister and heiress of Ranald MacRuari, descended from a younger son of Ranald, son of Somerled. On the murder of Ranald MacRuari, John of Islay acquired the southern half of the Outer Hebrides (North and South Uist, Barra and others.), Rum and adjacent isles, and the district of Garmoran (Moidard and Knoydart) on the mainland. He kept these extensive possessions and, having divorced his first wife in 1350, married the daughter of the future King Robert II, the first Stewart king. This second marriage brought him Kintyre and much of Knapdale after the accession of his father-in-law to the Scottish throne.

John of Islay was now the ruler of territories much larger than those held by the old Norse kings of the Isles.

Moreover, his castle of Finlaggan on Islay was strategically preferable to the Norse Isle of Man. In 1354 he bestowed on himself the title Dominus Insularum (Lord of the Isles). The Gaelic title was *Buachaille nan Eileanan* (Shepherd of the Isles).

The first Lord of the Isles had a son by each wife. Ranald was the elder, but by agreement the second son, Donald, the nephew of the king of Scots, succeeded as Lord of the Isles, while Ranald was given the MacRuari inheritance, as a vassal of his younger brother.

Donald, second Lord of the Isles, married the sister of the Earl of Ross, whose territories were in extent second only to his own. When the earl died his legal successor was his daughter, but she was set on a religious life and the Regent Albany secured the earldom for her maternal uncle, the Earl of Buchan, who happened to be Albany's son. This led to one of the most famous campaigns of the lords of the Isles, since it was clear that Donald's wife had a prior claim as a sister of the late Earl of Ross. Full of wrath, Donald gathered his men, including such famous subordinate chiefs as the MacLeod chief, Red Hector of the Battles, and swept across Scotland towards Aberdeen. They were met at Harlaw (1411) by the Regent's army, commanded by the Earl of Mar (Alexander Stewart, who was Donald's cousin, both being grandsons of King Robert II). The fight was ferocious, Red Hector was killed, and neither side could claim a victory. But Donald was forced to withdraw to his own territories, though he did not withdraw his claim to the earldom of Ross.

When opposed to the king of Scots it was natural though ultimately dangerous for the lords – or kings, as they sometimes styled themselves – of the Isles to seek alliance with England, which treated them as the sovereign lords they were in fact if not in law (the king of

KING EDWARD THE III.th

ABOVE *Edward I's policy towards Scotland was always devisive. The Treaty of Ardtornish between himself and John of the Isles in 1462 recognised the independence of the lords of the Isles. Once the Scottish king found out, John was stripped of his possessions on the mainland. When his successors tried to take them back by force, they were defeated and in 1493 the lordship was forfeited to the Scottish crown.*

Scots being their overlord). This alliance had been renewed as recently as 1408, but the English provided no assistance at Harlaw and subsequently made peace with Albany.

Donald died in 1423 and was succeeded by his son Alexander, who eventually acquired the huge Ross earldom, for which his father had fought, by grant of King James I.

The lordship of the Isles now reached its greatest extent. Perhaps it was too large: the lord of the Isles confronted similar problems to the king of Scots in asserting his authority in distant and inaccessible regions.

The lordship of the Isles, spoken of by its enemies as if it were an association of savages, was a centre of Gaelic culture which to some extent went into decline when the lordship ceased to exist.

The MacDonald lords governed with the advice of their council from Finlaggan. The administration of justice was good: local judges existed in every major district, and the lord's council acted as a court of appeal. Although the great chieftains were the lord's feudal vassals, this was essentially a Gaelic state in which ties of kinship were strong. As long as it existed the rivalries and feuds of the developing clans were at least contained if not always prevented. In this respect too, the destruction of the lordship was a disaster.

From a wider, national viewpoint, however, the lordship of the Isles was always a potential and sometimes an actual menace. King James I was determined to assert the authority of the Crown and in 1427, having summoned the Highland chiefs to parliament, he arrested 40 of them, including Alexander, third Lord of the Isles. Some were executed, including at least one of the lord's kinsmen, and on his release he promptly raised a rebellion and burned Inverness. But he was later defeated and imprisoned again. The result of this was

another western rising, led by Alexander's cousin Donald Balloch, though it was suppressed after early success. King James I then sensibly changed his policy, releasing Alexander who was restored to the lordship and soon after succeeded to the earldom of Ross on the death of his mother.

Nothing was permanently solved thereby, and in 1462 the fourth Lord, John, together with the Earl of Douglas and others, was involved in a conspiracy with the English to divide the country between them. The terms of this treaty of Ardtornish (or Westminster) soon became public knowledge, and in 1476 the Lord of the Isles was deprived of much of his territory, including Kintyre and the earldom of Ross.

This was unacceptable to Angus Òg, illegitimate son of John, who was married to a daughter of the Earl of Argyll, and the result was a serious split, with Angus Òg and his father on opposite sides. The MacDonalds themselves were willing to follow Angus Òg, but the non-MacDonald vassals, notably the MacLeods and Mackenzies, remained loyal to the fourth Lord. At the battle of Bloody Bay (Mull) in 1480 Angus Òg was victorious, capturing his father as well as two MacLean chieftains. He was about to execute MacLean of Ardgour on the spot but was prevented by MacDonald of Moidart, who protested, 'If MacLean were gone, who should I have to quarrel with?'

Angus Òg was murdered by his own harper in 1490, but almost immediately the conflict was renewed. The Islemen's leader now was Alexander of Lochalsh, nephew of the fourth Lord of the Isles, who captured Inverness and ravaged the lands of the Mackenzies until defeated by them at Park.

John of the Isles was now an old man and though he had played no active part in the recent rebellion, he had again been intriguing with the English. The lordship

ABOVE *A peaceful scene in Moidart, MacDonald country.*

of the Isles was therefore annexed to the Crown in 1493, and John, fourth and last Lord of the Isles, died in a Dundee boarding house a few years later.

Unfortunately, this was not the end of the matter. For many years afterwards efforts were made to restore the lordship, most notably by Donald *Dubh* (Black Donald), son of Angus *Òg*. The young Donald was captured in 1506, not long after the Islesmen had yet again burned Inverness, but after almost 40 years in prison he escaped in 1545 and, though he must have been ill-fitted for warfare then, at once rose in rebellion in alliance with Henry VIII of England. With MacLean assistance he raised a force of 8,000 men and 180 galleys against the King of Scots. Loyalties die hard in the Highlands, as the descendants of Donald *Dubh*'s men were to prove exactly 200 years later.

Donald *Dubh* died in 1546 and the rebellion fizzled out amid mutual recriminations. The western clans held together by the lords of the Isles had now become quarrelsome and independent units, though they were at last prepared to forget their heritage as 'auld enemys to the realme of Scotland' and to acknowledge the Stewart dynasty as their rightful sovereigns.

MACDONALD OF SLEAT

NAME AND PLACE: see MacDonald

ORIGINS: see MacDonald

After the downfall of the lords of the Isles the individual clans which had come into being during the lordship became effectively independent. Their chiefs were tenants of the Crown, holding their land on leases rather than as vassals of the lord of the Isles. The chiefship of Clan Donald, disputed between various rivals, was no longer a force for union, rather the reverse, and since the Crown was initially unable to supply the authority of the forfeited lordship clan feuds were a frequent cause of disorder.

Alexander, third Lord of the Isles, had three sons, including his successor John. The youngest of them was Hugh, who inherited the barony of Sleat, on Skye, as his share of his father's estate. He lived until 1498, after the abolition of the lordship.

The remains of his castle at Dunskaith can still be seen, although it was finally abandoned in the 16th century by his descendant Donald *Gorm* in favour of the impregnably situated Duntulm, standing near Kilmuir.

The MacDonalds of Sleat were known as *Clann Uisdein* (children of Hugh) and sometimes Clan Donald

BELOW *Remains of the strategically sited castle of Duntulm, Skye, headquarters of Donald Gorm, fifth MacDonald of Sleat, and not far from the great Macleod stronghold at Dunvegan.*

North, to distinguish them from the MacDonalds on Islay (Clan Donald South). The early chiefs were invariably – and later chiefs often – called Donald, which is apt to cause confusion. Donald *Gorm*, fifth of Sleat, was involved in an attempt to recover the lordship of the Isles in 1539. He drove the MacLeods out of Trotternish and invaded Kintail, but while besieging the Mackenzie castle of Eilean Donan during his attempt to recover the earldom of Ross he was killed by a chance arrow.

After the death of Donald *Dubh* the MacDonalds of Sleat represented the senior male line of Clan Donald. Donald *Gorm Mór*, seventh of Sleat, was last in the direct line from Hugh and a still more formidable warrior than his earlier namesake. He assisted the Irish rebels against Elizabeth of England with a force of 500 men and at a later date, offering his aid to the same queen, he described himself as 'Lord of the Isles of Scotland and chief of the whole Clan Donald Irishmen wheresoever'. By that time he had made peace with King James VI, whose government secured his release after he had been captured while raiding the MacLeans of Mull. Although there were a few little upsets in this new relationship, Donald *Gorm Mór* appeared in Edinburgh together with other Highland chiefs in 1610 and agreed to accept certain limitations on his household.

The MacDonalds of Sleat were generally loyal to the Stewarts. They supported Mary Queen of Scots, fought with Montrose during the civil war and under 'Bonnie Dundee' for King James VII/II at Killiecrankie. As a result of their support of the rising of 1715 the estates were forfeited, but later restored. In 1745, however, the chief, Sir Alexander MacDonald of Sleat, who was influenced by Forbes of Culloden and also appalled by the prince's lack of preparations, refused to bring his men out, despite his natural sympathies. He was in poor health anyway, dying in 1746.

The first baronet, created in 1625, was Sir Donald MacDonald, nephew and successor of Donald *Gorm Mór*. Sir Alexander, ninth baronet, was created Lord MacDonald in 1796. As a result of his marriage his successor became heir to the Bosville estates in Thorpe, Yorkshire, in 1832. By an arrangement which had to be ratified by act of parliament, his eldest son inherited the Bosville estates, adopting the Bosville name, while the chiefship and the MacDonald peerage went to a younger son. However, in 1910 Bosville's grandson regained the chiefship of MacDonald of Sleat, although Lord MacDonald, descendant of the third lord, remained Chief of the Name, ie of the Clan Donald. This unusual arrangement was confirmed by the Lyon Court in 1947.

MACDONALD OF CLAN RANALD

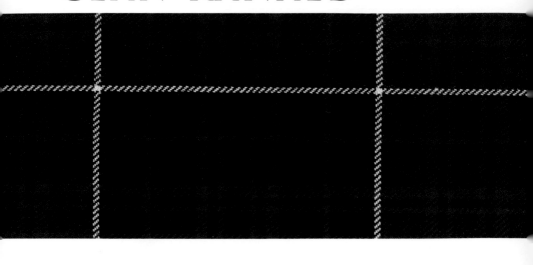

NAME AND PLACE: see MacDonald

ORIGINS:
see MacDonald; MacDonald of the Isles

The progenitor of the MacDonalds of Clan Ranald was Ranald, son of John, first Lord of the Isles. For about four centuries Clan Ranald's stronghold was the dramatic fortress of Eilean Tioram which commands Loch Moidart from its rocky island below Ardmolich. Ranald was the Lord of the Isles's eldest son, but the title went to his younger half-brother whose mother was a daughter of the future King Robert II, while Ranald received the MacRuari inheritance from his own mother.

THE CLAN

Clanranald (the chief) was a loyal vassal of the Lord of the Isles, and it was a member of his house, Donald Balloch, who attempted to rescue Alexander of the Isles from imprisonment in the fortress of Tantallon.

The history of the clan in the 16th century was notably turbulent. Dugall, the sixth Clanranald, was killed by his own kin for unspecified 'cruelties', and replaced as chief by his uncle, Alastair. When Alastair died in 1530 he was succeeded by his illegitimate son, John of Moidart (*Ian Mùideatach*), who fell foul of the royal government and was imprisoned along with other chiefs during King James V's visit to the Hebrides in 1540. An attempt was then made by the Frasers to assert the claims to the chiefship of a candidate amenable to them, Ranald *Gallda* (the Stranger), who was the son of the fifth chief by a Fraser wife and had been fostered by the Frasers. He proved unacceptable to Clan Ranald, and the controversy eventually led to one of the bloodiest battles in Highland history, *Blar-na-Léine*, 'the battle of the Shirts' (1544).

The Frasers had approached with a powerful alliance led by the Earl of

BELOW *Castle Tioram, which dominates Loch Moidart from its island, was the seat of Clanranald until the dispersion of the clan in the late 18th century.*

Huntly, but the Earl of Argyll, in his official capacity as the king's lieutenant in the west, intervened to prevent the battle. On their way home the Frasers unwisely separated from their allies and were ambushed by Clan Ranald on the north side of Loch Lochy. As it was a hot day both sides abandoned their plaids and fought in their shirts.

Legends have accrued around this famous conflict. It is said that over 300 Frasers were killed, including their chief, Lord Lovat, his son and Ranald *Gallda* himself, and that only five survived – also that all 80 of the Fraser 'gentlemen' who fell left pregnant widows who later without exception gave birth to sons! Clan Ranald are said to have suffered even worse casualties, with a dozen or so survivors out of 500, but among them was John of Moidart. Though Huntly returned to extract revenge, John of Moidart survived that as well and lived to gain royal recognition as chief of Clan Ranald and, surprisingly, the friendship of the next Lord Lovat. He died in 1584. His grandson Sir Donald, tenth chief, was knighted by King James VI.

Powerful and prosperous, retaining possession of their lands while other clans and families were losing theirs, Clan Ranald played an important part in the internecine conflicts of the 17th and 18th centuries, their activities recorded, not without understandable bias, in the *Leabhar Dearg*, the Red Book of Clan Ranald.

John, eleventh Clanranald, supported Montrose in 1644–45. Some 700 MacDonalds of Clan Ranald fought at Killiecrankie and the thirteenth Clanranald was killed at Sheriffmuir (1715). He was succeeded by his brother, who died in exile at the Jacobite court. The future seventeenth chief was one of the first to rally to Prince Charles in 1745, and many members of Clan Ranald played prominent roles in the ensuing campaign.

ABOVE *A peaceful scene on the shores of Loch Lochy, not far from the site of the frightful Battle of the Shirts in 1544. In spite of the name, which suggests something unusual, it was common practice for Highlanders to discard their plaids before a fight.*

The estates were forfeited after Culloden but later restored. Sadly, Clan Ranald's luck ran out when the seventeenth chief's grandson succeeded in 1794. This wretched fellow preferred the frivolity of Regency society in London and Brighton and managed to squander his vast resources (rents alone brought him the enormous sum of £25,000 a year) to such an extent that practically all the Clan Ranald territories were sold out to sheep-raising landlords. The clan disintegrated.

CLAN ASSOCIATION
Wester Lix Cottage, Killin FK21 8RD, Scotland

MACDONALD OF CLAN
RANALD 146–147

MACDONELL OF GLENGARRY

NAME AND PLACE

The MacDonells of Glengarry were a cadet branch of Clan Ranald (see page 146), descended from Donald, son of the founder of Clan Ranald. Their castle at Invergarry overlooking Loch Oich is today a grim, intimidating ruin. The Gaelic name of the chief, *Mac Mhic Alasdair*, derives from the fourth MacDonell of Glengarry.

The sixth Glengarry married Margaret, daughter of Sir Alexander MacDonald of Lochalsh, the senior surviving line of the lords of the Isles, and this gave his successors a questionable claim to the chiefship of Clan Donald. Since Margaret was not the sole heiress of Lochalsh, it also led to a long and bloody feud with the expanding power of the Mackenzies over that desirable property.

A number of the Glengarry chiefs adopted a high-handed attitude to the world at large which was excessive even by Highland standards. One example was Angus, ninth Glengarry, created Lord MacDonell and Aros at the Restoration (1660), who attempted to dictate humiliating terms to the burgh of Inverness after two of his men had been killed in a brawl in the marketplace there in 1665 (he did later obtain substantial damages).

Generally, Glengarry loyalties were the same as Clan Ranald's, and the future Lord MacDonell had earned his promotion by fighting with Montrose in 1644. His successor, Alasdair *Dubh* (he did not inherit the title as he came from another branch, MacDonell of Scotus), fought for King James VII/II in 1688–89 and carried the royal standard at Sheriffmuir.

According to General Wade, in 1716 Glengarry could put 500 men in the field, but rather more than that were present among Prince Charles's forces in 1745,

BELOW *Invergarry Castle, above Loch Oich, the uninviting stronghold of the MacDonells of Glengarry. In the miserable times after the Forty-Five, a militia company was formed of the starving clansmen. Many of them later emigrated to Ontario, where they prospered.*

under the chief's son Angus Òg.
Unfortunately, Angus was killed when
the musket of a MacDonald of Clan
Ranald went off while being cleaned –
the unfortunate perpetrator also being
killed according to the rough Old
Testament precepts accepted in the
Highlands. Dispirited by the loss of their
leader, many Glengarry men deserted (the
incident did not improve the morale of
Clan Ranald either) though there
remained 500 of them in the MacDonell
regiment at Culloden under the
command of the 18-year-old younger son
of the chief, who himself took no part in
the fighting though he was afterwards
imprisoned along with his son.

It is said, though not in front of a
MacDonell, that the thirteenth chief
subsequently changed sides, acting as a
spy for the government among the
Jacobites in France.

In the 1790s the Glengarry
Highlanders, mostly remnants of a
company of militia raised to ease their
poverty, received assistance to emigrate
to Canada, where they founded
Glengarry, Ontario, each family naming
their homestead after their old farm in
Glengarry. In the war of 1812 with the
United States, they were summoned by
the fiery cross to combat an American
raid. The Glengarry immigrants were
perhaps the most influential in rooting
the idea of clanship in Canada where it
has prospered to this day.

The headstrong behaviour noted in an
earlier chief was also unfortunately
evident in the notorious fifteenth chief,
the friend of Scott and subject of
Raeburn, Colonel Alasdair MacDonell of
Glengarry. At a time when his clansmen
were close to economic extinction he
strutted about with a 'tail' of attendants
in the manner of a Highland chief of an
earlier and very different period. This
'tiresome poseur', as a recent historian of
the Highlands described him, put every
possible obstacle in the way of Telford's

ABOVE *Detail of Raeburn's portrait of
Colonel Alasdair MacDonell of Glengarry
about 1812, the combative chief who had
all the pride and bravado of his ancestors,
but little statesmanship or common sense.*

Caledonian Canal project in spite of
receiving enormous compensation for
the very small part of his estates through
which it ran, and also carried on an
endless argument over precedence with
Clanranald.

His successor, beset by debts and
worried by evictions, sold out and
emigrated to the Antipodes.

MACDONELL OF
GLENGARRY 148-149

MACDONELL OF KEPPOCH

NAME AND PLACE

The MacDonells of Keppoch were descended from Alastair *Carrach* (the Warty), third son of John, first Lord of the Isles, who was a grandson of King Robert II. Their lands were on the mainland, in Lochaber, and they were sometimes known as Clan Ranald of Lochaber.

THE CLAN

Their history is decidedly eventful. Alastair *Carrach* was responsible for the burning of Elgin, one of the most plundered cities of the north, in 1402, only 12 years after the notorious assault of the Wolf of Badenoch. Alastair spared the cathedral, or what the Wolf had left of it, in memory of which act of forbearance the Little Cross was erected in Elgin. In 1411 the chief fought at 'Red' Harlaw with his brother, Donald of the Isles. For his part in the rebellion led by Donald Balloch on behalf of the imprisoned third Lord of the Isles he was forfeited and some of his lands in Lochaber given to the Mackenzies, leading to a rancorous feud. His son Angus, second MacDonell of Keppoch, lost the lordship of Lochaber, and John, fourth chief (or captain, the older name preferred by many of Clan Donald) was deposed because he had agreed to hand

BELOW *The east end of the much-plundered cathedral of Elgin, still an impressive ruin. A monument to Alastair* Carrach *stands in the town for his act in sparing what remained of it after the Wolf of Baddenoch had burned it 12 years earlier.*

over a clansman to the Mackintosh. He was succeeded by a cousin, Donald *Glas*, who built the old castle of Keppoch. His son Ranald, who fought in the battle of the Shirts with the MacDonalds of Clan Ranald, was executed as a rebel in 1547, along with Cameron of Lochiel, by the Earl of Huntly. The ninth MacDonell of Keppoch, also Ranald, spent most of his life as an outlaw. His son, tenth chief, was father of the ancestor of the Canadian line of MacDonells, *Seigneurs de Rigaud*, in Quebec.

The murder of Alastair, the twelfth chief, in 1663 is commemorated at 'the Well of the Heads' near Invergarry. The heads of seven of his murders were washed by the clan bard Ian *Lom* MacDonell and presented to Glengarry, who had failed to respond with the requisite spirit of vengeance (exacted later by MacDonald of Sleat). The sculpture commemorating the event was erected in the 19th century by Colonel Alasdair MacDonell of Glengarry.

The last clan battle in the Highlands was fought between MacDonell of Keppoch and Mackintosh of Mackintosh in 1688. The Mackintosh had obtained what Highland chiefs sometimes scornfully called a 'sheepskin charter' for the lands of Glenroy. The affronted MacDonells met the Mackintoshes in a pitched battle in Lochaber, defeated them, and captured the Mackintosh himself, who was forced to surrender his claim to Glenroy.

However, times had changed, and MacDonell's lands were subsequently ravaged by government troops with Mackintosh assistance. The fifteenth chief, known as 'Coll of the Cows', held on to his lands by the sword for 40 years, evading all attempts to capture him. Together with his son Alexander, he fought for the Jacobites at Sheriffmuir.

The MacDonells of Keppoch provided many heroes in the Jacobite risings of the 18th century. Though an elderly man by

1745, the sixteenth chief was one of the first to join Prince Charles. He intercepted the government force at Highbridge on their way to the gathering of the clans at Glenfinnan, where the prince raised his standard, and thus initiated the first action of the Forty-five. Keppoch had only 200 men with him at Culloden and like many others, including Lord George Murray, he doubted the wisdom of giving battle at that time and place (he was practically the only Highland chief with military experience, having fought in France). He fell during the retreat and was left for dead, but his son Angus *Bàn* found him and, calling some of his men, carried the old chief in his plaid to a nearby bothy, where he breathed his last. The estates of Keppoch were subsequently forfeited. The last chief in the direct line from Colonel Alexander MacDonell died in 1889.

MACDONALD OF GLENCOE

NAME AND PLACE: see MacDonald

ORIGIN

The MacDonalds came to Glencoe when a brother of John, first Lord of the Isles, settled in Lochaber in the early 14th century. His name was Iain *Abrach*, and the chiefs of the MacDonalds of Glencoe were subsequently known as MacIain. By the 17th century they were a small, more or less independent clan, who were notorious cattle thieves. Despite the proximity of the powerful and perhaps understandably hostile Campbell of Glenorchy, they were survivors, their men renowned for brawn, and secure in their natural fortress of Glencoe.

They are, of course, chiefly remembered for the disaster that overtook them on the night of 12–13 February 1692.

After the resistance in the Highlands following the flight of King James VII/II and the accession of William III and Mary II, a free pardon was promised to all chiefs who took an oath of submission to the Crown before 1 January 1692. The elderly MacIain MacDonald set off in reasonable time to perform this, but he was delayed by snowstorms and then found when he got to Fort William that he would have to go on to Inveraray. As a result he was six days late, but nobody appeared troubled by this and he returned home feeling perfectly secure. He was not even suspicious when a company of troops was billeted on him at the end of the month.

After a fortnight's amicable residence the soldiers attacked their hosts in the middle of the night. MacIain was shot dead in his bed and his wife thrown naked into the snow where she died hours later. Altogether, 38 men, women and children were killed, and probably more died in the snow. The remainder, fewer than 150, escaped up the glen.

As the orders had been to massacre the entire clan, the operation cannot be called successful. Moreover, it gave rise to a feeling of horror and revulsion not

BELOW *Inhospitable Glencoe in winter. Even driving along the modern highway in summer sunshine, there is a certain grimness in the scenery.*

only in the Highlands but throughout the British Isles and even in Europe. Such a massacre was not unique in Scottish history; it was not even particularly uncommon. What made this incident so shocking was that it happened at a date when clan wars and feuds had virtually disappeared, that it was perpetrated not by a rival clan but by the forces of the government under orders approved at the highest level, and that it was carried out in such a particularly treacherous manner. Who was responsible?

The chief villain was undoubtedly the Master of Stair, Lord Advocate and William and Mary's Secretary of State. He wrote down quite plainly that the intention was 'to extirpate that set of thieves', adding, 'Let it be secret and sudden'. (Stair wished to annihilate the MacDonells of Glengarry as well but was discouraged by the formidable defences of Invergarry Castle.) King William signed the order and although he may not have understood exactly what was intended, he cannot be excused on that account. His public denial of all foreknowledge was clearly a falsehood. Campbell of Glenorchy, first Earl of Breadalbane, who had suffered from the activities of the MacDonalds of Glencoe during Montrose's campaign and on other occasions, appears to have had no idea of what was afoot and later condemned the massacre (see page 43).

The intense unpopularity of the Campbells in many parts of the Highlands was certainly exacerbated (there are still old men who will spit on the floor at the mention of the name Campbell though perhaps only in front of tourists), and they were unjustly blamed for the deed itself. The troops were commanded by Campbell of Glenlyon (a minor sept), who was in fact related to MacIain by marriage. His men came from Argyll's regiment but that does not mean they were Campbells; most apparently had other names.

The order to carry out the massacre was signed by Campbell of Glenlyon's superior officer, Major Duncanson, and given only a few hours in advance. Moreover, it seems not to have been carried out with great efficiency. So many escaped chiefly because the additional troops (not Campbells) assigned to block the glen on the night did not arrive in time (snowstorms again). But some of Campbell of Glenlyon's men dropped hints to their hosts, and others made sure their approach was noisy enough to give the victims a chance of escape.

A government inquiry was later held into the affair but, not surprisingly it failed to probe too deeply. Stair was removed as Secretary of State but later received an earldom. The MacDonalds of Glencoe were not exterminated but survived to fight in MacDonell of Keppoch's regiment in the Forty-five.

MACDONALD OF KINGSBURGH

NAME AND PLACE: see MacDonald

ORIGIN

This family was not a clan, scarcely even
a sept of Clan Donald, but it achieved
fame at the time of the last Jacobite
rising. The MacDonald of Kingsburgh
tartan is said to be copied from a
waistcoat given to Prince Charles during
his flight after Culloden by Alexander
MacDonald of Kingsburgh.

THE FAMILY

When Prince Charles arrived in Scotland
he no doubt expected the great chiefs of
Skye, MacDonald of Sleat and MacLeod
of MacLeod, to rally to his banner. But,
influenced by Forbes of Culloden (who
had once done him a good turn in
suppressing awkward facts about a group
of alleged 'emigrants', tenants of Sleat,
who were apparently forced on to a ship
after being evicted), Sir Alexander of
Sleat held aloof, as did MacLeod.
Nevertheless it was to Skye that the
prince came during his dramatic flight
after the final defeat.

While there may be doubts about the
chief, his wife, Lady Margaret (a
daughter of the Earl of Eglinton) was a
very popular figure in Skye, though not a
fervent Jacobite (nor were the others
involved in this romantic episode).

BELOW 'Raising of the Standard'. The
overlords of the MacDonalds of Kingsburgh
did not rally to Prince Charles's banner, but
various members of the Kingsburg family
were instrumental in his escape.

One of Sir Alexander's tacksmen, or lessees, was his relative Hugh MacDonald of Armadale, whose wife was connected through an earlier marriage with the MacDonalds of Clan Ranald. Her daughter by this marriage was the famous Flora MacDonald (1722–90), who was to marry (in 1750) Allen MacDonald of Kingsburgh. Allen's father, Alexander of Kingsburgh, was factor to MacDonald of Sleat.

In 1746, when the prince was moving westward, Hugh of Armadale was in government service in south Uist in the Outer Hebrides, where Flora was able to visit him without arousing suspicion. The prince arrived there in due course, but the trail was getting hot and he was warned by Hugh, despite the latter's official allegiance, that the island was no longer safe. A family conference decided that he should travel with Flora to Skye, disguised as her Irish maidservant, 'Betty Burke'. If this tale were fiction, one would scoff at such unlikely plotting, but 'Betty Burke' arrived safely and was conducted to Sleat, where at that moment government soldiers were quartered. Lady Margaret and the laird's factor were drawn into the business, and the prince spent the night at Kingsburgh's house. A great many other people must have known what was going on by the time Prince Charles said goodbye to Flora at Portree, but no one talked.

Both Flora and Alexander of Kingsburgh were imprisoned after their activities had been uncovered, but both were fairly soon released. Flora married Alexander of Kingsburgh's son Allen and they later emigrated to North America. Allen fought for the government in the American War of Independence and was taken prisoner. Flora returned to the Hebrides in 1779 (her husband following later) but the Kingsburgh property had gone and they were poor. Fortunately they had five sons, one of whom became a successful military engineer.

ABOVE *Flora MacDonald. The Prince's escape has been built into a romantic episode. What is most extraordinary about it is that, in spite of prevailing poverty and the large price on his head, he was never betrayed. Yet many of those who helped him were not committed Jacobites.*

MACDONALD OF
KINGSBURGH 154–155

MACDOUGALL

NAME AND PLACE

The MacDougalls, tracing their descent
from Dugall, son of Somerled by the
daughter of the Norse King Olaf of Man,
are an example of a race that once held
great, indeed royal, authority who
survived the vicissitudes of the early
modern period, although in reduced
circumstances, and still hold a small part
of their ancient lands in Lorne.

ORIGINS

The MacDougalls were senior to Clan
Donald, and their progenitor, Dugall,
held Argyll and Lorne, Mull, Jura and
other Hebridean islands. He was the
senior sub-king of the Isles under the
king of Norway. His son was known as
Duncan 'of Argyll' and that name was
used by his immediate descendants.

THE CLAN

The MacDougalls were a considerable
sea power, with fortresses on several
islands. Their main bases, however, were
Dunstaffnage, which later passed to the
Campbells, and Dunollie Castle, which
still overlooks Oban Bay and still belongs
to the MacDougall chief. Sir Iain
Moncrieffe pointed out its similarity in
design to the castle of Bergen in Norway.

The son of Duncan, Ewen of Argyll,
Lord of Lorne and third chief, was faced

BELOW *Dunstaffnage Castle was originally
built by the MacDougall, Lord of Lorne,
seized by Bruce and made over to Campbell
of Argyll, becoming a centre of royal
authority in the west. Severely damaged in
the civil wars, it was later restored to the
Campbells. Flora MacDonald was briefly
held here after assisting the escape of
Prince Charles.*

with a difficult decision in 1263 when King Haakon of Norway made his cruise through the Western Isles in an attempt to re-establish Norwegian sovereignty. He decided to support Alexander III, King of Scots, but first requested permission from his Norwegian overlord and formally surrendered the lands he held of him. Such feudal gallantry was not very common, but it proved wise, since Haakon was repulsed at Largs and the MacDougall King of Argyll remained in full possession.

Events during the Scottish wars of independence brought changes from which the MacDougalls were never to recover. Alasdair of Argyll, Lord of Lorne and fourth MacDougal chief, married an aunt of the Red Comyn, who was killed by Bruce in the church at Dumfries in 1306. As a result the MacDougalls were involved in the blood feud between the Comyns and Bruce, and became Bruce's most dangerous opponents. At one moment they almost captured him in the Pass of Brander: he escaped but left the them in possession of his cloak pin, 'the Brooch of Lorne'. Later the MacDougalls were defeated, Dunstaffnage captured, and the estates forfeited.

The sixth chief partially retrieved the position. He married a granddaughter of Bruce and regained the lordship of Lorne from King David II. He had no sons and the lordship passed to the Stewarts through the marriage of his daughters to two Stewart brothers. The chiefship passed to his cousin Iain, son of Duncan, the fourth chief's brother, who had taken the opposite side in the wars of independence and had gained Dunollie Castle as a result of his support for Bruce. In 1451 the Stewart Lord of Lorne confirmed the then MacDougall chief (the first, incidentally, to be known as the MacDougall) in the possession of lands around Oban as well as in the island of Kerrera in the Firth of Lorne.

The MacDougalls did not lose hope of regaining their former lands, and for a brief period following the attainder and execution (in 1686) of the Earl of Argyll, it looked as though they might succeed. However, the Campbells were soon back in favour and the MacDougalls had to remain content with Dunollie. They nearly lost that during the Jacobite rising of 1715, when the twenty-first chief fought with the Jacobites while his wife successfully defended the castle against siege. It had undergone an earlier siege in 1647 when, as in 1715, the estates were temporarily forfeited.

CLAN ASSOCIATION

Port Na Mairt, Ganavan, Oban
PA34 5UT, Scotland

18 Teresa Drive, Mendon,
MA 10756-1176, USA

MACDOUGALL 156–157

MACDUFF

NAME AND PLACE

In the days before the clan system had
come into recognisable existence the
MacDuff earls of Fife were the greatest
family in Scotland. They represented the
ancient Celtic royal house to which the
MacBeth and Lady MacBeth known
chiefly through Shakespeare's play both
belonged. The MacDuff of that play,
however, who assists Malcolm (IV) to
defeat MacBeth, is fictional, though
something similar may well have
happened.

ORIGIN

The wife of King Malcolm III (*Ceann
Mór*) was an English princess. They had
five sons, four of whom became kings of
Scots in their turn. Strangely enough the
one who did not was the eldest, although
the reasons why he was passed over are
no longer apparent. His name, no doubt
chosen by his English mother, was
Aethelred. He is the first historically
documented Earl of Fife and was also
hereditary Abbot of Dunkeld (perhaps
this office barred him from the throne).
His wife was a granddaughter of Queen
Gruoch (Lady MacBeth) and sister of the
King of Moray (Malcolm's authority had
not advanced into that region).

BELOW *Duff House in Banff was built
between 1735 and 1741 by William Adam
in a Baroque style. It is now an outstation
for the National Galleries of Scotland.*

THE CLAN

So far as is known Aethelred, or *Aedh* as he was called in Gaelic, caused no trouble, though the men of Moray, that is to say, Clan MacDuff, rose on several occasions in attempts to gain the throne for his son before they finally accepted the status quo.

The earls of Fife, first subjects of the king, enjoyed particular privileges known as the Law of Clan MacDuff. Chief of these was the right to enthrone the king of Scots on the Stone of Scone at his coronation. They also included the right to lead the vanguard in battle (a dubious honour, we 20th-century cowards might suppose), and the right to be absolved from a charge of homicide by taking sanctuary at the Cross of MacDuff (north of Newburgh) and paying a fixed fine. This extended to fairly remote kindred.

The first chiefs of Clan MacDuff on whom anything is known for certain were successive earls of Fife named Constantine and Gillemichael MacDuff, who lived in the early 12th century. They were probably brothers, and possibly grandsons of Aethelred (their father having predeceased their grandfather).

The centre of MacDuff power was the kingdom of Fife, but they also held extensive lands in the north-east and in the Lowlands, south of the Forth. A number of clans claim descent from them and there are many families named Duff or MacDuff who may have originated in some branch of the ancient royal house. The name MacDuff was not generally used as a surname, and there is no proof that the modern earls and (since 1889) dukes of Fife were related to the old Celtic earls, whose line came to an end in the 14th century. The earls of Wemyss were recognised in the 18th century as representing the ancient line, with reasonably authenticated descent from Gillemichael MacDuff, the 12th-century

ABOVE *The famous round tower at Abernethy, which offered a useful refuge in the event of attack, dates from the time of the Celtic MacDuff earls of Fife. Aethelred succeeded to the hereditary position of Abbot of Abernethy when he gained the earldom of Fife. Abernethy was the ancient Pictish capital and the round tower remains from the Columban church of that time.*

Earl of Fife. The Wemyss family is still resident in what used to be known as 'Wemysshire' in Fife because of its former size. See also Wemyss.

CLAN ASSOCIATION

4528 Greenhill Way, Anderson, IN 46012 USA

MACEWEN

NAME AND PLACE

According to a 15th-century genealogy the MacEwens were connected with the MacNeills and MacLachlans as member of *Siol Gillevray*, all of them being neighbours in Cowal and allegedly sharing a common ancestor. They seem to have been fairly numerous. The name is quite common today although there are no certain links between contemporary MacEwen (or Ewing and other possible variants) families and the old Clan MacEwen of Otter.

ORIGIN

Since the Clan MacEwen was 'broken' in the 15th century, little is known of its history. In the records of the parish of Kilfinnan, Argyll, an entry from the end of the 18th century remarks on the remains of a building on a rocky promontory of Loch Fyne below the church which was called 'MacEwen's Castle', after a MacEwen who was the chief of a clan and held a district called Otter, which means a spit of land. It is clear that practically all memory of the MacEwens in their homeland had been lost by this time.

THE CLAN

The first recorded chief of the clan was Ewen of Otter, probably the source of the patronymic, who held land on Loch Fyne in the early 13th century. About a century later Gillespie was the fifth chief from Ewen, and the names of his successors are known down to Swene, ninth and last chief.

The manner in which he lost the clan territory suggests that he was a victim of the Campbell facility in exploiting the law to their own benefit and the detriment of their simpler neighbours. In 1432 Swene granted land to Sir Duncan Campbell of Lochow and surrendered the barony of Otter to King James I. He received it back from the king but with remainder to Campbell's heir. Thus the MacEwen chief signed away his territory to the Campbells, who took over on Swene's death. In 1493 the grant of the lands to the second Earl of Argyll was confirmed by royal charter.

What happened to the MacEwans? Probably a large proportion of them became followers of the Campbells. The hereditary bards of Campbell of Argyll and Campbell of Glenorchy were MacEwens, and in 1602 a number of them were listed as vassals of the earl of Argyll, who was to be responsible for their good behaviour. Some apparently followed the MacLachlans, their kin; others scattered across the Highlands and, eventually, the Lowlands: a group

of MacEwens were later to be found in
Dumbarton and Galloway, Loch Tayside,
Comrie and Crieff.

The name often appears in criminal
records, a sadly inevitable result of the
loss of a clan's territory. According to
General Wade, 150 MacEwens crossed to
the mainland from Skye to take part in
the Fifteen, but whether these men were
connected with the MacEwens of Otter it
is impossible to say.

ABOVE *MacEwen Hall, where graduates of
Edinburgh University receive their degrees.
Designed by Robert Rowand Anderson
and opened in 1897, it is named after the
wealthy brewer, Sir William MacEwen, who
provided most of the finance.*

CLAN ASSOCIATION

Bellcairn Cottage, Cove, Argyll
G84 0NX, Scotland

Saraland Apartments 105B, 8010
Highway 49, Gulfport, MS 39501, USA

P O Box 3, St Peters, Nova Scotia,
B0E 3B0, Canada

88 Laura Street, Tarragindi, Brisbane,
Queensland, Australia

MACFARLANE

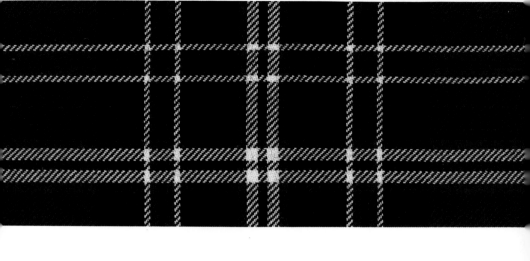

NAME AND PLACE

MacFarlane country lay among the soft glens and lochs of the Trossachs which on a summer day present a lovely and peaceful scene, as millions of visitors would testify. But things were not always so: 'a land of savage sheep, tended by savage people', said Burns. The savage sheep sound a little unlikely, but the people – certainly. The clan name was derived from *Pàrlan* (Bartholomew), the descendant of Gilchrist (see below) and accounted fourth chief.

ORIGIN

Clan MacFarlane is well documented. They were a branch of the family of the old Celtic earls of Lennox, descended from Gilchrist, younger brother of Earl Malduin (a common name in the ancient royal house of Munster, from which the earls of Lennox were probably descended).

THE CLAN

Gilchrist received from his brother the lands of Arrochar, north of Loch Long and west of Loch Lomond, territory expanded through marriage in the 14th century. The seventh chief's possession of Arrochar was confirmed by a charter of 1420. A predecessor, Malduin, third chief, supported Bruce during the wars of independence. Later chiefs were killed at Flodden (1513) and Pinkie (1547).

The Lennox earls came to an end when the last of them, Duncan, was executed in grisly circumstances by the vengeful King James I in 1425. The MacFarlane chief, as senior male descendant, claimed to be his heir, but the earldom was subsequently conferred on Sir John Stewart of Darnley, descended from a daughter of Earl Duncan. This might have caused serious trouble, but it was averted by the marriage of Andrew MacFarlane of Arrochar to the Stewart Earl's daughter. Thereafter, the MacFarlanes remained loyal subjects of the Stewarts.

The murder of Mary Queen of Scots' husband (and cousin) Lord Darnley (as he is generally known today) in 1567 turned the MacFarlanes against the queen, as their first loyalty was to the Earl of Lennox, Darnley's father. Moreover, they had become Protestants. Their action against her at Langside, after she had escaped from captivity in Loch Leven Castle, is said to have been decisive in the final defeat of that unfortunate lady.

The MacFarlanes were a notably warlike clan, frequently raiding their neighbours by the light of 'MacFarlane's lantern', the moon. Their pipe tune is

appropriately called 'Lifting the Cattle'. They were involved in ferocious feuds at various times with the Buchanans, Colquhouns and other neighbours on Loch Lomond. (The gruesome revenge taken on a Colquhoun chief who had seduced MacFarlane's wife is mentioned under Colquhoun.) In 1594 some MacFarlanes were listed among the 'broken' clans.

Walter MacFarlane of MacFarlane, sixteenth chief, fought under Montrose during the civil war and was subsequently fined by the Covenanters. His castle of Inveruglas, a small island in Loch Lomond whose remnants are overlooked by the modern power station, was twice besieged by Cromwellian forces and on the second occasion destroyed by fire. The chief moved to a house at Arrochar (later rebuilt).

The twentieth chief, also Walter (died 1767), was a famous antiquary, one of the few people before the 19th century who made a serious effort to preserve the Scottish heritage by collecting and transcribing documents. He was a friend of Boswell, who recorded that General Wade, the famous builder of roads in Highlands after the Fifteen, addressed the chief as 'Mr MacFarlane' since, in English custom, plain 'MacFarlane' would have been discourteously

ABOVE Loch Lomond, today untroubled by the clash of weapons and the war cries of the MacFarlanes and their neighbours.

informal. The chief was incensed, 'Mr MacFarlane', he said, 'may with equal propriety be said to be many; but I, and I only, am MacFarlane)'. He was succeeded by his brother William, who was an Edinburgh doctor.

The arrival of a black swan among the MacFarlane's white swans was a grim omen, since that had been forecast as presaging the loss of Arrochar. Not long afterwards the twenty-first chief was forced to sell the lands. The twenty-fifth chief, who died in 1886, was the last of his line.

CLAN ASSOCIATION

17715 Guld Boulevard #144, Reddington Shores, FL, USA

(MacFarlane of Arrochar)
207 Brian Drive. Ardmore, AL 35739, USA

MACGILLIVRAY

NAME AND PLACE

The presumed progenitor of Clan
MacGillivray (that the progenitor was
Gillebride, or Gillivray, the father of
Somerled, seems rather far-fetched), was
Gillevray, who was responsible for their
association with what became Clan
Chattan in the 13th century. During the
15th century the MacGillivrays became
established in what was to be their home
for four centuries, Dunmaglas in
Strathnairn.

ORIGINS

The MacGillivrays are of ancient origin
and according to one account sat on the
council of the lord of the Isles. Mull is
usually suggested as their original
homeland, but at some point in the 13th
century, probably as a result of King
Alexander II's campaigns in Argyll, they
split up. Some remained in the west,
becoming followers of MacLean of
Duart, others, under Gillevray, sought
protection from the Mackintosh chiefs.
There was no connection by blood so far
as we know, the MacGillivrays and the
Mackintoshes being of different racial
origin, and the association seems to be an
early example of a small, independent
clan seeking safety in numbers.

BELOW *Garron ponies. These small
Highland horses have an 'eel stripe' down
the flanks. Ponies were used for centuries in
Scotland in preference to larger horses.*

THE CLAN

Possibly the first MacGillivray of
Dunmaglas (the patronymic was not yet
in use) was one Iain Ciar (the Brown),
mentioned in Mackintosh documents of
the 15th century.

They prospered and increased,
forming many cadet branches and
becoming one of the major constituents
of Clan Chattan. Three MacGillivrays
signed the Clan Chattan bonds of union
in the early 17th century, when the clan
was probably at its height. The name
crops up frequently in the accounts of the
many disputes in which Clan Chattan
was involved, and also, more pleasantly,
in unlikely tales of ladies kidnapped by
fairies and retrieved by magic.

The MacGillivrays were prominent in
the Jacobite risings of the 18th century.
In 1715 the two sons of the current chief
were officers in the Clan Chattan
regiment, and in Prince Charles's rising
Clan Chattan was led by Alexander
MacGillivray of Dunmaglas, appointed
to the command (consisting mainly of
Mackintoshes, Farquharsons and
MacBeans, besides MacGillivrays) in the
absence of the Mackintosh, who had
remained loyal to his commission in
government service. At Culloden they
made a famous charge which all but
annihilated Cumberland's left wing
before they were pushed back, tearing up
stones from the heather to hurl at the
enemy. Their casualties were frightful.
Iain *Mór* MacGillivray killed 12 men
before he died, the red-haired Dunmaglas
about as many. When he fell, with many
wounds, he managed to drag himself to a
well, where he died as he drank. A stone
marks the spot today.

Times were hard after Culloden and
Alexander's successor was forced to enlist
in the army. He died in 1783 and was
succeeded by his son, John Lachlan, chief
for nearly 70 years, who when he died
bequeathed his capital and lands to his

ABOVE *The MacGillivray memorial stone at
the Well of the Dead on the field of
Culloden marks the spot where the
MacGillivray chief died in 1746.*

tenants. A fine gesture, but after
numerous legal disputes, the estates were
broken up.

CLAN ASSOCIATION

7233 North Denver Avenue, Portland,
OR 97217, USA

MACGREGOR

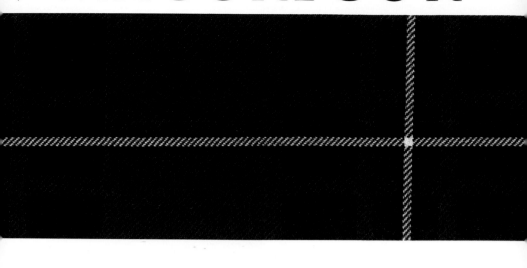

NAME AND PLACE

Probably the patronymic derives from an early 14th-century chief, but no one would dispute that the MacGregors were the principal members of *Sìol Ailpein*. Their home was Glenorchy and adjacent glens.

ORIGIN

The MacGregors' motto is translated as 'Royal is my blood'. According to legend the original Gregor was the brother or son of King Kenneth MacAlpin. The original chiefly line descended from Iain, the first known chief.

THE CLAN

It was the loss of their land that led to the persecution of the MacGregors in the 17th and 18th centuries. There is no doubt that the MacGregors were violent and troublesome (so, invariably, were other landless clans), but it would be hard to prove that they were any worse than others, at least until circumstances forced them into a life of outlawry.

As a result of their marriages the Campbells established a foothold in the MacGregor lands in the early 14th century, which by one means or another they were able gradually to extend.

The new line of MacGregor chiefs descended from a younger son of Iain and included Gregor 'of the Golden bridles', from whom the clan is thought to have taken its name. Unwilling to submit to another chief, the MacGregors held on to their lands for as long as possible. The Campbells continued to foment trouble by trying to undermine the authority of the MacGregor chiefs (their own feudal tenants) among their clansmen, and in 1519 they set up their own nominee as Chief of MacGregor. He was a junior chieftain who had married Campbell of Glenorchy's daughter (having begun his courtship by raping her). However, the landless MacGregors, 'the children of the mist' (a name which it has been waspishly remarked, might equally be translated as 'the fog folk') continued their lawless existence, in which even the imposed chief became

BELOW *The original homeland of the MacGregors, Glen Orchy and Glen Strae - too near the Campbells for comfort.*

involved, and several commissions of fire and sword were issued to neighbouring chiefs, including the much-injured Colquhoun of Luss. The latter feud culminated in the battle of Glenfruin, when the Colquhouns were massacred in large numbers.

King James VI, furious at this latest example of the failure of his policy of pacification in the Highlands, then issued the Privy Council edict in which Clan Gregor was proscribed (it was practically his last act before leaving for London in 1603). This made it illegal even to bear the name MacGregor, and the clansmen were compelled to adopt pseudonyms (often, ironically, Campbell) to the confusion of later genealogists. They were not allowed to carry weapons, except a blunt-ended knife to cut their meat, and no more than four were allowed to gather in the same place. The chief and a number of leading clansmen were executed in Edinburgh, and by a new commission issued to Argyll against them in 1611 the women were to be branded in the face with a red-hot key.

Such laws could not be, and were not, effectively enforced, but they remained current, with brief intervals, until 1774. At times MacGregors were hunted down with bloodhounds, though at other times they were largely left alone.

Many of the Highlanders were sympathetic to them, most notably the Grants and the Mackenzies, and were prepared to aid and shelter them even at considerable risk to themselves. At one time a merger was discussed between MacGregors and Grants, though it was to founder on the prickly question of the chiefship. Huge fines were levied against those who succoured the MacGregors, the proceeds of these fines going straight into Argyll's coffers.

MacGregors fought with Montrose for Charles I and for his son at Worcester (1651), and as a result the proscription of the clan was lifted at the Restoration

ABOVE *King George IV enters Holyrood Palace, the first non-Stewart monarch to do so, during a famous visit to Edinburgh in 1822 that symbolised the final acceptance of the Hanoverian monarchy by the majority of Scots.*

(1660), but it was reimposed after the rebellions against William III. Some MacGregors fought in the Jacobite risings of 1715 and 1745 and one of the Seven Men of Glenmoriston, the outlaws who sheltered the prince in 1746, was named Gregor MacGregor.

The proscription was finally lifted in 1774, and when the Honours of Scotland were paraded before George IV in Edinburgh in 1822 the MacGregors were among the guard of honour.

CLAN ASSOCIATION

Mo Dhachaidh, 2 Braehead, Alloa
FK10 2EW, Scotland

9800 Pinebrake Court, Pensacola,
FL 32514-5768, USA

316 Bedford Highway, Halifax, Nova
Scotia, Canada

41 Boomerang Road, Collaroy Plateau
NSW 2098, Australia

4 Laud Avenue, Ellerslie, Auckland 5,
New Zealand

MACGREGOR
(ROB ROY)

NAME AND PLACE: see MacGregor

ORIGIN

The tartan known as Rob Roy is the oldest of the MacGregor tartans and its simple sett of red and black dice was no doubt worn in the 18th century, though whether by Rob Roy himself it is impossible to say.

ROB ROY

Rob Roy, the famous outlaw who has been romanticised by Sir Walter Scott, was born in 1671. His father was Donald MacGregor, fifteenth chief of the 'children of the mist', and his mother was a Campbell. At that time the penal laws against the MacGregors had been temporarily lifted, following the Restoration of Charles II and the disgrace and execution of the MacGregors' enemy, the Marquess of Argyll. Nevertheless Rob Roy, an exceedingly powerful young man although not tall, probably learned the MacGregor techniques of lifting cattle and extracting blackmail. However until he fell out with the Duke of Montrose he seems to have been a law-abiding figure.

In 1693, the year in which the penal acts were renewed, or thereabouts, Rob Roy, whose father had led the MacGregors in the Jacobite forces in

BELOW *Rob Roy in the Tolbooth, Edinburgh, during one of his, usually quite short, periods in captivity. In 1722 he was sent to Newgate prison in London and sentenced to be transported, but was pardoned before the ship sailed.*

1689, became acting head of the clan, probably by sheer force of character. He had to go into hiding in 1712, adopting his mother's maiden name of Campbell, to avoid arrest on charge of defrauding Montrose. This charge seems to have been false, at least in a moral, if not strictly legal sense, and Rob Roy nursed his resentment.

In the Jacobite rising of 1715 he led a collection of Buchanans and others in the Jacobite cause and captured Falkland Palace in an independent action. Thereafter he was mainly engaged in his depredations against Montrose and those who could be considered Montrose's allies. Stories of his exploits are numerous, and no doubt a few of them are more or less true. He was captured twice, but effected a dramatic escape, and eventually made some sort of truce with Montrose through the mediations of Argyll, who, of course, was no friend of Montrose and may well have assisted Rob Roy on certain occasions. In 1722 he submitted to General Wade, commander in Scotland. In his later years he lived quietly at Balquhidder, adopting Roman Catholicism and dying peacefully in 1734, practically a national hero. He had five sons, at least three of whom were convicted of treason after the Forty-five, though only one was executed.

Scott's Rob Roy may be a largely fictional figure. Nevertheless, the man was romantic enough in actuality, the hero of excellent yarns of derring-do, an outlaw and brigand who was also a man of fine sensibilities, excellent education and a considerable musician.

ABOVE *A statue of Rob Roy in Stirling. It has become difficult to disentangle the historical figure from Sir Walter Scott's largely mythical hero.*

MACINNES

NAME AND PLACE

Mac Aonghais means 'son of Angus', and the chief of MacInnes was known as Kinlochaline, after the castle of which he was hereditary constable.

ORIGINS

Clann Aonghais is of ancient Celtic origin; their ancestors were probably among the earliest settlers of Dalriada. They were probably members of *Siol Gillebride*, or *Gillevray*, A traditional tale has the MacInneses being favoured by the lord of the Isles or, in one version, by King Somerled himself. A MacInnes was still in command of Kinlochaline, it seems, when the castle, today a picturesque ruin, was besieged by Alasdair MacColla, the leader of Montrose's Irish MacDonalds, in 1645.

The clan was probably dislocated by the campaign of Alexander II in Argyll in the 13th century, and perhaps by the murder of a MacInnes chief in the late 14th century. At about that time the clan came under Campbell protection. They were first associated with the Campbells of Craignish, and in the conflicts of the 17th century followed the Marquess of Argyll, supporting the Covenanters, while in the Jacobite risings they adhered to the government party.

However, this appears to have been true of only one part of *Clann Aonghais*. A family of hereditary bowmen to the Mackinnon chief named MacInnes was said to have been descended from Neil *a' Bhogha*, who is claimed as an ancestor by the MacInneses of Rickersby, possibly related to the MacInneses of Kinlochaline.

Another group were followers of the Stewarts of Ardshiel and may have split away from the Kinlochaline branch in about the 15th century. They were probably among the 300 'men of Appin', led by Stewart of Ardshiel at Culloden.

CLAN ASSOCIATION

8232 Kay Court, Annandale, VA 22003, USA

BELOW *Kinlochaline Castle from which the chief of MacInnes, as its hereditary constable, took his name, stands above Loch Aline off the Sound of Mull.*

MACINTYRE

NAME AND PLACE

MacIntyre is perhaps more correctly spelt Macintyre. The Gaelic name *Mac an t-Saoir* means 'the Carpenter' and was probably applied to others not connected with the clan, which was settled in Glenoe, near Bonawe on Loch Etive, in the 14th century.

ORIGINS

The MacIntyres were closely associated with the MacDonalds, though their war cry 'Cruachan!' is the same as the Campbells'. According to one tale their ancestor was a MacDonald who acquired his nickname 'the Carpenter' when he cut off his thumb to plug a leak in his boat so that he might wave his arms for help.

Another tradition says the MacIntyres came to Lorne from the Hebrides in a galley, bringing with them a white cow.

THE CLAN

MacIntyres were hereditary foresters to the Stewart lords of Lorne, later to the Campbells. They were hereditary pipers to the Mackenzies and produced a famous Gaelic bard of the 18th century, Duncan *Bàn* MacIntyre (1724–1812), whose monument stands in Greyfriars churchyard, Edinburgh.

The Glenoe chiefs are numbered from Duncan, who died in 1695, although

ABOVE *The Scottish broadcaster and former head of Radio Three, Alastair MacIntyre.*

there were many generations before him. His last direct descendant died in London in 1808, after the lands of Glenoe had been lost. Things had never been the same since the MacIntyres' landlord, Campbell of Glenorchy (Breadalbane), had commuted their rent of a snowball to a cash payment.

With the loss of the clan territory many of the MacIntyres of Glenoe emigrated to the United States.

CLAN ASSOCIATION

214 West College Street, Mount Olive, NC 28365-1622, USA

MACKAY

NAME AND PLACE

The Mackays for many centuries held a large dominion in the north-west corner of the Scottish mainland centred on Strathnaver. They were called *Clann Aoidh*, or alternatively Clan Morgan (*Morgund*).

ORIGIN

They claimed descent from the old royal house of MacEth, *mormaer*s (earls) of Moray. It has been said that 'Morgan' was son of King Magnus of the Northern Isles and that *Aodh* (Hugh) was his grandson, though this remains doubtful.

THE CLAN

Assuming that the Mackays really did originate in Moray, they probably reached Strathnaver when King Malcolm IV drove them 'beyond the Scottish mountains' in the 12th century. Clearly they prospered there. It was said that in 1427 the current chief of Mackay, Angus *Dubh* (d. 1429) could command as many as 4,000 fighting men.

The Mackays are noted both for the martial qualities of their men and the beauty and intelligence of their women. The historian of the chiefs of Mackays, Ian Grimble, has pointed out that up to the 17th century every traceable marriage of a Mackay chief was with another

BELOW The Pass of Killiecrankie, site of a battle during the campaign of 1689 when the Jacobites led by Viscount Dundee (Graham of Claverhouse) ambushed the government (pro-William III) troops led by William Mackay and soundly defeated them, though at the cost of Dundee's death.

member of the old Celtic aristocracy. The most notable of these marriages was that of Angus *Dubh* to a daughter of Donald, second Lord of the Isles. He had possibly met her while he was the lord's prisoner, for he had opposed Donald's attempt to gain the earldom of Ross which culminated in the famous battle of 'Red' Harlaw (1411).

In 1626 Donald, chief of Mackay, created Lord Reay in 1628, took a regiment of 3,000 men to fight on the Protestant side in the Thirty Years War, a memorable episode commemorated in well-known prints of 1631 which provide useful evidence of Highland dress at that time (vast plaids and floppy bonnets), and by an account of the expedition which was published in 1637.

Another famous warrior was Hugh Mackay of the cadet branch of Scourie, who served in Holland and accompanied William III to England in 1688. He commanded the army defeated by Bonnie Dundee at Killiecrankie (1689) and was killed in a later engagement.

Strategically the Mackays' country appears well placed to avoid the problems faced by clans nearer the centre of power, but from the 14th century if not earlier they were frequently hard pressed to preserve their lands from the earls of Sutherland. Early in the 16th century that earldom passed to the Gordons of Huntly and by the end of the century the chief of Mackay was a vassal of the Gordon Earl. Subsequently the Mackays became involved in the efforts of the Gordons to expand their power in the far north at the expense of the Sinclair earls of Caithness.

As Whigs and Protestants the Mackays survived the 18th-century troubles comparatively unscathed. In the late 18th century the Earl of Sutherland (raised to a duke in 1833) was an absentee English millionaire – the largest landowner in Britain – with no feeling for the country or its inhabitants. The Sutherland Clearances in which vast numbers were removed from the interior to the coast (and beyond) are infamous: their effect is visible to this day.

The seventh Lord Reay sold his estates, including the House of Tongue, his ancestral home, in 1829. The old way of life, destroyed forever by the Clearances, was celebrated in the poetry of Rob Donn Mackay (1714–78), said to be the Gaelic poet most nearly comparable to Burns.

A younger son of the second Lord Reay, who was also a nephew of General Hugh Mackay, followed his uncle's example and entered Dutch service in the 17th century. His grandson, Aeneas (an anglicised form of Angus) married the heiress to a Dutch barony and his son, Barthold Mackay, was created a baron of the Netherlands in his own right. His nephew, another Aeneas, was Prime Minister of the Netherlands. The Dutch Mackays inherited the Mackay chiefship when the senior line died out in 1875.

CLAN ASSOCIATION

807 Pinehurst, Woodstock, GA 30188, USA

P O Box 1176, Auburn, NSW 2144, Australia

MACKENZIE

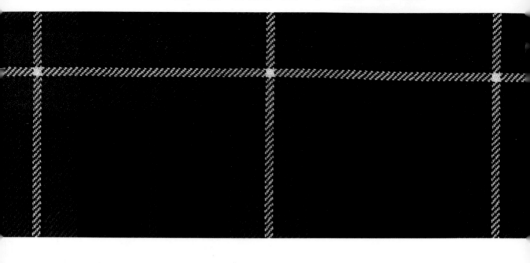

NAME AND PLACE

The old Gaelic name is *Mac Cainnigh*, a name anglicised as Kenneth. At least one early 15th-century Mackenzie chief in Wester Ross was called *Cainnech Mór*.

ORIGIN

Their origins are disputable. One tradition holds that their ancestor was an Irish chieftain who came over with his forces to take part in the battle of Largs and was rewarded with lands in Kintail in Wester Ross. A more probable one asserts that the Mackenzies were descended from Gilleon of the Aird, a scion of the ancient royal house of Lorne, who lived about 1100.

THE CLAN

Allegedly the 15th-century *Cainnech Mór* could command 2,000 men in 1427. His predecessor Murdoch Mackenzie is the first to appear in a surviving charter, in 1362, and he is described as son of Kenneth, son of John, son of Kenneth, son of Angus, son of Christian, son of Adam, son of Gilleon of the Aird. He was confirmed in the lands of Kintail by King David II.

His descendant Alasdair (Alexander) of Kintail was among the chiefs summoned to parliament (with disastrous results for some of them) by King James I

in 1427. He must have been a young man then, for he lived until 1488. He supported the Crown against the MacDonald Lord of the Isles and benefited immensely as a result, not least by gaining legal title to his land, old and new, the lack of which created so many problems for other Highland clans. His son Kenneth defeated the MacDonalds in battle in 1491 but died soon afterwards and was succeeded by his son Iain.

Some Mackenzies fought at Flodden in 1513 under Iain who, like his grandfather, was a natural survivor. Though at least one Mackenzie chieftain fell in that disastrous battle, the chief was one of comparatively few Scottish leaders who survived. Moreover he lived to fight again at Pinkie 35 years later and emerged from that battle unscathed also. His grandson Colin supported Mary Queen of Scots and was probably among her forces at Langside (1568), but he avoided retribution by making fairly prompt submission to the Earl of Moray, Regent for the young King James VI. Nevertheless the Mackenzies' loyal adherence to the Stewart dynasty, which assisted their rise, was eventually to become a serious disadvantage.

By this time the Mackenzies were becoming very powerful. They had benefited, first, from the decline of Clan

Donald, while avoiding the usual
concomitant of creating many dangerous
enemies. In the reign of King James VI
they bought out the Fife Adventurers,
who had attempted to settle Lewis but
had been thrown out by the affronted
MacLeods. The Mackenzies, who had
already absorbed MacLeod lands on the
mainland, had more success and soon
became dominant in Lewis too. They also
prised Lochalsh away from the
MacDonells of Glengarry.

Their territories now extended in a
wide swathe across Scotland from the
Outer Hebrides to the Black Isle, in total
acreage unchallenged by any clan except
the Campbells. Kenneth of Kintail
became Lord Mackenzie and his son by
his Grant wife was created Earl of
Seaforth in 1623.

So far the story had been one of
constant expansion. However, the loyalty
of the Mackenzie chiefs to the unlucky
remnants of the Stewart dynasty was
their undoing. The fourth Earl of
Seaforth, one of the original Knights of
the Thistle, died in exile with King James
VII/II. The fifth earl took part in the
rising of 1715 and was attainted, losing
lands and title. He was also a leader of
the abortive Spanish-assisted rising of
1719, being wounded at Glenshiel. He
was pardoned in 1726 thanks to General
Wade, who threatened to resign if this
were not done. He regained some of his
lands but not the title and died peacefully
in Lewis in 1740. The Mackenzies did
not fight as a clan in 1745–46, although
many cadet branches were 'out'.

For the fifth earl's grandson, who
repurchased the family estates from the
government, the earldom of Seaforth was
recreated in 1771. In gratitude (it is said),
the earl raised the Seaforth Highlanders
in 1778, made up mostly of Mackenzies
and MacRaes, old allies of the
Mackenzies. They were sent to India in
1781 – a disastrous voyage on which one
man in three died (mostly of scurvy).

ABOVE *Many Mackenzies have played
important parts in Canadian history.
Alexander Mackenzie (1822–92, above),
emigrated in 1842, won a seat in the first
Dominion House of Commons, and became
Liberal prime minister in 1873–78.*

The estates but not the title passed to
another branch in 1784 and after that
line had failed they passed through
various heiresses, constantly diminishing,
along with other Mackenzie families,
though the foremost of them, the earls of
Cromartie, hung on to at least a remnant.

The decline of the house of Seaforth
was foretold by the 'Brahan Seer'
(Brahan was a Mackenzie castle near
Dingwall, once chief residence of the
Seaforths) in the 16th century. The
details of this prophecy were written
down before the events they foretold,
so cannot be dismissed as the result of
someone reworking the prophecy to suit
the circumstances. Their accuracy is
certainly remarkable, and that some of
the events forecast have yet to occur is
more disquieting than consoling.

The Kintail estate today is owned by
the National Trust for Scotland.

CLAN ASSOCIATION

Farm Cottage, Wester Moy, Urray, Muir
of Ord IV6 7UX, Scotland

4522 Bond Lane, Oviedo,
FL 32765-9600, USA

580 Rebecca Street, Oakville, Ontario
L6K 3N9, Canada

P O Box 282, Punchbowl, NSW 2196,
Australia

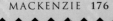

MACKINLAY

NAME AND PLACE

This was not a common name in Scotland. It comes from the Gaelic *Mac Fhionnlaigh* (son of Finlay), which was the title of the Farquharson chiefs, deriving from Finlay, grandson of Farquhar, who was killed at Pinkie in 1547. Finlayson is another form of the name, and Clan Finlayson in Lochalsh also claimed descent from Finlay.

ORIGIN

It is probably that the Mackinlays, or some of them, came from the same stock as the Farquharsons of Braemar, for although the name was not known in that district, it may have been adopted by those who moved away.

THE CLAN

The early 18th-century account by Buchanan of Auchmar ascribes to the Mackinlays a descent from a Buchanan chieftain named Finlay, and according to Sir Thomas Innes, 'there can be little doubt the country of this clan was in the Lennox district'; there was a colony north of Callandar. According to Buchanan of Auchmar some Mackinlays were to be identified with MacFarlanes.

Besides the sept of Farquharson and Buchanan, the Mackinlays have also been connected with Stewart of Appin.

ABOVE *Mount McKinley, Alaska, the highest mountain in North America, was named after William McKinley, 25th President of the United States, from 1897–1901.*

Several variants of the name appear in the 17th century (including McKandlay and McYndla), especially in Glenlyon and Balquhidder, and a family of Mackintoshes from Glenshee were described as 'alias Macinlies'.

There are possibly more Mackinlays, or MacGinleys, in Co. Antrim than anywhere else, the result of the plantation of Ulster by Protestant Scots in the 17th century. From one of these David McKinley (whose ancestors spelt their name McKinlay), descended a president of the United States, William McKinley (1843–1901).

MACKINNON

NAME AND PLACE

The Mackinnons claimed kinship on the one hand with King Kenneth MacAlpin though his brother Fingon, and on the other with St Columba, 'the apostle of Caledonia'. The original homeland of the Mackinnons was the Isle of Mull, at first apparently in the south, then from the 15th century, at Mishnish in the north.

ORIGIN

Although, as with other clans claiming membership of *Sìol Ailpein*, the descent there is speculative, the Mackinnons' kinship with St Columba is more certain.

THE CLAN

In the 14th century the brother of the Mackinnon chief was Fingon, Abbot of Iona, known as the Green Abbot. His grandson (Celtic clergy could marry), who was also called Fingon, was said to have made free with the monastery's property. A fine Celtic cross at Iona was erected by Lachlan Mackinnon, father of the last abbot, Iain Mackinnon, who died in 1500. His effigy has survived at Iona.

Although the clan was not a large one, it was of some note (and probably more numerous than generally supposed) during the time of the lords of the Isles.

The Mackinnons seem to have lost their original territory through some

BELOW *Castle Moil (formerly known as Castle Dunakin), near Kyleakin, the gateway to Skye. Although their original homeland was Mull, the Mackinnons were also found in several places in and around Skye, including Strathaird and the island of Scalpay.*

trouble created by the Green Abbot,
described by the chroniclers as 'subtle
and wicked', as a result of which the
Mackinnon chief was executed and the
lands in the south of Mull were taken
over by the MacLeans.

By the 16th century the Mackinnons
also held (probably through a marriage
with the MacLeods) Strathaird in Skye,
comprising over 150 square miles and
rather more significant than their lands in
Mull, together with the isle of Scalpay.

The Mackinnons took part in efforts
to restore the lordship of the Isles after its
suppression in 1493. Ewen Mackinnon
of Strathaird was a member of Donald
Dubh's council during his last rising in
1545. The clan was regarded as
troublesome by the government, and
early in the 17th century the chief, along
with other Highland leaders, submitted
to the restrictions of the Statutes of Iona.

Subsequently the Mackinnons were
loyal adherents of the Stewarts. Sir
Lachlan Mackinnon, twenty-eighth chief,
was knighted by Charles II before the
battle of Worcester (1651). His successor
John *Dubh* was 'out' in the Jacobite
rising of 1715, his estates being forfeited
but later restored, and again in 1745.
After Culloden the Mackinnons of Mull
were harassed by troops and the chief
spent some time in prison at Tilbury. He
was eventually released on account of his
age and sent home. When the attorney
general emphasised the king's generosity
in so releasing him, Mackinnon replied,
'Had I the King in my power as I am in
his, I would return him the compliment
of sending him back to his own country'.

He died in 1756 and was succeeded
by his son Charles, who had the sad
experience of seeing the estates sold to
pay off debts. His own son inherited
nothing except the chiefship and died 'in
humble circumstances' in 1808, the last
of his line. The chiefship passed, via some
convolutions, to a cadet branch.

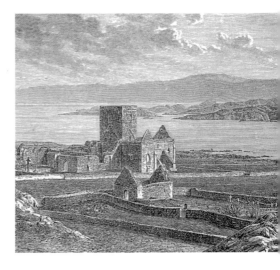

ABOVE *The church of the abbots of Iona
was rebuilt in about 1200. The Chapel of St
Oran is said to have been founded by that
great ecclesiastical patron, Queen Margaret,
wife of Malcolm III Ceann Mór.*

The ruins of the great Mackinnon
castle of Moil (Dunakin) still command
the passage between Kyleakin and Kyle
of Lochalsh on the mainland.

MACKINTOSH

NAME AND PLACE

Mac an Tòisich means 'son of the chief'
or 'thane', and some Mackintoshes are
not connected with the famous clan
whose chief became also the captain of
Clan Chattan in the central Highlands
south of.Inverness.

ORIGIN

The ancestor of the Mackintoshes,
according to a tradition which has not
been seriously questioned, was a younger
son of MacDuff, ancestor of the old earls
of Fife. He, or perhaps one of his
immediate descendants, married the
heiress of Clan Chattan, which was
named after a 13th-century chief,
Gilliechattan *Mór*.

THE CLAN

Mackintosh is first referred to as captain
(chief) of Clan Chattan in 1442. By that
time he was established on an island in
Loch Moy, Strathdearn.

During the wars of independence the
Mackintosh chiefs supported Bruce in
spite of the dominance of the Comyn
family, at feud with Bruce, in their
district. They also chose the right side in
1411, fighting with the Regent's forces at
Harlaw under the Earl of Mar. Their
lands in Lochaber were obtained in the
14th and 15th centuries at the expense of
the Camerons and the MacDonells of
Keppoch, which led to feuds that
continued off and on for centuries.

No clan was more often embroiled in
violent quarrels than the Mackintoshes,
though that was probably due more to
unavoidable circumstances, including
their wide responsibilities, the difficulty
of getting Clan Chattan to act together,
and their very complicated landholding

BELOW *The modern (19th-century) castle of
Inverness, capital of the Highlands. The
Mackintoshes resided at the earlier castle
from 1163 to 1496.*

arrangements, than to their alleged short tempers. The feud with the Comyns (Cummings) over lands in Strathnairn may have lain behind the famous clan battle at Perth in 1396, a sort of mass duel witnessed by the king himself. Some mystery surrounds the precise identity of the participants, but Sir Iain Moncreiffe believed that they were the Mackintoshes and the Cummings.

An ultimately more dangerous opponent was the Gordon Earl of Huntly, who was feudal overlord for some Mackintosh lands in Badenoch, and had the advantage of government backing for most of his activities. It was probably through Huntly that the Shaws (members of Clan Chattan and kin to the Mackintoshes) lost Rothiemurchus to the Grants in the 16th century. The Mackintosh tried to get it back, at first by purchase and, when that was rejected by the Laird of Grant, by force – which was no more successful. One 16th-century Mackintosh chief was judicially murdered by Huntly. His successors had the satisfaction of taking part in the battle of Corriechie (1562) where the Gordon Earl was killed, and at Glenlivet (1594), where they fought less successfully for Argyll against the rebellious Catholic earls.

The feud with the MacDonells eventually came to a head in what is usually described as the last great clan battle, at Mulroy in 1688. Despite the assistance of a company of regular soldiers and contingents from their allies, the Mackintoshes were defeated.

In the 17th century Clan Chattan generally supported the Stewarts (though not King James VII/II in 1688–89) and that allegiance continued during the Jacobite risings of the 18th century. Lachlan (a favourite name among the Mackintosh chiefs) brought his men 'out' in 1715, but the most notable Mackintosh leader in that campaign was William Mackintosh of Borlum, known

as 'Old Borlum', who had served in the French army. He led a Jacobite force into the Lowlands and, prevented from taking Edinburgh by Argyll, continued south as far as Preston in Lancashire, where he was forced to surrender. He was released in plenty of time to participate in the stillborn rising of 1719 and was captured again. While in prison he wrote a book on agricultural management.

The Mackintosh regained his estates and died in 1731. He had no direct heir and the chiefship passed to a cadet branch; not a single father-son succession occurred during the next hundred years.

Angus, twenty-third chief, was an officer in the British army at the time of the Forty-five and remained loyal to his commission. However, the clan was raised by his young wife 'Colonel Anne', whose strategy was responsible for the 'Rout of Moy', when several hundred redcoats were repulsed by half-a-dozen Mackintosh retainers (see Farquharson).

On the death of the twenty-third chief the chiefship migrated first to a merchant in the West Indies then to a Canadian businessman. But eventually it returned, and today the Mackintosh resides in the lands of his forefathers, now in a fine modern house besides Loch Moy.

CLAN ASSOCIATION
Moy Hall, Moy IV13 7YQ, Scotland

9812 Bronte Drive, Fairfax,
VA 22032-3910, USA

46 Donvegan Drive, Chatham, Ontario
N7M 4Z8, Canada

Coraki Road, South Gundurimba,
NSW 2480, Australia

Clan Chattan Society, P O Box 14010,
Edinburgh EH10 7YD, Scotland

MACLACHLAN

NAME AND PLACE

The MacLachlans of Strathlachlan in Argyll are named after Lachlan *Mór*.

ORIGIN

The descent of the MacLachlans from the Ulster royal family of O'Neill is as well attested as these things can be. According to the old Celtic genealogists five generations separated King Aodh O'Neill in the 11th century and Lachlan *Mór*. There is independent evidence from a charter of about 1238 of the existence of Lachlan *Mór*'s father, Gilpatrick.

THE CLAN

The MacLachlans have a good fairy, the Brounie, who has watched over them since ancient times, and it is said that when the first marriage between a MacLachlan and a Campbell (the first of many) occurred, the Brounie was so angry that he made the wedding feast laid out at Castle Lachlan disappear. This seems misguided, for it was largely through their alliance with the Campbells, the seat of whose chief at Inverary was only a few miles away from the MacLachlan stronghold, that this clan preserved their lands and independence into modern times.

In 1292 Gillescop, son of Lachlan, was named as one of the 12 barons

BELOW *The crumbling remains of Castle Lachlan on the shore of Loch Fyne. Some say the fire some years ago at Inveraray, seat of the Campbell chief ten miles to the north, was not unconnected with the misguided machinations of the Brounie.*

whose lands formed the new sheriffdom of Argyll. His son (or grandson) of the same name supported Bruce, at least from his coronation, and attended King Robert's first parliament at St Andrews in 1308. The same chief made a grant to the friars of Glasgow, an example of the numerous connections of the MacLachlans with the Church in the Middle Ages.

The territory of the MacLachlans ran for about ten miles on both sides of Loch Fyne, extending in the west at one time as far as the Sound of Jura. Cadets held other estates; the MacLachlans of Craiginterve were established near the head of Loch Awe and were once physicians to the Campbells of Argyll, when they were sometimes called Leech. Another MacLachlan family held the castle of Inchconnel on Loch Awe in the 17th century.

The MacLachlans' ability to stay on the right side of the Campbells did not extend to other neighbours in Cowal. With the Lamonts there were frequent feuds, though also alliances. They seem to have been involved in the dreadful massacre of the Lamonts by the Campbells in 1646. Subsequently, Lachlan MacLachlan of that ilk held office under the Protectorate, but despite the dominance of the Campbells, the chiefs of MacLachlan retained their freedom of action to such an extent that they were zealous Jacobites in the 18th century. They were with Bonnie Dundee at Killiecrankie in 1689, and in the rising of 1715 Lachlan MacLachlan was with Mar's somewhat stationary army at Perth. He died in 1719, possibly shot by Campbell of Ardkinglas.

In 1745 his son, accounted seventeenth chief and bearing the same name, was an early supporter of the prince, although he was able to raise only 180 men because there were Campbells all around. They joined the MacLeans at Culloden and most of them were killed,

cut down by grapeshot and musket fire before they could engage the foe. The elderly chief, leading his men, died as he made his way forwards, shot off his horse by a cannon ball. His son, Prince Charles's aide-de-camp, though hardly more than a boy, was already dead, killed by a chance shot before the charge began. It is said that the news of the terrible defeat was brought to Strathlachlan by the dead chief's riderless horse.

During the harassment of the Highlands after Culloden, Castle Lachlan was bombed into ruins from a ship in Loch Fyne. The estates, though forfeited, were returned comparatively quickly thanks to the good offices of the Duke of Argyll. A new castle was built in the 19th century in the Scots-baronial style. This slightly whimsical edifice is today the seat of the chief of the MacLachlans.

CLAN ASSOCIATION

18 South Craig, Bowness-on-Windermere LA23 2JH, England

119 Wrightwood Place, Sterling, VA 20164, USA

MACLAREN

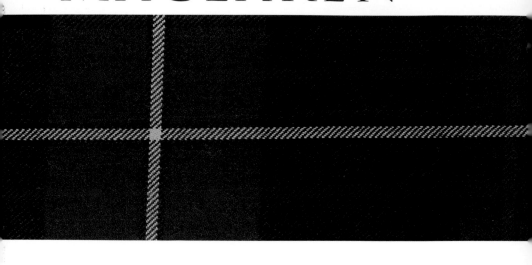

NAME AND PLACE

The general supposition is that the homeland of the MacLarens was, as it still is, the Braes of Balquhidder, the district around Loch Voil.

ORIGIN

Sadly the history of the MacLarens is shrouded in Highland mists. Their origins are a matter for speculation: Sir Thomas Innes accepted there were two distinct clans, those of Perthshire and the MacLarens or MacLaurins of Argyll. The war cry and the gathering place of the clan was *Creag an Tuirc* (the Rock of the Boar) near Achleskine, where the chiefly family resided, in Balquhidder. Heraldic evidence supports this. The MacLarens were probably kin to the Celtic earls of Strathearn, who died out in the mid-14th century.

THE CLAN

The Maclarens were at their height around the end of the Middle Ages, when they had spread beyond their original homeland throughout Strathearn and to other parts also. The disappearance of their former landlords, the earls of Strathearn, brought problems, but since the MacLarens never held their land by charter, they were perhaps fortunate to survive as long as they did.

BELOW *Clan MacLaren cairn above Loch Voil in the Braes of Balquhidder. The MacLaren clan badge of a mermaid represents the water spirit of Loch Voil.*

About the middle of the 16th century they were overrun twice in the same generation by the MacGregors. A great many people died and the clan never really recovered, subsequently seeking the protection of Campbell of Glenorchy. It was probably at about this time that all the clan records were, unfortunately, completely destroyed.

The prominence of the MacLarens in foreign military service may have been partly due to difficulties at home, and the warlike reputation of the clan equally a necessary characteristic to preserve their existence (the chiefs were said to have been 'all grand, strong men'). There were MacLarens in French service in the 15th century, and they fought for the Swedes in the Thirty Years War.

In later times many MacLarens followed Stewart of Appin. This resulted from a romantic marriage in the 15th century between a younger son of the Stewart Lord of Lorne and a notably beautiful daughter of a MacLaren chieftain. Their son, born out of wedlock but legitimised after his parents' marriage, became the founder of the Stewarts of Appin.

MacLarens fought alongside the Stewarts of Appin for the royal Stewarts in the civil war and in 1689, and they took part in the Jacobite risings of 1715 and 1745. One of their officers at Culloden was Donald MacLaren of Invernenty, who was afterwards captured and sent for trial at Carlisle. He made a dramatic escape in the mist at the Devil's Beef Tub in Annandale, hiding in a bog for several days and living off the flesh of a dead (long dead, apparently) sheep. He then made his way back to Balquhidder, where he lived for the next two years disguised as a woman. Scott made use of the episode in *Redgauntlet*, and it is said to have been some business connected with the MacLarens that first brought the great novelist, then a lawyer's clerk, into direct contact with the Highlands.

By that time the clan had virtually disintegrated, but the chiefship was later re-established and some of the original clan territory, including *Creag an Tuirc*, has been regained by purchase.

CLAN ASSOCIATION

6 Riding Park, Edinburgh EH4 6ED, Scotland

825 East Main Street, Salem, Illinois, USA

152 Ramsgate Road, Ramsgate, NSW 2217, Australia

MACLAINE OF LOCHBUIE

NAME AND PLACE: see MacLean

ORIGIN: see MacLean, MacLean of Duart

The rivalry between the MacLeans of Duart and the MacLaines of Lochbuie, descended from two brothers, gave rise to many tales of dark and dirty doings. The most famous concerns the temporary eclipse of the Lochbuie chiefs at the hands of their kinsmen and rivals.

Iain Òg, or Iain the Toothless, was chief of Lochbuie. His only son Ewen rebelled against him. Hector *Mór* of Duart supported the father, and Ewen was killed in a battle (his ghost, the Headless Horseman, appears ominously shortly before the death of a MacLaine of Lochbuie). Hector imprisoned his now childless kinsman of Lochbuie on a small island and, to stop him begetting a new heir, the only female companion allowed him was a hideous hag. In due course, however, she gave birth to Murdoch *Gearr* (Stunted), who later sought refuge in Ireland, while Duart attached the estates of Lochbuie to his own.

After various adventures Murdoch *Gearr* returned and regained his inheritance by force. He was legitimised in 1538 and subsequent MacLaines of Lochbuie were descended from him.

Despite these family difficulties the MacLaines of Lochbuie were generally allied with their kinsmen in national conflicts, just as they had been as vassals of the lords of the Isles (both Duart and Lochbuie sat on the Lord's council at Finlaggan). They fought with Montrose for Charles I, and 300 of Lochbuie's men fought at Killiecrankie under Bonnie Dundee, but they were not with MacLean of Drimmin in the Forty-five.

While Duart was lost, the MacLaines hung on to Lochbuie. When they were visited by Dr Johnson and Boswell, the chief no longer lived in the castle but in a house nearby. Johnson was not impressed by the house or the chief: 'a true Highland Laird, rough and haughty, and tenacious in his dignity'.

The estates would have been sold for debt in the 19th century but for the fortune amassed by Donald, twentieth Chief of Lochbuie, as a merchant in Java. A century later, however, it was lost, ironically a few years after Duart had been regained.

CLAN ASSOCIATION

4744 Casper Drive, Roanoak, VA 24019, USA

MACLEAN OF DUART

NAME AND PLACE: see MacLean

ORIGIN

Fierce argument has waged over which brother, Lachlan, founder of the MacLeans of Duart, or Hector, founder of the MacLaines of Lochbuie, was the elder and therefore which house is the senior. It is rather a pointless argument, since the old Celtic law made inheritance a family matter rather than an individual one, and it was quite in order for the chiefship to be inherited by a younger son, whose house subsequently became the senior line.

THE CLAN

Lachlan, even if younger, was the more successful, mainly through his marriage to the daughter of the lord of the Isles. This was effected by unconventional techniques, involving an affray in which the Mackinnon chief was killed and the girl's father kidnapped, but the lord of the Isles was impressed by his future son-in-law's boldness and from then on the MacLeans were in high favour. At the expense of the Mackinnons they received a large part of Mull and other islands. A more modest version of the great dark fortress of Duart, commanding the Sound of Mull and the Firth of Lorne, probably already existed at that time.

ABOVE *Duart Castle as it looked before the restoration of 1911–12. The curtain walls are 3m (3½yd) thick and nearly 10m (11yd) high.*

There was some rivalry between the houses of Duart and Lochbuie, but in major matters the MacLeans acted together. They repaid the favour of the lord of the Isles with great loyalty. Red Hector of the Battles, the second MacLean of Duart, was killed at Harlaw in 1411 fighting for the lord in his attempt to gain the earldom of Ross. MacLean chieftains held many military (especially naval) commands and administrative posts, including seneschal of the Isles and chamberlain of the household.

The fall of the lordship was no doubt inevitable but it was certainly assisted by the disastrous career of Angus Òg, son of the fourth lord, who was supported in his revolt against his father by the MacDonalds but opposed by the MacLeans and other clans who remained loyal to his father. In the gruesome sea battle of Bloody Bay in 1481 the MacLeans were defeated. Some 50 of them were butchered in cold blood after being smoked out of the cave in which they had taken shelter.

The MacLeans supported the lords of the Isles until the death of Donald *Dubh* in 1546, but thereafter came to terms with the Stewart dynasty. MacLean of Duart received royal confirmation of his lands and titles as early as 1496.

From the time of Angus Òg the MacLeans were frequently at odds with the various branches of Clan Donald. However, though not yet fully apparent, the ultimate winner of this particular power struggle was neither the MacLeans nor the MacDonalds, but Clan Campbell, waiting in the wings and not at all inclined to discourage their rivals' mutual animosity. The MacLeans did intermarry with the Campbells on several occasions, but this did not affect the outcome. In one notorious case, instead of cementing MacLean-Campbell relations, it had quite the opposite effect.

Lachlan MacLean of Duart married Lady Catherine Campbell, sister of the Earl of Argyll, early in the 16th century. He grew tired of her and marooned her on the Lady Rock in the Sound of Mull, which is submerged at high tide. MacLean hastened off to inform his brother-in-law of how his wife had met with an unfortunate accident at sea. He should have waited, for the lady was rescued by some fishermen who restored her to her brother's house. Later, on a visit to Edinburgh, MacLean was surprised by Campbell of Cawdor, another brother, who stabbed him to death in his bed.

That was not the end of the revenge of the Campbells. One way or another, not least through their efforts on behalf of the Stewarts during the civil wars, the MacLeans of Duart fell heavily into debt. Argyll, with his characteristic ingenuity, and through brazen employment of public office in private interest, bought up all the outstanding claims and eventually obtained a judgement

BELOW *Duart today, commanding the lovely waterway of the Sound of Mull. Castles sited for strategic command have the happy asset of providing superb views.*

authorising him to take over Duart's
territory (which his predecessor had
briefly held during the civil war).

The MacLeans resisted by the only
means available – force. English warships
were brought in to bombard Duart
Castle from the sea, but its massive walls,
some 10 feet thick, resisted successfully.
Meanwhile, Duart himself was fighting
with Bonnie Dundee, and the ultimate
defeat of the Jacobites in the 1688–89
rebellion gave Argyll the opportunity to
invade Duart with a sizable army, driving
the chief into exile.

Though landless, the MacLeans of
Duart were active in the Jacobite cause in
1715 and 1745. The last chief of the line
was captured in 1745 and the clan was
led at Culloden by MacLean of Drimmin.

The chief was allowed to return to
the exile from which he had emerged to
lead his men for Prince Charles, though
he was not, of course, restored to his
lands and castle.

Nevertheless, against the odds, the
MacLeans did eventually return to Duart.
Sir Fitzroy MacLean, a survivor of the
Charge of the Light Brigade, regained
possession of the castle, which the
Campbells had allowed to fall into ruins,
in 1911 and set about restoring it. As he
was 77 years old when he finally gained
possession after a lifetime of endeavour
to that end, he was not expected to enjoy
his success for long, but he lived to pass
his 101st birthday, and his grandson,
twenty-sixth chief, flies his banner from
the ramparts of Duart today.

ABOVE *A room in Castle Duart, now again
the home of the chief and an international
clan centre. Restored early in the 20th
century, it nonetheless has an authentic
atmosphere.*

CLAN ASSOCIATION
12 Elie Street, Glasgow
G11 5HJ, Scotland

5 Sandalwood, Laguna Hills,
CA 92656, USA

Clan Gillean USA, P O Box 4061, Alvin,
TX 77511, USA

MACLEAN

NAME AND PLACE

The Gillean from whom the clan takes its name was Gillean of the Battle-Axe, who lived in the 13th century. The original home of the MacLeans was probably Morvern, though they were more widely spread in the west at an early date.

ORIGIN

The MacLeans became a powerful clan under the lords of the Isles, of whom they were loyal adherents. After the extinction of the lordship – few fought harder than the MacLeans to maintain it – the main divisions of Clan Gillean became virtually independent clans. The two senior branches, the MacLeans of Duart and the MacLaines (they preferred the phonetic spelling) of Lochbuie were descended from two brothers, Hector (Lochbuie) and Lachlan (Duart), whose grandfather fought at Bannockburn.The two houses at times feuded with each other as well as with the MacDonalds.

THE CLAN

Gillean of the Battle-Axe is said to have fought at the Battle of Largs (1263). No doubt he was a warrior as fierce as he sounds, though his nickname arose from the peaceful use of that instrument: he became lost while hunting, and after wandering for days lay down to die,

hanging his axe on a laurel tree where it was seen in time to save him. He was probably descended from the royal house of Lorne and therefore from the kings of Dalriada, the ancient kingdom of the Scots corresponding roughly with Argyll.

Originally followers of the lord of Lorne they transferred their allegiance to the lord of the Isles in the 14th century probably after Lachlan married the daughter of the lord of the Isles, reputedly a love match.

Loyalty apart, the MacLeans benefited territorially from the collapse of the lordship of the Isles and reached perhaps their greatest power and influence in the 16th century.

BELOW *The ruins of the castle at Breacachadh (Breachacha), original headquarters of the MacLeans of Coll, and of the later Georgian house. The great number of these ancient strongholds, often in remote parts of the Highlands and Islands means that many are neglected.*

Besides Duart and Lochbuie, two cadet branches of the MacLeans of Duart came to be recognised as distinct clans.

The MacLeans of Ardgour, in Morvern, were founded in the 15th century by Donald MacLean, son of Lachlan, son of Red Hector of the Battles, son of Lachan the progenitor of the house of Duart. Donald wrested Ardgour from the MacMasters, whom he slaughtered to the last man, and since 'MacLean's Towel', the waterfall that descends the hillside at the back of (18th-century) Ardgour House has not yet run dry, his descendants are there still. Sir Fitzroy Maclean of Strachur, traveller, writer, soldier, politician and farmer, belonged to the Ardgour family.

The MacLeans of Coll were descended from Iain, brother of Donald of Ardgour. They quarrelled with the senior house of Duart in the 16th century and MacLean of Duart attacked them, taking over their lands and castle of Breacachadh, which, however, were restored after government intervention. 'Young Coll' the chief's son, was host to Johnson and Boswell when they visited the island on their Hebridean tour of 1773 and was drowned soon afterwards. At that time the MacLeans of Coll also held land in Mull and Rum. The lands were sold in 1848 by the last MacLean of Coll, who emigrated to South Africa. In Johnson's time there were a thousand or so people on Coll. Two centuries later there were fewer than 200, mainly of Lowland origin.

The MacLean of Duart hunting tartan is of particular historical interest because as long ago as 1587, in a charter of land in Islay then held by a son of MacLean of Duart, a feudal duty was payable in cloth of white, black and green – the colours of the modern MacLean hunting tartan. The same colours were mentioned in 1630. In 1527, between the two dates, when the lands were temporarily held by a different landlord, the 'green' becomes 'grey'.

ABOVE *A MacLean chief in formal Highland dress, complete with basket-hilted broadsword, before World War I. The three eagle feathers in his cap denote his rank.*

MACLEOD

NAME AND PLACE

The MacLeods were descended from Leod (said to derive from an old Norse word meaning ugly), son of Olaf the Black (d. 1237), who was King of Man and the Isles.

ORIGINS

Leod acquired Harris, Lewis and part of Skye, including Dunvegan, by marriage to the heiress of the Norse seneschal, or steward, of Skye. His sons Tormod (often called, a shade incongruously, Norman) and Torquil were the founders of the two main branches of the clan, respectively the MacLeods of Harris, whose chiefs became known, as the senior line, as the MacLeods of MacLeod, and the MacLeods of Lewis. The two main branches, known as *Sìol Thormoid* (Tormod) and *Sìol Thorcail* (Torquil) indulged in an intermittent dispute over seniority, but the chief of *Sìol Thormoid* was widely acknowledged as paramount by the 16th century.

THE CLAN

The motto of the MacLeods is 'Hold Fast', and it seems an appropriate one. They certainly held fast to Dunvegan Castle, at the head of the sea loch facing towards Harris, for it has remained the seat of their chiefs for about 700 years.

BELOW *Dunvegan, Skye, seat of the senior chiefs of MacLeod for about seven centuries. Architecturally no great gem, its collection of historical treasures makes it perhaps the most satisfying of all great Highland homes.*

This, the most famous clan chief's castle in the Highlands, could be entered only by the sea gate (built by Leod himself) until after the Forty-five, which signifies the importance of the sea in the history of the MacLeods. Thanks to this security of tenure, despite the absence of a charter until about 1500, the archives of Dunvegan are a treasure trove for historians of the Highlands, and the history of the MacLeods is comparatively well documented. There is a fine modern history of the clan by the well-known Highland historian, Dr Isabel Grant.

Among other treasures at Dunvegan is the Fairy Flag, to be unfurled only in case of extreme danger, which is now thought to be nearly a thousand years old and of Byzantine origin. MacLeod tradition says it was the gift of a fairy princess to Iain, fourth chief. Sir Iain Moncreiffe suggested with characteristic ingenuity that it is the banner brought back from Constantinople by King Harold of England (who later the same year fought less successfully against another invader, William of Normandy).

Siol Thormoid supported Bruce in the wars of independence although they do not seem to have benefited significantly from doing so. Under Malcolm, grandson of the original Tormod, Glenelg on the mainland was confirmed by a charter of King David II in about 1343, the first official confirmation of any MacLeod landholding. Early chiefs were known as 'of Glenelg' rather than, as later, 'of Dunvegan'. They were vassals of both the king of Scots and the lord of the Isles, with whom there were disputes, though the sixth Chief of Glenelg fought with Donald of the Isles at Harlaw (1411). His successor, the first to be described as 'of Dunvegan', was killed in the very nasty battle of Bloody Bay by Angus Òg's MacDonalds.

The eighth chief was the famous Alasdair *Crotach* (Hump-backed – the result of an accident), who had a charter of Trotternish (the northern peninsula of Skye, later lost to the MacDonalds of Sleat) and built the Fairy Tower at Dunvegan and the church of Rodel in Harris, where his fine tomb can still be seen. He married the alleged tenth daughter of Cameron of Lochiel, the previous nine having all refused him because of his deformity. In desperate battles with Clan Ranald he was twice compelled to resort to the ultimate weapon (unfurling the Fairy Flag). He died in 1547.

Alasdair *Crotach* was probably the MacLeod chief who figures in a famous story: dining at the royal court, a snooty Lowland courtier patronisingly remarked that the simple Highland chief must be impressed by the grandeur of his surroundings. MacLeod contradicted, saying he had finer halls, tables and candlesticks at home. A wager was made and subsequently MacLeod entertained the court to a banquet on the flat-topped hills opposite Dunvegan known as 'MacLeod's Tables', lit by torches held by statuesque clansmen. The Lowlander conceded the bet.

The most celebrated chief of *Siol Thormoid* was Sir Roderick (knighted by King James VI), better known as Rory *Mór*, who commanded that high degree of devotion from his followers that many MacLeod chiefs have shared up to present times. He is remembered in the famous lament of Patrick *Mór* MacCrimmon, of the family of hereditary pipers at Dunvegan.

After the collapse of the lordship Dunvegan became perhaps the chief centre of Gaelic culture (Gaelic is still spoken). The MacLeod court, attended by the chieftains of numerous septs of *Siol Thormoid*, was entertained by harpers (including the great Blind Harper

of Dunvegan, Roderick Morrison), pipers and jesters, as well as bards. Some of the learned families of the Beatons came to Dunvegan, and Rory Mór and his descendants spent freely on social and economic improvements such as schools and roads. In years of bad harvests they imported grain for their tenants. They even maintained an Edinburgh post.

Though they were not active in Montrose's campaign the MacLeods of Harris and Dunvegan supported the Stewarts in the 17th century. They provided about 700 men for the battle of Worcester (1651), of whom about three-quarters were killed. After this disaster no MacLeod chief ever took the field on behalf of the Stewarts again. Some were 'out' in 1715, but in 1745 the chief not only held aloof (though there were many MacLeods in Glengarry's and other regiments), but raised a company in government service.

He had been implicated along with his brother-in-law MacDonald of Sleat some years earlier in forcibly deporting some clanspeople to the American colonies. He had interests in a wider world than the Hebrides – ominous in a Highland chief. Within a generation much of his lands

had to be sold, though not until after the visit of Dr Johnson and Boswell in 1773. They were 'so comfortably situated' at Dunvegan they did not want to leave. Boswell rejoiced in the wine and venison and in 'the sight of a great Highland Laird surrounded by so many of his clan'. The visitors combined to dissuade Lady MacLeod from leaving the castle into a comfortable house more suited to a lady of 18th-century 'sensibilities'.

In the 19th century, inevitably, the clan dwindled and scattered, though the chiefs generally did their best. In 1935 Dame Flora MacLeod of MacLeod became chief and revived the life and spirit of the clan in an extraordinary way, making Dunvegan a kind of miniature United Nations assembly.

CLAN ASSOCIATION
10 Victoria Gardens, Newtongrange
EH22 4NL, Scotland

7909 Lock Lane, Columbia,
SC 29223-2531, USA

MACLEOD OF LEWIS

NAME AND PLACE: see MacLeod

ORIGIN

Sìol Thorcail trace their descent from
Torquil, brother of Tormod, progenitor
of the MacLeods of Harris and
Dunvegan on Skye (see MacLeod).

THE CLAN

By the reign of David II the MacLeods
of Lewis had also gained Assynt in
Sutherland, presumably by marriage. It
went to a younger son and became one of
several powerful, quarrelsome septs of
the clan. A 17th-century chieftain, deep
in debt, betrayed Montrose in 1650.
Another cadet branch held the island of
Raasay, between Skye and the mainland,
from the 16th century.

Like the senior branch, the MacLeods
of Lewis supported their overlord, the
MacDonald lord of the Isles, up to the
final rebellion of Donald *Dubh* in 1545,
but after came to terms with the royal
government but they soon became
involved in one of the worst conflicts in
Highland history, resulting in the
extinction of the chiefly house and the
loss of their lands.

The main source of trouble was the
Mackenzies who had a (phoney) claim
to Lewis through the marriage of a
Mackenzie lady to Rory MacLeod of
Lewis. The MacLeods had no formal title
to their lands so King James VI granted
Lewis to a Lowland commercial
company called the Fife Adventurers, his
object being to suppress the Lewis
MacLeods. But they were not so easily
dislodged. They resisted by force under
Neil *Mòr*, an illegitimate son of Rory,
and sent the Lowlanders packing. The
disillusioned Fife Adventurers sold out to
Mackenzie of Kintail. He had already
acquired Gairloch and other MacLeod
territories on the mainland, and he
moved into Lewis in force. Neil *Mòr* was
executed in 1613, and the entire chiefly
family was massacred.

The Mackenzies thus acquired
virtually all the lands of *Sìol Thorcail*
except for Raasay, whose chieftain
subsequently represented the Lewis
family. Trouble was largely avoided
during the civil wars, though Malcolm of
Raasay took part in the rising of 1745. In
1773 Samuel Johnson and James Boswell
found him a 'perfect representation of a
Highland gentleman'. Though his son,
was £40,000 in debt Raasay was not sold
until 1846, when the chief and his family
emigrated. Today, *Sìol Thorcail* have no
chief of their own.

MACMILLAN

NAME AND PLACE

The name MacMillan comes from the Gaelic *Mac Mhaolain*, generally translated as 'son of the tonsured one', ie, a monk, though it could conceivably mean merely bald. (The tonsure in the old Celtic Church was different from the Roman one, requiring the whole front of the scalp to be shaved.) Although there is no more substantial evidence, it is generally agreed that the ancestor of the MacMillans was a monk. In that case he would probably have been of high social rank and would have been free to marry and beget heirs.

MacMillans were to be found in many different parts of the country and the connection between them, if there was one, would be hard to trace.

ORIGIN

The most eminent, chiefs of a substantial clan, were the MacMillans of Knap (Knapdale) in the late medieval/early modern period, but earlier than this there were MacMillans around Loch Arkaig, in Lochaber. According to tradition they were moved during the reign of King Malcolm IV to Crown lands by Loch Tay, though in fact they seem to have been still established in Lochaber centuries later.

BELOW *The MacMillan Cross, one of several old Celtic memorials, at the Chapel of St Maelrubha at Kilmory, a mile or two north of the Point of Knap in Knapdale.*

THE CLAN

The MacMillans are said to have bound themselves to the Mackintoshes in the 15th century, probably in return for lands at Murlagan so they were thus placed between the Camerons and the Mackintoshes, eventually transferring their allegiance to Cameron of Lochiel. There is a legend that Lochiel, having been wounded at Culloden, was carried from the field by two MacMillans. The Seven Men of Glenmoriston, who sheltered Prince Charles in a cave for a week, included for a time an eighth man named Hugh MacMillan.

The MacMillans of Knap, possibly descendants of the MacMillans of Loch Tay, acquired their extensive holdings in that peninsula by a marriage to an heiress of the MacNeils. They held a charter from the lord of the Isles which promised that the land should be theirs 'while the sea beats on the rock', a promise engraved on a rock that sat beside Loch Sween. The charter has gone now, allegedly removed by the Campbells after they had acquired Knapdale in the 18th century. (Since the rock itself had disappeared, thrown into the sea by Campbell of Cawdor according to one story, the promise cannot be said to have been proved false.)

There are other memorials of the MacMillans in the district still surviving: MacMillan's Tower at Castle Sween, and a fine Celtic cross in the churchyard of Kilmory, which is carved on the reverse with a hunting scene, MacMillan himself (presumably) wielding an axe.

In the 18th century Duncan MacMillan of Dunmore was described as the representative of the vanished MacMillans of Knapdale. There were also MacMillans in Galloway and Ayrshire. The well-known publishing family originated in Arran and Ayrshire, gaining extra fame for the family and name when a political scion became British prime minister in 1957.

ABOVE *Sir Harold Macmillan outside Number 10, Downing Street, his residence as British prime minister in 1957–63.*

The estates of Macmillan of Dunmore passed to MacMillan of Laggalgarve whose descendant, the present MacMillan of MacMillan, is chief of the clan.

CLAN ASSOCIATION

Ardtalla, Glebelands, Rothesay
PA20 9HN, Scotland

Finlaystone, Langbank PA14 6TJ
2023 Medhurst Drive, Greensboro,
NC 27410, USA

3056 Oak Creek Drive N, Clearwater,
FL 34621, USA

Valleys Mills, River Denys RR2,
Inverness, Nova Scotia B0E 2Y0

MACNAB

NAME AND PLACE

The number of clan names with an ecclesiastical origin is not surprising as the higher ecclesiastical offices among the Celtic clergy were usually held by leading families and they, unlike those of the Roman Church, could marry. *Clann-an-Aba* means 'children of the abbot', and the MacNabs were descended from the abbots of Glendochart, possibly from the 7th-century St Fillan. Glendochart, west of Loch Tay, was the MacNabs' homeland.

ORIGINS

The MacNabs, members of the ancient *Siol Ailpein*, were traditionally connected with the MacGregors and Mackinnons, whom in a clan bond of 1606 they recognised as their kin.

THE CLAN

During the Scottish wars of independence the MacNabs supported the losing side and their lands were confiscated by the victorious Bruce. However, a feudal charter of 1336, restoring the barony of Bovain in Glendochart, shows that they were reconciled with King David II at that date.

Raeburn's famous portrait *The MacNab* shows a figure of marked individuality, tough, uncompromising, eccentric; and the MacNab chiefs were renowned as men of forceful character. It is not hard to guess that a MacNab chief called Iain *Min*, or Smooth John, owed his nickname to the same spirit in which Robin Hood's giant comrade was called Little John.

The MacNabs were not a large clan and as they were never inclined to be dictated to their fortunes were decidedly mixed. Among their neighbours were the MacNeishes, a sept of Clan Gregor, whose base was on an island in Loch Earn. One of the most famous incidents in clan warfare occurred in 1612 when Smooth John, at that time not yet chief, led his 11 brothers against the MacNeishes, carrying their boat on a winter's night from Loch Tay over the steep hills to Loch Earn. Anyone familiar with that country would say such a feat was impossible, but in fact it was repeated by a party of Black Watch territorials in 1965. The MacNeishes, greatly reduced in numbers since a recent battle with the MacNabs, were surprised sleeping and slaughtered (except for the obligatory single survivor, necessary to tell the tale). The MacNabs carried their enemies' heads home in a sack, but were forced to abandon their boat in the hills.

During the 16th century the MacNabs expanded considerably, but by the end of the century most of their lands were officially mortgaged to Campbell of Glenorchy, and they were listed among the 'broken' clans in 1594. Nevertheless, they were a considerable force by the time of Smooth John. As chief he joined Montrose in 1644 when the royalist commander arrived in Glendochart on his way to harry the Campbells, and he died fighting with his clansmen at the battle of Worcester in 1651.

The Campbells were then able to dispossess the MacNabs, but the estates were regained after the Restoration, when the Campbells were going through a rare phase of royal disfavour. In the risings of 1715 and 1745 the MacNabs were not eager Jacobites. Although the clan was 'out' for Prince Charles, the MacNab himself adhered to the government.

Francis, twelfth and last chief of his line (the subject of Raeburn's portrait), held considerable estates at the end of the 18th century, augmented by an inheritance through his mother. However, by the time he died in 1816, he had amassed large debts and although he is said to have 'left the MacNab country littered with bastards', he failed to produce a legitimate heir.

He was succeeded by his nephew Archibald, hitherto better acquainted with the salons of Paris and London than the hills of Perthshire. One morning he went out for a walk with his dogs and gun and disappeared. His creditors traced him to London and he fled to Canada, where he attempted to set up a little feudal empire among the MacNabs who had emigrated earlier. His exploitation of his clansmen led eventually to criminal prosecution, but he later returned to settle in Orkney, for by that time the MacNab lands had all been sold to the Earl of Breadalbane (Campbell of Glenorchy). The descendant of one of the Canadian MacNabs, Sir Allan MacNab, became prime minister of Canada.

ABOVE *A magnificent portrait of the MacNab, Francis MacNab (1734–1816) in the uniform of colonel of the Royal Breadalbane Volunteers.*

Part of the old MacNab lands were recovered a century later, and the present MacNab lives in Kinnel House, which, after the castle of Eilean Ran had been destroyed by Cromwellian troopers in 1654, was the home of his predecessors in the 17th and 18th centuries.

CLAN ASSOCIATION

8610 Lurline Avenue, Canoga Park, CA 91306, USA

MACNAUGHTON

NAME AND PLACE

The MacNaughtons (MacNachtans, etc, 'sons of Nechtan') were of ancient Pictish stock, and their homeland was between Loch Awe and Loch Fyne in Argyll.

ORIGINS

Gillechrist MacNaughton, son of Malcolm, was made hereditary keeper of the royal castle of Fraoch Eilean in Loch Awe in 1267. He also held Dunderave, on Loch Fyne, the residence of the chiefs of MacNaughton for many centuries.

THE CLAN

As adherents of the MacDougall lords of Lorne the MacNaughtons supported Balliol against Bruce and after Bruce's victory lost many of their lands to the Campbells. They changed sides later and received other lands from David II. Sir Alexander MacNaughton died fighting for James IV at Flodden in 1513.

As they no longer held lands on Loch Awe, Dunderave became the home of the MacNaughton chiefs in the 14th century. Relations with the Campbells were then untroubled, and the MacNaughtons seem to have recovered their 13th-century position. The chiefs continued loyal to the Stewarts through the 17th century, incurring periodic Campbell hostility. The sixteenth Laird of MacNaughton fought under Bonnie Dundee in 1689 at Killiecrankie, and lost his estates.

A bad situation deteriorated beyond recall in about 1700 when the next chief, John of Dunderave, seventeenth and last of his line, fell out with Campbell of Ardkinglas, who married him off to his uglier daughter by getting him so drunk he couldn't see straight. MacNaughton then vanished to Ireland, taking with him the prettier sister whom he had intended to marry, but leaving the estates to Ardkinglas. The chiefship became vacant, and the clan, chiefless and landless, virtually ceased to exist. But in the 19th century MacNaughton genealogists discovered a direct descendant in the male line of Sir Alexander MacNaughton who died at Flodden: Edmund MacNaughton lived in Co. Antrim. He was recognised as chief by the Lyon Court in 1818, and the title is held by his descendants, still resident in Antrim.

CLAN ASSOCIATION

82 Greenbank Crescent, Edinburgh EH10 5SW, Scotland

4444 Blackland Drive, Marietta, GA 30067, USA

MACNEIL OF BARRA

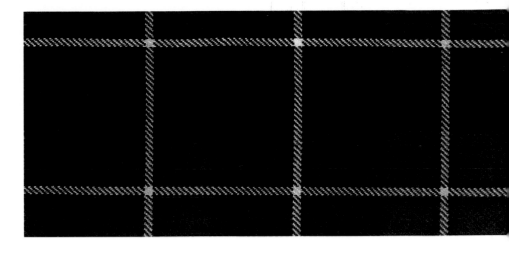

NAME AND PLACE.

The MacNeils were of the same stock as
the MacLachlans, Lamonts and
MacEwens, and took their name from
Niall, a descendant of Anrothan, the Irish
prince who married into the royal house
of Argyll in the 11th century. They were
confined almost exclusively to the smaller
islands of the Hebrides, chiefly Barra,
Gigha and Colonsay.

ORIGIN

The MacNeil chiefs, famous for being
even prouder than they were poor,
claimed descent from Niall of the Nine
Hostages, High King of Ireland at about
the end of the 4th century. This is about
as far back as even the old Celtic
genealogists could go.

THE CLAN

In the 16th century the MacNeils made
their living largely from piracy. A famous
story relates how Rory the Unruly of
Barra got into trouble in the late 16th
century by attacking English ships, which
provoked a sharp protest from Queen
Elizabeth to her kinsman, King James VI.
Mackenzie of Kintail was commissioned
to bring in the culprit, which he
accomplished by some sort of trick and
the king demanded of MacNeil, an
amiable-looking old gentleman with a

ABOVE *Kisimul Castle, home of the
MacNeil chiefs, on its rock opposite
Castlebay, Barra. Its present excellent
state is because of the restoration,
completed in the 1960s, by an American-
born chief – a romantic tale to rival that
of the MacLeans' Duart.*

long white beard, what the devil he meant by harassing the Queen of England's ships. MacNeil replied that he had thought to do His Majesty a favour by annoying the woman who had murdered his mother.

The Irish Niall lived in about 1300, but the first O'Neill chief known from historical records is a century later. He had a charter of Barra from the Lord of the Isles in 1427. Kisimul Castle, on a rock in a land-locked bay on the south of Barra, was the home of the chiefs for many years. The mooring place for MacNeil's galley can still be seen in the rock on which the castle stands.

An old ceremony said to have been conducted there illustrates the extraordinary self-importance of the old island chiefs, and also the amazing cultural exchanges that took place in those distant times – since the ceremony is believed to be of oriental origin and was presumably introduced by the far-sailing Norsemen. In the evening a trumpeter ascended the ramparts of Kisimul and blew his horn to all corners of the compass, before declaring to all the nations that since the great MacNeil of Barra had finished eating, the princes of the earth might now sit down to dine. Poor or not, the MacNeils of Barra lived at Kisimul in some style.

The MacNeils remained loyal to the lords of the Isles and, after their disappearance, to the Stewart dynasty. The chief was 'out' in 1688–89 for King James VII/II and in 1715 for his son. After the Forty-five Roderick, 'the dove of the west', was imprisoned for Jacobite sympathies although he appears to have taken no part in the events of 1745–46. His great-grandson, the last of his line, was forced to sell Barra in 1838. The chiefship continued in exile and in 1914 passed to Robert Lister MacNeil of

ABOVE *The statue of Our Lady of the Sea stands on the slopes of Heaval on Barra.*

Barra, an American who fulfilled his childhood dream by repurchasing Kisimul Castle and much of Barra. He restored the ruined castle, making many fascinating discoveries in the process, and spent much time endeavouring to restore prosperity to the islanders.

CLAN ASSOCIATION
Kisimul Castle, Isle of Barra
HS9 5XA, Scotland

1824 Stonyridge Drive, Charlotte,
NC 28214-8341, USA

MACNEIL OF COLONSAY

NAME AND PLACE

According to tradition the MacNeils of Colonsay (who generally spelt their name MacNeill) and the MacNeils of Barra descended from two brothers. Of their common origin there can be no doubt. Since their lands were much closer to the centre of Campbell power, however, the territorial history of the MacNeils of Colonsay is less stable.

ORIGIN

Their ancestors were called the MacNeils of Taynish and Gigha. In 1449 Torquil MacNeil of Taynish was keeper of Sween Castle (it went to the MacMillans through marriage with a MacNeil heiress after the main line failed).

THE CLAN

Torquil was the father of numerous minor branches, and the genealogy of the family of Taynish and Gigha is very complicated. Right up to modern times there was a great deal of exchanging of lands and responsibilities. It is said that on Sundays the children of the MacNeils of Colonsay were compelled to recite their genealogy backwards: one pities the poor creatures.

The island of Gigha was sold in 1554 but two brothers, descendants of Torquil named Neil and John Òg, revived the failing fortunes of their house and Gigha was repurchased from the Campbells before the end of the 16th century.

Torquill MacNeil of Gigha was described as 'Chief and principal of the clan and surname of MacNeils' by the Privy Council in 1530, but this seems to have been a temporary anomaly (and in any case it is not certain that he did belong to this branch).

Colonsay and Oronsay, where the MacNeils had been established since early times, were acquired by Donald MacNeil of Crear, in exchange for his own estates, from the Earl of Argyll in 1700. His descendant Alexander, sixth of Colonsay, sold it to his brother Duncan and himself acquired Gigha from his cousin – a characteristic MacNeil transaction, confusing to the historian.

The early 19th century was a time of prosperity in the islands thanks to the kelp industry and, on Colonsay, to the reforms of 'the Old Laird'. But the demand for kelp collapsed and the prosperity was short-lived. After more complicated exchanges, the island was eventually sold to pay off debts in the late 19th century, while the chiefship passed to a New Zealander.

MACPHEE

NAME AND PLACE

The probable Gaelic original of
MacPhee, or MacFie, is *Mac Duibh-sidhe*
(son of the black fairy), and MacDuffy
was an early form of the name. The
original homeland of the MacPhees, as
far as can be traced, was the fertile island
of Colonsay, with the adjacent isle of
Oronsay, in the Inner Hebrides.

ORIGIN

The name has prompted speculation that
this undoubtedly ancient clan sprang
from pre-Celtic stock. Another legend
ascribes the origin of the MacPhees to a
union between a mortal and a mermaid,
or seal-woman. The more recent
association of MacPhee with the trade of
the tinker tends to encourage the belief in
their ancient association with the elves,
though more realistically this was due to
their misfortune in losing their lands and
livelihood.

THE CLAN

The MacPhees held their lands under the
lord of the Isles and were hereditary
keepers of the records of the lordship,
which, sadly, have almost totally
disappeared.

A MacPhee sat on the lord's council at
Finlaggan in 1463, though apparently
not earlier, and after the fall of the

BELOW *Colonsay House. After the death of
MacPhee of Colonsay in 1623, the
MacPhee lands passed into the hands of
first Alasdair MacColla, then to the Earl of
Argyll and finally to a MacNeil. The 18th-
century house is now the home of Lord
Strathcona.*

lordship the clan was active in support of efforts to restore it. A fine tombstone in Oronsay commemorates the death in 1539 of 'Murchardus' MacPhee, and he was presumably the same chief who had been charged with treason eight years earlier in connection with his support of the lordship. Later chiefs generally followed MacDonald of Islay, and Sir Iain Moncreiffe suggested that the 'elfin bolt' which killed the MacLean of Duart Chief when his clan invaded Islay in 1598 was fired not by a *dubh-shidh* (a black fairy) but by a *Mac Duibh-sidh* (a MacPhee). There is a story too, from about this time, of a MacPhee chief who was killed by one of the MacLeans.

A MacPhee was among the Highland chiefs who consented (under duress) to the Statutes of Iona (1609), an attempt by the government of King James VI/I to restrain the independence of the chiefs by generally conciliatory means which, however, included drastic reduction of their authority.

The MacPhees' support for the MacDonalds of Islay eventually led to their downfall. Malcolm MacPhee of Colonsay joined the MacDonald rebellion of 1615 with 40 men, probably all the fighting men of his clan. Another Clan Donald chieftain, Alexander MacDonald, known as Colkitto from his Gaelic nickname meaning left-handed (he was the father of Montrose's war leader Alasdair MacColla, who is sometimes given his father's nickname), acting on behalf of the Earl of Argyll, defeated MacPhee of Colonsay, and later killed him when the MacPhee chief attempted to hide under a heap of seaweed. Colonsay passed into his possession, then to the Earl of Argyll, who exchanged it in about 1700 for the lands of Donald MacNeil of Crear, in Knapdale.

The MacPhees, deprived of their chief and of their lands, became a 'broken' clan. Some of them settled in Lochaber and became a sept of Cameron of

ABOVE *The isle of Colonsay is stunningly beautiful on calm summer's days, belying the violent pasts of its lairds.*

Locheil, fighting with notable courage at Culloden. Others remained with the MacDonalds of Islay.

In the 1840s Ewen MacPhee held out for some years on an island in Loch Phee (since named after him) with his wife, as good a shot as himself, and their children, paying no rent, acknowledging no authority, and keeping intruders at bay. The outlaw is said to have been expelled after, as an elderly man, he was caught stealing sheep.

MACPHERSON

NAME AND PLACE

MacPherson means 'son of the parson' and there may have been others so named who were not connected with the famous clan resident in Badenoch.

ORIGINS

The MacPhersons of Badenoch were important members of Clan Chattan, for a long time rivals for its captaincy with the Mackintoshes. Like them, they claimed descent from Gillechattan in the 13th century, but the origins of the MacPhersons have not yet been fully elucidated. Among other names, they were known as *Clann Mhuirich*, after Muriach (or Murdoch), great-grandfather of Duncan (the) Parson, who was imprisoned at Tantallon Castle with the Lord of the Isles in 1438. He was hereditary parson of Kingussie, and descended from Gillechattan.

They are also known as the Clan of the Three Brothers, who were sons of Ewen, a 14th-century chief said to have been son of Muriach. There are problems in fitting all these ancestors together chronologically however. Of the three brothers, Kenneth was the ancestor of the Cluny MacPhersons, who eventually came to be recognised as overall chiefs, Iain of the MacPhersons of Pitmain, and Gilles of the MacPhersons of Invereshie.

THE CLAN

The conflict between the Mackintoshes and the MacPhersons was particularly unfortunate in view of the proximity of powerful neighbours, by no means friendly. The Comyns (Cummings) were their overlords until destroyed by Bruce in the early 14th century; then the Stewarts, among them the notorious Wolf of Badenoch, and finally the Gordon earls of Huntly, generally backed by royal commissions and not averse to exterminating their opponents if an opportunity presented itself. Huntly naturally exploited the Mackintosh-MacPherson rivalry on the time-honoured principle of 'divide and rule'

From the 15th to the 17th century there were occasions of which evidence survives when the paramount status of the Mackintosh chiefs was acknowledged by the MacPhersons, but on the whole there was little co-operation, and the

BELOW *Loch Laggan, Badenoch, MacPherson country.*

MacPhersons were seldom eager to support the Mackintoshes in their feuds. Andrew MacPherson of Cluny, with other MacPherson chieftains, signed the Clan Chattan bond of union in 1609, but Cluny MacPherson's claim to the captaincy of the confederation of the Cat was reasserted in 1672, only to be overturned by the Privy Council, which pronounced the Mackintosh to be 'the only and true representer of the ancient and honourable Clan Chattan'.

Duncan of Cluny, the rejected claimant of 1672, had no sons and proposed to settle the chiefship on his daughter Anne, who was married to Sir Duncan Campbell (of the Cawdor house). This was opposed by William MacPherson of Nuid, the nearest male heir, and others, and their opposition prevailed. When Cluny died he was succeeded by Nuid's brother, Lachlan.

The MacPhersons were strong royalists during the civil wars of the 17th century, Ewen of Cluny leading a Badenoch contingent under Montrose. But, although they were an ancient clan and not insignificant numerically, but partly as a result of their own divisions they did not play a great part in national affairs until the 18th century, when their record of zealous support for the Stewart dynasty continued.

Sir Aeneas MacPherson of Invereshie, whose father died of wounds sustained in Montrose's campaign, was a Jacobite agent after 1688 and, following a spell in prison in vile conditions, departed under sentence of banishment to the Jacobite court in France.

Duncan of Cluny was 'out' with his clan in the Forty-five, and the greatest of MacPherson Jacobite heroes, Ewen of Cluny (son of William of Nuid who died in 1746), also made his reputation in that sad affair. He joined Prince Charles at an early stage of the campaign in 1745, bringing 600 men, and fought with great dash and bravado. Campaigning elsewhere, he arrived at Culloden too late to take part in the fighting.

Afterwards, with a large price on his head, he hid in 'Cluny's Cage', a specially constructed hide-out on Ben Alder in Badenoch, for nine years, protected and supplied by his men, even receiving rent regularly from his tenants. Eventually he escaped to France. His forfeited estates were restored to his son Duncan in 1784 and Cluny, which had been destroyed after Culloden, was rebuilt.

Duncan's son Ewen (d. 1885) was one of those Victorian Highland chiefs who maintained the old style and traditions in an age when they had become sadly redundant. But in spite of difficulties Cluny was not sold until the 1930s.

James MacPherson (1736–96), who was born in Kingussie, caused a tremendous stir with his alleged translations of Ossian, the Celtic bard of the 3rd century. The work was in fact mostly his own invention, as many suggested at the time, and modern Gaelic scholars find it hard to understand how anyone could have believed otherwise. Nevertheless, his *Works of Ossian* is powerful poetry, which gave a stimulus to the Romantic movement in Europe.

The MacPhersons have a red tartan but the grey hunting tartan is generally preferred, being of some antiquity. It is said to be identical with the 'grey plaid of Badenoch' copied by in 1745 Lady Cluny-MacPherson, the chief's wife, from an old plaid at Cluny, which makes it one of the oldest, perhaps the oldest, authentic clan tartan. The clan museum at Newtonmore opened in 1952.

CLAN ASSOCIATION

81 Runnymede, London
SW19 2PG, England

227 Amelia, Royal Oak, MI 48073, USA

MACQUARRIE

The MacQuarries' badge of the pine marked them as members of *Sìol Ailpein*. The name was derived from *Guaire*, meaning noble. They were native to the isle of Ulva, off Mull.

ORIGIN

The original *Guaire*, tradition says, was the brother of Fingon (beloved), ancestor of the Mackinnons. The first of them to appear in historical records was Iain of Ulva, who lived in the mid-15th century and was probably a member of the council of the lord of the Isles.

THE CLAN

When Samuel Johnson and James Boswell visited Ulva, off Mull, in 1773 they found a small, barren island and an ancient but small clan. The chief impressed them rather more, with his intelligence and worldliness.

The MacQuarries also held Staffa, later famous for 'Fingal's Cave', and part of Mull. It is said that a chief supported King Alexander II in his campaign in Argyll in 1249, and his successor fought under Bruce at Bannockburn. They were associated with MacLean of Duart and active in efforts to restore the lordship. In 1609 the MacQuarrie chief was one of the Highland chiefs inveigled into agreeing to the Statutes of Iona.

BELOW *Lachlan MacQuarrie, born on the Isle of Ulva, was an officer in the Black Watch who became governor of New South Wales at a low point in the colony's existence and raised it largely through his own enterprise and good administration into a prosperous community, earning the honourable title, 'Father of Australia'.*

In the train of the MacLeans, the MacQuarries were caught up in debilitating feuds, and they never recovered from the disaster at Inverkeithing (1651) when the chief and many of his men died, along with Duart and many MacLeans, fighting for Charles II. The MacQuarries were also involved in resisting Campbell encroachments in Argyll in the 1670s and in Bonnie Dundee's victory at Killiecrankie in 1689.

The chief who entertained Johnson and Boswell was later forced to sell his lands. He entered the army, though allegedly 63, and died in Mull in 1818. He was the last of his line and there have been no MacQuarrie chiefs since, although no doubt some family from North America, where they are more numerous, will one day succeed in establishing their claim.

The most famous member of the clan was a cousin of the last chief, Lachlan MacQuarrie (1762–1824), a soldier who as governor of New South Wales in 1810–21 turned a chaotic penal settlement into a prosperous colony.

ABOVE *Fingal's Cave, on the geologically fascinating island of Staffa (now uninhabited), which was the inspiration for Mendelssohn's 'Hebrides' overture.*

MACQUEEN

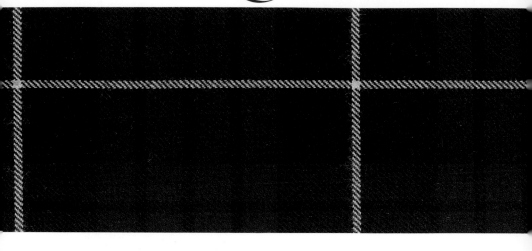

NAME AND PLACE

There are numerous, often highly dissimilar derivations of this name, the principal one of which is from the Gaelic *Suibhne*, meaning 'going well'. Preceded by Mac, the S is aspirated, giving rise to something very like 'MacQueen'. Some writers suggest that the origin is *Mac Cuinn* (son of Conn, ie the semi-legendary Conn of the Hundred Battles), but this was denied by George Black (*The Surnames of Scotland*, 1946). The Gaelic name in turn perhaps derived from the Norse *Sweyn*.

ORIGIN

The Macqueens (the more 'correct' spelling) were of Hebridean origin, and were associated with the MacDonalds. In 1778 Lord MacDonald of Sleat wrote in a letter to the Macqueen chief that the Macqueens 'have been invariably attached to our family, to whom we believe we owe our existence'.

THE CLAN

It is therefore at first sight somewhat surprising that the clan of this name should have been a member of the confederation of Clan Chattan. They were there known as the Macqueens of Corribrough (the chiefly family), or alternatively as Clan Revan.

BELOW *Castle Sween in Knapdale, one of the oldest castles on the Scottish mainland, probably built by MacSweens in the 12th century, which later passed to the Campbells and, for a time, was held by MacNeils as hereditary constables under the Crown.*

The traditional explanation is that the Clan Chattan Macqueens came from Moidart on the west coast early in the 15th century when Mora MacDonald of Moidart married the Mackintosh, and brought with her the usual train of her kinsfolk. Among them was one Revan, the ancestor of the Macqueens of Corribrough, who settled in Strathdeath. Revan apparently fought with the Mackintoshes against the Lord of the Isles at the battle of Harlaw in 1411.

The first Macqueen known to be styled as 'of Corribrough' was Donald, who signed the Clan Chattan bond of union in 1609, taking responsibility also for Macqueen of Little Corribrough and Sweyn Macqueen of Railbeg.

There were Macqueens and MacSweens also in Argyll (MacSweens held Sween Castle in the 13th century), and the Hebrides, notably at Garafad in Skye. The Rev. Donald MacQueen, who in 1773 so impressed Dr Johnson ('There must be great vigour of mind to make him cultivate learning so much in the isle of Skye, where he might do without it'), was the fourth generation of Macqueen ministers of the church at Snizort.

Robert MacQueen, Lord Braxfield, the late 18th century judge notable for the savagery of his prejudices and equally of his sentences, came from a Lanarkshire family whose connection with the clan, if any, no one is particularly anxious to make.

The Macqueen lands appear to have been lost in the late 18th century, when a great number of the clan emigrated. A later chief followed their example and the chiefship is now in New Zealand.

ABOVE *Robert MacQueen, Lord Braxfield (1722–99), a notorious 'hanging judge' known as 'the Scottish Jeffreys', the model for Lord Weir in Robert Louis Stevenson's unfinished book,* Weir of Hermiston *(1896).*

MACRAE

NAME AND PLACE

The name *Mac Rath* means 'son of grace'. MacRae is one of many anglicised forms, which include Macrea and the Irish form Magrath, which is closest to the original. It is basically a forename (like MacBeth), and may or may not have something to do with the number of MacRaes who entered the Church in the early modern period.

When surnames first became common in Scotland towards the end of the Middle Ages, MacRaes cropped up in various parts of the Lowlands and the modern MacRaes are not necessarily related to the clan that is for ever associated with Kintail and the castle of Eilean Donan.

ORIGIN

The original home of the MacRaes was near Inverness. They had a long-standing association with the Frasers, and there was once an inscription carved above the gates of Lord Lovat's castle asserting that no MacRae should ever have to wait without while there was a Fraser within. However, by the end of the 14th century they were established on the other side of the country in Kintail, Wester Ross, and attached to the rising star of the Mackenzies.

ABOVE *Loch Duich, the eastward extension of Loch Alsh, with the Five Sisters beyond.*

THE CLAN

Later a branch of the MacRaes acquired Inverinate from the Mackenzie Earl of Seaforth. They became constables of Eilean Donan castle – not a hereditary office since it was sometimes held by others – more-or-less permanently. They also held other honoured posts under Mackenzie of Seaforth, whose chamberlain was often a MacRae, and were ministers of surrounding parishes. In the 17th century the same man was constable of Eilean Donan and minister of Kintail. This was Farquhar MacRae (1580–1662) of Inverinate, whose grandson Duncan of the Silver Cups

compiled the invaluable Gaelic poetry
anthology known as the Fernaig
Manuscript, containing works by himself
and other MacRaes.

The MacRaes' loyalty to the
Mackenzies and their stout defence of
Eilean Donan castle, commanding the
entry to Loch Duich and the route to the
Isles, earned them the name 'Mackenzie's
shirt of mail'. In 1539 when Donald
Gruamach of Sleat was besieging the
castle (at that time commanded by a
Matheson) in his effort to restore the
lordship of the Isles in his own person,
Duncan MacRae, son of a previous
constable, shot him in the knee with an
arrow fired from the battlements. The
wound might not have been so bad but
Sleat impatiently wrenched out the
arrow, and the barbs fatally ripped an
artery. There are other tales of the
individual military prowess of 'the wild
MacRaes', one of whom, when
Cromwellian troops occupied Eilean
Donan, slew a soldier with one stroke of
his sword.

During the unsuccessful Jacobite
rising of 1719 Spanish troops who
landed with the exiled Mackenzie chief
were billeted at Eilean Donan, and the
castle was subsequently blown up. It was
restored in the 1930s to its present
picturesque state, and it remains in the

ABOVE *The castle of Eileann Donan,
probably the best-known image of the
Highlands thanks to biscuit tins and other
commercial images. It was painstakingly
restored from almost total ruin by Colonel
John MacRae-Gilstrap.*

hands of descendants of the MacRaes of
Conchra, an important branch of the
clan since the 17th century, and is the
headquarters of Clan MacRae.

CLAN ASSOCIATION
5 Craigard Place, Inverness
IV3 6PR, Scotland

P O Box 3145, Wilmington,
NC 28406, USA

1/23B Albert Parade, Ashfield,
NSW 2131, Australia

MALCOLM

NAME AND PLACE

It is said that the names Malcolm and MacCullum are interchangeable (see MacCullum). An 18th-century Chief of the MacCallums, Alexander of Poltalloch, changed his own name to Malcolm, assuming them to be identical. However, the two may have been quite different. Malcolm means 'servant' or 'devotee of Colm' (Columba). The Gaelic *Maol* ('shaven-headed', therefore 'monk') is similar, as a prefix, to the more familiar 'Gille-'. The 'devotee' of Colm is not the same as the 'son of Colm' (ie MacCallum), and the implication is clearly that no such blood relationship existed. The argument is strengthened by the scarcity of evidence that, before the 18th-century MacCallum chief, the two names were used interchangeably. However, it must be said that this evidence is not altogether lacking, and also that it would be surprising if it could be found in convincing quantity, whatever the situation was. According to the famous work of Dr George Black (*Surnames of Scotland*, New York, 1946), MacCallum is a version of *Mac Gille Chaluim*, of which there are 15th-century examples, which means 'son of the devotee of Calum'. This seems to weaken the original argument! It is true, however, that as a surname Malcolm is comparatively recent.

There are, anyway, both MacCallum and Malcolm tartans. Take your pick!

THE CLAN

See MacCullum

CLAN ASSOCIATION

See MacCallum

BELOW *Sir John Malcolm (1769–1833), born in Eskdale, had a distinguished career in India, culminating in the governorship of Bombay (1827–30).*

MATHESON

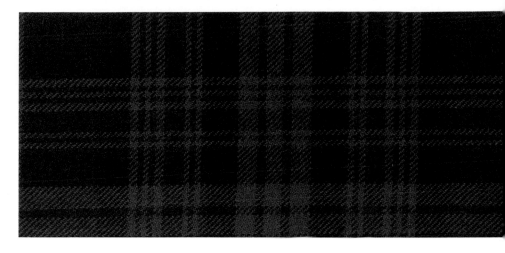

NAME AND PLACE

The name comes from the Gaelic *Mac Mhathain*, though Mathesons in the south were 'Matthew's sons' and not connected with the northern clan whose home was Lochalsh.

ORIGIN

The clan was traditionally descended from Gilleon of the Aird, who was also the ancestor of the Mackenzies. An early chief, Cormac, fought with the Earl of Ross against Haakon of Norway, receiving 20 cows from the earl for services rendered.

Subsequently the Mathesons supported the Lord of the Isles. They were present at Harlaw in support of the lord's claim to the Ross earldom. The chief, Alasdair, or his successor, was among those arrested at Inverness by King James I in 1427. At that time he was said to have 2,000 fighting men at his call, but the Mathesons, as allies of the MacDonalds, were soon to decline, their hold on their lands was further weakened by clan feuds.

At times Mathesons appear to have held Eilean Donan (usually the prerogative of the MacRaes) on behalf of Mackenzie of Kintail. A Matheson chief, Iain *Dubh*, was killed in 1539 at the time of MacDonald of Sleat's siege.

Iain *Dubh*'s grandson, Murchadha (or Murdoch) *Buidhe*, was ancestor of the Mathesons of Bennetsfield in the Black Isle who included the historian of the clan. His descendants became the present chiefly family. Other branches settled in Sutherland, until driven to emigrate in the Clearances.

By the early 19th century practically all the Matheson lands had been lost, but fortune was restored to the name by two merchant princes, James Matheson and his nephew Alexander, of the Mathesons of Shiness, Sutherland. Both amassed fortunes in the Eastern trade which they invested in property. Alexander gained Lochalsh, the old clan homeland, spending about a million pounds on purchase and subsequent land improvements. Sir James bought Lewis in 1844 and spent generously to alleviate the disaster of the potato famine.

CLAN ASSOCIATION

Croxton Old Rectory, Eltisley, Huntingdon PE19 4SU, England

MAXWELL

NAME AND PLACE

The origin of the name of this prominent
Border clan is of English, possibly Norse,
origin. Its earliest known leader was
Maccus, son of Underweyn, who lived in
the 12th century and gave his name to
Maccuswell (*wael* meaning 'pool' in old
English), near Kelso on the Tweed.

ORIGIN

His grandson John of Maccuswell
(Maxwell) was Chamberlain of Scotland
about ten years before his death in 1241
and he was probably the first to hold the
great Maxwell stronghold of
Caerlaverock, whose impressive ruins
stand today in the marshy fields of lower
Nithsdale. He was succeeded as
chamberlain by his brother Sir Aymer,
from two of whose sons, Herbert and
John, many of the numerous branches of
the Maxwells descended.

The position of Border lords like the
Maxwells 'between the hammer and the
anvil', was not an easy one, though on
the whole they tended to make the most
of the situation. During the wars of
independence Caerlaverock was besieged
and changed hands on more than one
occasion. Herbert, son of Aymer,
recognised John Balliol as king and
Herbert's grandson, Sir Eustace, held
Caerlaverock for the English in 1312. But

he subsequently dismantled the
fortifications – before Bruce knocked
them down – and was one of those who
signed the Declaration of Arbroath,
sometimes called Scotland's declaration
of independence, in 1320. The castle was
rebuilt on a triangular plan in the 16th
century. Sir Eustace reverted briefly to
(Edward) Balliol in 1322 and Sir John
Maxwell, his brother and successor,
accompanied King David II on the
expedition which ended in defeat at
Neville's Cross in 1346.

The Maxwells became increasingly
powerful in the 15th century after the
eclipse of the Black Douglases. The chiefs
bore the title Lord Maxwell from 1424,
and often held the office of warden of the
Western Marches. After Flodden (1513),
where John, fourth Lord Maxwell, was
killed fighting for the king, this office
became almost a Maxwell monopoly.

Feudal ties as well as the many
branches of the clan, contributed to
Maxwell hegemony, and surviving bonds
of manrent show them to have been very
successful in securing loyalty and support
by that means.

It was never an easy task, however.
John Maxwell of Terregles, brother of
the fifth Lord Maxwell (who later
became Lord Herries through his wife's
inheritance), resigned as warden in 1553

because he could not deal with proliferating local feuds. Later, however, he resumed the office. Meanwhile his brother had served briefly as regent during King James V's absence from the kingdom and was later captured by the English at Solway Moss (1542).

The Maxwells were naturally involved in feuds themselves, notably with the Johnstons, who also at times held the office of warden of the Marches. The rivalry was particularly fierce towards the end of the 16th century, and in 1593 the sixth Lord Maxwell, who had become Earl of Morton after the execution of the Douglas holder of that title in 1581, was killed in a battle with the Johnstons near Lockerbie. The seventh lord eventually gained revenge, killing Johnston of that ilk in 1608. Afterwards he fled abroad, but unwisely returned a few years later and was executed in 1613.

By this time the union of the Scottish and English Crowns had brought the Border wars to an end and the Maxwells, lost their traditional role. Nevertheless, they did not retire into obscurity. Robert, eighth Lord Maxwell, was created Earl of Nithsdale and on the death of his son the title passed to Lord Herries, descendant of the first Lord Herries.

The fifth Earl of Nithsdale embraced the Jacobite cause and was captured at Preston in 1715. He was tried for treason and sentenced to death, but his wife, a lady of some mettle, secured his escape from the Tower of London disguised as a maidservant. They got away to Rome where the earl died in 1744.

Among the prominent branches of the Maxwells were the Maxwells of Monreith, the barony held in the 15th century by a grandson of the first Lord Maxwell. Sir Herbert Maxwell (1845–1937), writer, statesman and expert salmon fisherman, and his son the writer-naturalist Gavin Maxwell (1914–69) belonged to this line.

ABOVE *The stunning Maxwell stronghold of Caerlaverock, despite its ruined state, is one of the finest medieval buildings in Scotland. Like most Border castles, it had a hectic history before the elegant Renaissance additions were made by the 1st Earl of Nithsdale, not long before the place was wrecked by the Covenanters in 1640.*

CLAN ASSOCIATION

Kirkconnell House, New Abbey
DG2 8HL, Scotland

246 de Lee Drive, Kingsport,
TN 37663, USA

111 Bruce Street, Suite 416, Kirkland,
Quebec, H9H 4B7, Canada

MENZIES

NAME AND PLACE

The name Menzies is of Norman origin.
It probably comes from Mesnières, and
the English version of the surname is
Manners. An early spelling in Scotland
was Meyners, and the name is usually
still pronounced (and sometimes spelled)
Mingies. The family was apparently first
settled in Lothian, but Clan Menzies
belongs to Atholl.

ORIGIN

In the reign of King Alexander II, Robert
de Meyners, who was the Royal
Chamberlain, held Culdares (Culdair). A
charter from him (regarded as the first
chief of the Atholl Clan Menzies) to Sir
Matthew Moncreiffe of that ilk,
confirming him in the lands of Culdares
and Duneaves (Glenlyon) is still in the
possession of the Moncreiffes.

THE CLAN

Sir Robert's son Alexander held Weem,
Aberfeldy, Fortingale and Glendochart in
Breadalbane as well as Durisdeer in
Nithsdale. His son supported Bruce and
was rewarded with further territories,
making the family one of the largest
landholders in the southern Highlands. In
the early 15th century a David Menzies
was governor of Orkney and Shetland
under the king of Norway.

BELOW *Colonel James Menzies, a kinsman
of Sir Alexander Menzies (the first baronet),
held the estate of Culdares in Glenlyon, and
it was here that a member of his house
intruduced the larch tree from the Austrian
Tyrol in 1737, which now flourishes
throughout the Highlands of Scotland. The
Culdares branch is now extinct in the male
line, and* Am Mèinnearach *descends today
from its heiress.*

Sir Robert Menzies, descendant of the first Sir Robert, had his properties erected into a barony by King James IV, and at about this time the great Castle Weems (later renamed Castle Menzies) was built.

The Menzies were involved in various feuds. There was trouble with the Campbells despite various bonds and marriage alliances, and in a quarrel with the Stewarts of Garth, who had taken over the former Menzies property of Fortingale, the castle was burned early in the 16th century. It was rebuilt later on the Z-plan, designed for effective fire against raiders. During the various civil conflicts of the 17th and 18th centuries Menzies were to be found on both sides. The Weems family were allied with the Campbells but the Pitfoddels branch fought with Montrose.

The senior house was again active on behalf of William III, but Pitfoddels was 'out' in the Fifteen for James Edward. During the 1745 rising Clan Menzies, or at least some members of the clan, were raised by Menzies of Shian, though it was said that the summons of the fiery cross was not obeyed with great enthusiasm by the clansmen.

The last member of the Pitfoddels family is remembered for founding the Roman Catholic college of Blairs, on Deeside. A member of the senior line of Weems was the first, or one of the first, to introduce what is now a tree characteristic of the Highlands, the larch, from the Tyrol, in 1737.

The tartan illustrated is a so-called hunting tartan (their war cry is 'Up with the White and Red!'). The Menzies also have a black and white 'mourning' tartan of the same sett .

The Menzies of Menzies, chief of the clan, whose Gaelic title is *Am Mèinnearach*, is a member of a branch of the Culdares family, the senior line having ended in 1910. During the 19th century Castle Menzies ('the place of Weems') was enlarged and embellished with baronial turrets, but without obliterating the original structure. Later it fell into ruins, but it has been restored by the Clan Menzies Society, which bought it in 1957, and remains the clan headquarters.

CLAN ASSOCIATION

110 Seaview Terrace,
Edinburgh EH15 2HG

323 Roughwater Point, Canton,
NC 28716-8196, USA

MONCREIFFE

NAME AND PLACE

The name Moncreiffe comes from a
Gaelic place name, *Monadh Craoibhe*,
meaning 'hill of the sacred bough', or
'tree', which overlooks the valleys
harbouring Scone and other centres of
the ancient Pictish kings.

ORIGIN

Sir Iain Moncreiffe of that ilk, a notable
Highland historian, surmised that the
Moncreiffes themselves were descended
from the Pictish kings in the female line.

Very few of Scotland's ancient families
have remained ensconced in their original
home and district for so long. There were
Moncreiffes of Moncreiffe at the time of
the earliest surviving records, and they
are still there today.

THE CLAN

Sir Matthew of Moncreiffe, brother-in-
law of one of the regents of Scotland, had
a royal charter of that estate in 1248, and
a year later another charter from Sir
Robert Menzies (founder of Clan
Menzies) for the lands of Culdares and
Duneaves, in Glenlyon.

For such an ancient and distinguished
family the Moncreiffes did not play a
major part in national affairs generally,
which no doubt helps to explain why
they have managed to hold on to their

BELOW *Tayside, looking towards
Moncreiffe Hill. That the clan has held onto
these beautiful lands for so long is unusual,
but may be because on the whole they
managed to stay out of other people's
quarrels and played only a small part in
national affairs.*

patrimony. Though various conflicts could hardly be avoided, the Moncreiffes, as Sir Iain wrote, 'have always had a firm reputation of loyalty to the Sovereign's person.' One was chamberlain to King James III and two fell at Flodden. However, one took part in the murder of Rizzio, Mary Queen of Scots' secretary.

In 1312 Sir John Moncreiffe of that ilk, who is said to have once sheltered Wallace in a cave on Moncreiffe Hill, gave Easter Moncreiffe to his younger son Matthew, founder of that house. In 1592 Easter Moncreiffe was erected into a free barony, giving the laird the same powers of life and death as those of the Laird of Moncreiffe himself, but in the late 17th century it was acquired by Thomas Moncreiffe of Moncreiffe, who as the first baronet later became Sir Thomas.

The old tower house of Easter Moncreiffe fell into ruins about this time, presumably because no one lived there, but a house was built to replace it early in the 18th century. It was much extended in Victorian times by Sir Robert, eighth baronet and twenty first Laird of Moncreiffe. Later it was the home of the ninth Duke of Atholl, from whom it was acquired by Sir Iain, a cousin of the twenty-third Laird of Moncreiffe. He also gained the old tower and the barony (no longer with powers of life and death, however).

The House of Moncreiffe was built in the late 17th century to replace a medieval tower house by Sir William Bruce, who went on to build Holyrood Palace. It was destroyed in a terrible fire in 1957 in which the twenty-third laird lost his life. Bruce's doorway is incorporated in the new house which, though of more modest scale, owes much to its predecessor.

The three main branches of the Moncreiffes are distinguished by the way the name is spelt. The Moncreiffes of Tulliebole have produced many distinguished churchmen. A number of other cadet branches, descended from the lairds of Moncreiffe, are called Moncrieff. They include the Scott-Moncrieffs, one of whom gained great literary fame as the translator of Proust.

The Moncreiffe tartan is a recent one, designed by Sir Iain Moncreiffe of that ilk, who chose a simple diced pattern of the kind which seems to have been common in the days before tartans became popular emblems. Previously Moncreiffes wore the Murray of Atholl tartan, having been closely connected with the Murrays for centuries.

MONTGOMERY

NAME AND PLACE

Montgomery is a Norman name. Roger de Montgomerie (d. 1094) was one of those left in charge while the Duke of Normandy was absent on other business in 1066. The following year he came to England and was made Earl of Arundel.

ORIGIN

The first in Scotland was Robert de Mundegumri (d. c. 1177), a grandson of the Earl of Arundel, who arrived with Walter fitzAlan, Steward to King David I and received Eaglesham in Renfrewshire, which remained the property of his descendants until the 19th century.

THE CLAN

His descendant John Montgomerie of Eaglesham was a warrior of great renown for his feat at the battle of Otterburn (1388), where he fought single-handed with Henry Percy (Hotspur) and defeated him. He is said to have built the castle of Polnoon with the ransom, and he also made a profitable marriage to the heiress of Sir Hugh de Eglinton. His grandson became Lord Montgomery and the second Lord Montgomery was created Earl of Eglinton (1507).

Hugh, second Lord Montgomery and later Earl of Eglinton, was one of those who conspired to replace the unpopular King James III with his son, and he fought at Sauchieburn (1488), where the king was wounded and afterwards killed in miserable circumstances. He held Brodick Castle and the Isle of Arran until replaced there by the Hamiltons. He was succeeded by his grandson Hugh, second earl (d. 1546), whose son the third earl was a loyal supporter of Mary Queen of Scots and fought for her in the final battle at Langside. Thereafter he was imprisoned for a time and after his release endeavoured to secure toleration for Roman Catholics in that unpromising time when Calvinism was rampant.

One of the longest private feuds in Scotland was that between the Montgomerys and the Cunninghams. It

BELOW *Brodick Castle, Arran, an imposing Victorian residence of the Hamiltons. A few parts of the earlier building, which was for a time held briefly by the Montomery earl of Eglinton, remain.*

originated in some relatively minor
dispute over jurisdiction, and several
times apparently seemed to have been
settled by legal judgement or government
intervention, but on each occasion broke
out once more after an interval. Eglinton
manor house was burned early in the
16th century and in 1586 the fourth earl
was killed by the Cunninghams. Finally
the royal government persuaded the
rivals to shake hands in 1609, and three
years later the fifth earl died childless,
which no doubt helped to cool the ashes
of the old conflict.

He was succeeded in his estate and
title – though not without objections by
various people, including for a time the
king, who took his time in assenting to
the necessary charter – by Alexander
Seton, through his mother, Lady
Margaret Montgomery (daughter of the
third earl), who had married the Earl of
Winton. Seton took the name
Montgomery and became chief.

His son, sixth Earl of Eglinton, was a
Presbyterian who sided with the
Covenanters in the civil war and
subsequently supported Charles II. He
was imprisoned for his royalist
sympathies by General Monk in 1659 a
matter of months before Monk himself
took the initiative in restoring the
monarchy to his throne.

Of the later members of this family,
the tenth Earl of Eglinton was shot by a
poacher in 1769, and the thirteenth earl
(from another branch, the Montgomerys
of Coilsfield) was responsible for that
ultimate piece of Victorian medieval
romanticism, the Eglinton Tournament
(1839), an occasion somewhat spoilt by
the pouring rain.

ABOVE *Hugh Montgomery, 12th Earl of
Eglinton (1739–1813) in the uniform of the
Black Watch, from a portrait by Sir John
Singleton Copley.*

FAMILY ASSOCIATION
25 Glencairn Crescent, Edinburgh
EH12 5BY, Scotland

Erngath, 31 Dean Road, Bo'ness
EH51 9BH, Scotland

409 Paddock Lane, Montgomery,
AL 36109, USA

MORE (MUIR)

NAME AND PLACE

According to Black's *Surnames of Scotland* (1946) More, Moor, Muir, Mure, etc, are all variants of the same name, originally deriving from the English word moor, a type of heathland.

ORIGIN

Early appearances of the name include de la More, del Moore and other forms indicating that the person concerned lived on or by a moor. However, one of the earliest of all appears as Dovenal le fiz Michel More de Levenaghes, and the absence of any genitive preposition suggests that this man's father Michael More, was in Gaelic known as Michael *Mór*, meaning big or great, which was of course frequently applied to prominent warriors, chiefs, etc. It is significant that other common descriptions of this sort became surnames. For example, Ogg comes from the Gaelic *Òg*, meaning young, Bain comes from *Bàn* (white or fair), and Begg from *Beag* (little).

As *Mór* was probably the most common suffix of all, it would be rather surprising if all Muirs, Mores, etc. were descended from heath-dwellers and none from great or large ancestors. It has even been suggested that the de or de la often appearing in front of the name in the early examples may as often as not have been a slip of the scribe, who would have been accustomed to such forms.

The variants of spellings of the name do show some regional identity. Thus, Moir is said to be characteristic of Aberdeen, Moar of Orkney and Shetland, etc. Anyone with the slightest familiarity with registers of the 17th and 18th century will feel a certain scepticism, and in fact it is quite easy to find families who themselves employed several variants of the name interchangeably. It was probably only coincidence that when the spelling of names became standardised, a particular form was adopted in a particular district.

FAMILIES

Strictly, there was no Clan More or Muir. Among notable families of the name were the Mures of Rowallan. They were sufficiently prominent in the 14th century for Elizabeth, daughter of Sir Adam Mure of Rowallan, to marry King Robert II in 1347. The family continued to prosper until the 17th century, and died out in the male line about 1700.

Sir William Mure was a notable 16th-century Scottish poet and religious propagandist.

The variant Muir is probably the most familiar, due to the prominence of several learned men who bore that name. They

included John Muir (1810–82), the orientalist who held the first chair of Sanskrit at Edinburgh University; his brother Sir William Muir (1819–1905), who shared his interests and was an expert on the early history of Islam; John Muir (1838–1914), the Scots-born US naturalist; Sir Thomas Muir (1844–1931), mathematician and educationalist, and Edwin Muir (1887–1959), the poet and translator. Sir John Moore (1761–1809), who died at Corunna, was one of Britain's most able and popular generals.

ABOVE *The Burial of Sir John Moore at Corunna. The son of a Scottish physician and well-known writer (also John), he was killed at the moment of an extraordinary victory against the odds in 1809.*

MORRISON

NAME AND PLACE

Morrison, 'son of Morris', is a name that crops up in many different regions in the period when surnames became common, and it is unlikely that all stem from a common source, although that has been asserted.

ORIGIN

Among notable families of this name were the Morrisons of Woodend in Kirkmichael, Dumfriesshire, the Morrisons of Dairsie in Fife and the Morrisons of Prestongrange, East Lothian.

The Morrisons of the Outer Hebrides may themselves have been of mixed origin – Gaelic and Norse – but among the ancestors of one branch were probably the Irish bards known as O'Muirgheasain, who settled in Mull in the 16th century. In the far north-west, where Morrisons are still numerous, the name is the anglicised form of the Gaelic *Mac Ghillie Mhuire* (son of the servant of Mary).

THE CLAN

The Morrisons were renowned as poets, musicians and scholars, and 'celebrated … for their independence of mind and sobriety of judgement.' For many generations the family held the office of *Britheamh*, or brieve, a kind of local judge, in Lewis under the MacLeods, from whom they held Habost in the district of Ness, at the northern end of Lewis. We know that a whole network of these judicial officials existed under the lord of the Isles, but the Morrisons are the only ones known by name. The first recorded holder of the office was Uisdean, who lived in the 16th century (comparatively late).

A later brieve made a confession on his deathbed that he was the father of the supposed eldest son of MacLeod of Lewis, and it was through a Mackenzie marriage to this child that that family later justified their campaign for possession of Lewis.

The Morrisons, or this branch of them at least, seem to have supported the Mackenzies, and two of them, Iain *Dubh* Morrison the brieve and Malcolm, his eldest son, were killed by the MacLeods early in the 17th century. However, the victory of the Mackenzies corresponded with the end of the brieve's authority, probably already in decline. When the Mackenzies gained a commission of fire and sword against the Morrison chief for resisting the Mackenzie takeover in 1616, he was described as the brieve, but there is no later reference to the existence of such an office.

The famous Blind Harper of Dunvegan, Roderick (*Ruaraidh*) Morrison, was born in Lewis about 1660 and died in 1712, and Morrisons were hereditary smiths to the MacLeods of Harris. John Morrison (Iain *Gobha*, the Smith), the religious poet who was an important figure in the Long Island (the chain terminating in Lewis) in the 19th century, was a member of this family. There were several branches of the clan in Harris and also on the mainland in Caithness, where they were associated with the Mackays. According to legend the Caithness lands were bestowed by the local bishop on a Morrison of Lewis, who brought 60 families to settle there.

It is interesting that the Morrison tartan is the same as the Mackays' with just an additional red line, though not much historical significance should be read into this as the Morrison tartan is of recent devising.

ABOVE *The beautiful coast of Lewis, where the Morrisons held the office of brieve. Their influence went much farther than their traditional homeland of the north of the island, extending far east as Caithness.*

MUNRO

NAME AND PLACE

The origin of the Munros is a matter of speculation, but a likely tradition, espoused by W.J. Watson in *The Celtic Place-Names of Scotland*, traces them to the River Roe, which flows into Lough Foyle in Northern Ireland. In Gaelic the Munros are *Clann au Rothaich*, and a Munro is a *Rotach*, or 'Ro(e)man'.

ORIGIN

In the 14th century they were already established in Ferindonald, as they called it after a supposed ancestor, the fertile land north of the Cromarty Firth dominated by the mighty summit of Ben Wyvis. The home of their chief was, as it still is, Foulis, from whose high tower (the medieval castle has long since been replaced) a fiery beacon summoned the clansmen with their war cry, 'Castle Foulis aflame!'.

The Munros held their lands from the old earls of Ross, in the 15th century from the lord of the Isles (as earl of Ross) and later from the Crown. Robert of Munro, Laird of Foulis, was killed in the earl's service in 1369. He was presumably the descendant of a Munro of Foulis said to have died in 1126.

From 1476 the Munros of Foulis were active in the king's service and in 1547 George Munro of Foulis was among the Scots killed at the battle of Pinkie. His successor Robert *Mór* was a Protestant (like his descendants) who held various royal posts in Ross and Invernesshire.

Hector Munro of Foulis (d. 1603), chief of the clan, despite a university education, employed witches when he became ill in 1589 to transfer what seemed to be his approaching death to his half-brother, George Munro of Obsdale. The spell, which involved the chief's midnight 'burial', seems to have worked, for he recovered from his illness and George died the following year. Munro, subsequently charged with witchcraft was acquitted. In a later generation the chiefship and estate of Foulis passed to the descendants of George of Obsdale.

BELOW *The mighty summit of Ben Wyvis, 1,046 metres (3,433 ft) above sea level, looms in the distance over the lands of Foulis, Easter Ross, homeland of the martial Munros.*

The Munros have long been noted for their martial spirit, and Hector's son and successor Robert, known as the Black Baron, went with many of his clan with Mackay's regiment to fight for the cause of Protestantism and the Winter Queen (sister of Charles I and wife of the king of Bohemia deposed by Catholic, imperial forces) in the Thirty Years War. The Swedish army is said to have included 27 officers above the rank of captain named Munro. The chief himself died of wounds in 1638, and another Robert Munro, of the Obsdale branch, wrote a famous account of the Scots' campaigning.

In the civil wars Munro loyalties were divided and, because there was no strong leadership for a long period owing to the minority of the chief and the termination of the original Foulis line, they were to be found fighting on both sides. Robert of Obsdale, who became chief in 1651, served as Sheriff of Ross in the Cromwellian period, though the sons of his predecessor fought against Cromwell at Worcester in the same year.

During the risings of the 18th century the Munros supported the government. In an incident at the battle of Glenshiel (1719) Munro of the cadet house of Culcairn was felled by rebel snipers but saved by two of his men, one of whom threw himself across the prostrate chieftain while the other charged the snipers single-handed and routed them.

Sir Robert Munro of Foulis, who had commanded the Black Watch at the battle of Fontenoy in 1745, was killed in the following year fighting the Jacobites at Falkirk. He was assailed, it is said, by six Camerons, slew two, broke his sword on a third, and was then felled by a pistol shot. Munros also formed the advance guard of General Cope's force defeated at Prestonpans.

Many Munros emigrated to the colonies and from their descendants (and from those of the Irish Munroes who sprang from the same stem) many

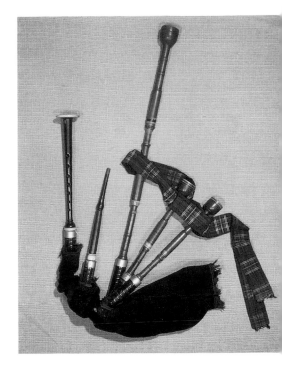

ABOVE *Bagpipes, from the National Museum in Edinburgh. Though now closely associated with the Highlands, bagpipes of different kinds are found throughout the world, and probably originated in the East*

notable leaders arose, including two Commonweath prime ministers and a US president, James Monroe (1758–1831), whose father is believed to have descended from the Munros of Foulis.

The old Castle Foulis was burned down in the 18th century, and the present impressive building was erected by Sir Harry (son of the gallant Sir Robert) Munro of Foulis (d. 1781).

CLAN ASSOCIATION

Fowlis Ferry Point, Easter Ard Ross
IV16, Scotland

3209 Alamance Road, Greensboro,
NC 27407, USA

MURRAY

NAME AND PLACE

The name comes from the great province, former kingdom, of Moray in north-east Scotland. Some families prefer the spelling Moray.

ORIGINS

Presumably the Murrays were of Pictish ancestry, but the man they claim as their ancestor, Freskin, may have been a Fleming, one of those adventurers who saw an opportunity to gain land for themselves by assisting the feudal Scottish monarchy to bring distant provinces under its control. Possibly he married a princess of the old royal house. His grandson was known in Latin charters as William de Moravia (of Moray), and he had lands in Moray from the Crown.

THE CLAN

His descendants were to prove remarkably numerous and successful. For a couple of centuries they held lands in Scotland ranging from Sutherland to the Borders. (One 15th-century Murray chieftain had 17 sons, most of whom founded substantial cadet houses.) So many locally powerful families dispersed over so wide an area naturally did not encourage close clan feeling, and in the 18th century Forbes of Culloden was to deny that the Murrays were a true clan at all. However, apart from the men of Atholl, there was undoubtedly a genuine clan spirit uniting the Murrays. On two

BELOW *Bothwell Castle, in Lanarkshire, perhaps the finest surviving example of a 13th-century castle, was once the seat of the senior Murray chiefs, and later held by many different families, including the Douglases and the Homes.*

occasions in the late 16th century Murray chieftains from all over the country (including the laird of Moncreiffe, closely associated with the Murrays through marriage) came together in a 'Bond of Association' in which they recognised Murray of Tullibardine as supreme chief and bound themselves to defend each other against 'the intrusions of Broken Men, and unthankful and unnatural neighbours.'

William de Moravia's eldest son came into large estates in Sutherland, and his followers took the name of the 'South land', as the Norsemen called it, for their own (see Sutherland).

Although the Murrays were essentially Highlanders, the first family to feature prominently in Scottish history were the lords of Bothwell in Larnarkshire. These estates were acquired through the marriage of William de Moravia's descendant Sir Walter, Chief of the Murrays, to an Oliphant heiress in 1253. (They later passed out of the family in the same way as they entered it, a Murray heiress carrying them with her marriage to the Black Douglas.) Sir Walter, first Lord Bothwell, was co-regent of Scotland in 1255.

Sir Andrew Murray of Bothwell was the associate of Wallace in resistance to the English in the late 13th century. Through scarcely more than a boy, some say he was the better general, for while Wallace was a first-rate guerilla leader it was largely Murray who engineered the smashing victory of Stirling Bridge (1297). Unfortunately, Sir Andrew fell in that engagement, and thereafter Wallace never won a pitched battle.

His son, also Sir Andrew, fourth Lord Bothwell, was no less active in resistance to the English. He was regent after Bruce's death and died in battle against the English at Halidon Hill (1333).

After the death of the last Murray lord of Bothwell in 1360 there was some doubt as to where the chiefship resided,

and it was not for many generations that the Murrays of Tullibardine were generally acknowledged. They were possibly descended from a younger son of William de Moravia, and they acquired lands near Auchterarder, Strathearn, by marriage, not long before the last Murray of Bothwell died. They were erected into a feudal barony in 1443 and in 1606 the twelfth laird was created Earl of Tullibardine.

There were numerous important cadets of this house, including the Murrays of Ochtertyre and the earls of Mansfield, who have the curious distinction of being earls of Mansfield twice over (of Mansfield in Nottinghamshire and of Mansfield in Middlesex – both titles held since the 18th century). The earl of Mansfield's seat is Scone Palace, a 19th-century structure.

The Morays of Abercairney, an older house, were descended from Sir John Murray of the house of Bothwell, who acquired the property when he married a daughter of the earl of Strathearn in about 1320. (It was his daughter who, on her second marriage, carried the lordship of Bothwell to the Earl of Douglas.) Sir John's sons, Maurice (killed at Neville's Cross, 1346) and Alexander, were successively earls of Strathearn, and the latter would seem to have been heir to the chiefship of the Murrays, although this honour eventually passed to the house of Tullibardine.

CLAN ASSOCIATION

129 Craigmount Avenue North, Barnton, Edinburgh EH4 8BS, Scotland

P O Box 119, Duluth, GA 30096, USA

P O Box 30, Albert Street, Brisbane, Queensland 4002, Australia

MURRAY 230–231

MURRAY OF ATHOLL

NAME AND PLACE: see Murray

ORIGIN

William, second Earl of Tullibardine, married the heiress of the Stewart Earl of Atholl, and their son John was confirmed as Earl of Atholl in 1629. The earldom of Tullibardine passed to his uncle.

THE CLAN

The Murrays were now a great power in the land, their possessions rivalling those of the Campbells. Moreover, the Campbells were about to go through a sticky patch, due to changing fortunes in the civil wars, and the Murrays on the whole benefited by supporting the Stewart dynasty against the Campbells. When the Campbells' position was restored after 1688 the Murray chief, now Marquess of Atholl, was unassailable. In 1703 the marquess became a duke.

In 1706 the duke raised 4,000 Athollmen in an effort to dissuade the Scottish parliament from assenting to its own dissolution, but his action was not imitated elsewhere so he disbanded his men, and to his great disgust the Act of Union was subsequently passed. However, in the Jacobite risings the duke remained loyal to the government, a fortunate decision for the future of his

house but one that presented some awkward problems at the time as the majority of the Athollmen (many of them Stewarts) were firm Jacobites.

In both risings the Athollmen were 'out' under William, Marquess of Tullibardine, son of the first duke (d. 1724) and elder brother of the second, who was created Duke of Rannoch in the Jacobite peerage. His younger brother was the famous Jacobite leader of whom it was said that if Prince Charles had stayed in bed for the rising of 1745–46 and left the conduct of military affairs to his able lieutenant he would have woken up as king of Great Britain.

BELOW *Blair Castle began as a 13th-century tower house and has been much altered and rebuilt over the centuries. It became an elegant Georgian villa after 1746 and was 'baronialized' in the 19th century.*

Lord George Murray (1694–1760), fifth son of the first Duke of Atholl, was a professional soldier from the age of 18. He took part in the Fifteen under the Earl of Mar and was wounded at the battle of Glenshiel, which ended the abortive Spanish-aided invasion of 1719. He escaped abroad but was later pardoned and settled down at Tullibardine in the 1720s, serving as Sheriff of Perthshire. On the eve of the Forty-five he was approached by the Jacobite leader, the Duke of Perth, but was at very reluctant to rise in the Jacobite cause, having accepted a pardon for his previous efforts on behalf of the exiled Stewarts. He is said to have been persuaded by a personal letter from James Edward.

He was a true Highlander who spoke Gaelic (unlike Prince Charles) and marched with this men, not all of whom, however, followed him with total satisfaction when summoned by the fiery cross. He was without doubt the most able Jacobite general of this or any previous campaign, and although he pressed for the retreat from Derby, at that stage the alternative, a dash on London, was probably impracticable.

Prince Charles, with whom his relations were never very warm, subsequently regarded him as little better than a traitor, but this was perhaps the reaction of a weak man seeking scapegoats. During the retreat Lord George found himself in a position which summed up the divided loyalties which made the Forty-five such a poignant episode, when he laid siege to Blair Castle, his family seat, then in government hands. (It had earlier been besieged by his brother Tullibardine; the siege of 1746 was the last of a castle in Britain.) After Culloden Murray again escaped abroad, He died at Medemblik in the Netherlands, where his tomb may still be seen, in 1760.

Blair Castle was repaired and considerably altered on two occasions,

ABOVE *Loch Arkaig, where John Murray of Broughton is reputed to have buried large sums of gold after the Battle of Culloden. He was Prince Charles's secretary, but after his capture was persuaded to turn king's evidence in order to save his own life and so is known as 'Mr Evidence Murray'.*

the latter one being largely an attempt to restore its original Gothic outward appearance. It remains luxuriously neo-classical inside. Its white walls, familiar to all tourists, contain many treasures of art and history.

The martial traditions of Atholl are still continued by the Atholl Highlanders, somewhat reduced in number nowadays, whose duties since the Forty-five have been confined to ceremonial. They are, however, the last private army in Britain.

It is said that the modern Murray of Atholl tartan is very similar to one worn by Murray of Pulrossie in the 17th century, but continuity would be hard to establish.

NAPIER

This is an English name which derives from the official in charge of the royal napery, or linen. Tradition says that the family was descended from the ancient earls of Lennox, but it is not impossible that some early descendant of that family should also have been the court 'naper'.

ORIGIN

We first find the family in a charter of the Earl of Lennox. John de Napier held lands from the earl in Dumbarton in 1280, and was present 23 years later at the defence of Stirling Castle.

THE FAMILY

Almost a century after that William de Napier was governor of Edinburgh Castle, and his son Alexander, a successful merchant in the wool trade, acquired the lands of Merchiston. His son, also Alexander, was wounded while helping to rescue the widow of James I and her second husband James Stewart (the Black Knight of Lorne) from the hands of a faction led by Sir Archibald Livingstone and others. As a result of this service he acquired some former Livingstone property as well as the office of comptroller of the household.

Several members of the Napier family died in battles in the 15th and 16th centuries. John Napier of Merchiston died fighting for James III against the victorious rebel earls at Sauchieburn (1488). His grandson Alexander was killed at Flodden with James IV in 1513, and Alexander's son fell at Pinkie.

The most famous family member is John Napier (1550–1617), eighth Laird of Merchiston, grandson of the casualty of Pinkie and son of Archibald (d. 1608), who was master of the Mint under King James VI. He was man man of many interests, a ferocious anti-papist, but is remembered for his efforts to make mathematical calculations easier, which resulted in his invention of logarithms.

His son Archibald, first Lord Napier from 1627, was related by marriage to Montrose and was a royalist during the civil war, as was his son, the second Lord Napier, who died in exile in 1658. The third Lord Napier was the last of the line.

Since the 17th century the Napiers have been remarkable for outstanding military achievements. During the Napoleonic wars there were six generals and an admiral named Napier.

CLAN ASSOCIATION

Kilmahew Route 2, Box 614, Ramer, AL 36069, USA

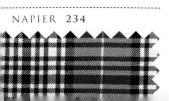

NICOLSON (MACNICOL)

'Sons of Nicol' appear in feudal rolls as far back as the 13th century, but there is no reason to suppose that all of them belong to the clan who, in modern Gaelic, are called *Mac Neacail*. The MacNicols of Portree in Skye anglicised their name to Nicolson, though there are many MacNicols in Argyll today.

ORIGIN

MacNicol of Portree is said to have been a member of the council of the lord of the Isles. The Nicolson chiefs held the land of Scorrybreck for many centuries: legend speaks of over a hundred chiefs buried in Snizort churchyard.

Another tradition traces the origins of the Nicholsons further back, to Assynt, on the northern-western mainland, and Ullapool. Presumably the clansmen then moved to Skye, although perhaps others of their descent were already there.

THE CLAN

The name often appears in the history of Skye (one of whose modern historians is a Nicolson), and the Nicolsons of Scorrybreck were notable for producing churchmen and Gaelic bards. Donald of Scorrybreck was a famous minister who eventually retired in 1696 under pressure from Presbyterianism, which he loathed. A contemporary, Thomas Nicolson, a Roman Catholic convert who worked in the Scottish mission, compiled a valuable record of the Hebrides at the end of the 17th century.

Donald MacNicol, appointed minister of Lismore in 1766, made a valuable collection of Ossianic ballads, and his resentment of Samuel Johnson's derogatory remarks on Gaelic literature informed his *Remarks on Dr Samuel Johnson's Journey to the Hebrides*.

Sir Thomas Innes recorded a press report of 1813 on the death at Scorrybreck at the age of 86 of 'Malcolm Nicholson, Esq., who, with his predecessors, lineally and without interruption, possessed that farm for many centuries back'. A later chief emigrated to the Antipodes, and was commemorated in an Australian sheep station named Scorrybreck. A Lowland family, the Nicolsons of Lasswade, have become chiefs of the name although it is not clear why this honour should not still belong to the family of Scorrybreck.

CLAN ASSOCIATION

Almondbank, Viewfield Road, Portree, Isle of Skye, Scotland

OGILVIE

NAME AND PLACE

The territorial name is said to derive from the Ancient British *ocel fa* (high plain). The Ogilvie homeland is the old Celtic earldom of Angus.

ORIGIN

The Ogilvies are one of the most distinguished families in Scotland, descended from the ancient earls of Angus (the old Gaelic title, *Mormaer*, carried more weight than 'earl'). Continual historical records take us back as far as Dubhucan, Earl of Angus in the early 12th century, whose son Earl Gillebride, or Gilbert, is regarded as the founder of the Ogilvies.

THE CLAN

Gillebride bestowed the lands of Ogilvie and Easter Powrie on his younger son, also Gilbert, and for half a millennium those lands passed down in unbroken male descent in the same family, the Ogilvies of that ilk.

Another branch, ultimately more important, were the Ogilvies of Auchterhouse, who were hereditary sheriffs of Angus in the 14th century. One of them fought with Joan of Arc against the English; another, Sir Walter Ogilvie of Auchterhouse, died at the battle of Harlaw in 1411. He had two sons; from the leader sprang the house of Inchmartine and from the younger the house of Airlie (originally Eroly). The latter was Sir Walter Ogilvie, Lord High Treasurer, who married the heiress of Lintrathan and built the tower of Airlie. His grandson became Lord Ogilvie of Airlie in 1491, and the eighth Lord Ogilvie was created Earl of Airlie in 1639. He was recognised as overall chief of the Ogilvies and the present chief is his descendant.

Throughout the series of crises, civil wars and rebellions between 1639 and 1745 the Ogilvies were supporters of the Stewart dynasty, an allegiance which entailed much grief for them.

Like other clans, the Ogilvies had their feuds, which had the effect of

BELOW *The French relieve Orléans, inspired by Joan of Arc. A member of the Auchterhouse branch of Ogilvies fought in her forces against the English.*

bringing the many branches of the clan together. There was a tremendous battle with the Lindsays, their immediate neighbours to the north, in 1446, when (it is said) 500 Ogilvies were killed, and there was a later feud with the Campbells resulting from Campbell encroachments on Ogilvie lands in the late 16th century.

The later civil disturbances offered unparalleled opportunities for conducting private quarrels in the guise of public duty, which the Earl of Argyll was foremost in exploiting.

In 1640 Argyll was commissioned to proceed against the clans of Atholl and Angus who had risen to resist the Covenant. He commanded 4,000 Highlanders, 'well-timbered men', who carried out their commission of fire and sword with customary zeal, not sparing women and children. To this campaign belongs the famous destruction of the 'bonnie House of Airlie', memorably related in ballad. However, the ballad's attribution to Argyll of lecherous designs on the Countess of Airlie is probably false: neither she nor the earl was at home at the time. Their absence was fortunate, for Argyll did indeed leave scarcely 'a standing stone in Airlie' (nor a standing Ogilvie). It was this campaign which turned Montrose against Argyll for good and all.

James, second Earl of Airlie, was captured at the battle of Philiphaug (1645), which put an end to Montrose's great campaign. He was incarcerated in St Andrews Castle under sentence of death but, shortly before the execution was due, escaped disguised as a woman in clothes provided by his sister. (The number of times this unlikely ploy succeeded does make one wonder about the honour of prison guards.)

The Ogilvies were 'out' in all the Jacobite risings of the 18th century. At Culloden an Angus regiment was led by Lord Ogilvie, son of the fifth Earl of Airlie, 'a boy of twenty with a long straight nose, a heavy jaw and a calm eye', wrote John Prebble, who had probably been looking at the portrait in Winton Castle. He escaped and years later received free pardon on the grounds of his youth at the time of his offence; the title was restored to his descendants.

The eighth Earl of Airlie was killed in the Boer War in 1900 during a courageous action at Diamond Hill, his last words been a reminder to the distraught NCO bending over him to mind his language. In Scotland Lady Airlie heard the drumming of the ghostly drummer boy which always announced the death of an earl of Airlie.

Another branch of the Ogilvies became earls of Findlater (1638) and of Seafield (1701). The latter title continues, having passed via the Laird of Grant to Nina, the late countess who was such a notable figure in Highland society and to her son, the present Earl of Seafield.

The seat of the Ogilvie chief today is Cortachy, but the Ogilvies still also hold Airlie Castle (rebuilt on the site of the building destroyed during Argyll's famous raid). Having descended (without much doubt though without firm proof) from the royal Pictish house, the family replenished its royal blood this century when Angus Ogilvie married Princess Alexandra, the Queen's first cousin.

OLIPHANT

NAME AND PLACE

The name was spelt in many ways, and according to legend it derives from accounts of elephants brought back by the Crusaders.

ORIGIN

The founder of this Scottish family is believed to have been an Anglo-Norman, David de Holifard, who came north with King David I and received lands in Roxeburghshire from his friend the king.

THE CLAN

There is little evidence of a genuine Clan Oliphant, rather a fraternity among families of the name. Sir John Oliphant, a presumed descendant of David de Holifard, held the lands of Aberdalgie in the early 15th century, and his immediate descendants were prominent in Scottish affairs. His son Lawrence became a lord of Parliament, ambassador to France and keeper of Edinburgh Castle (1493). His son, the second lord, was killed at Flodden in 1513 and his grandson fought at Solway Moss (1542), where he was captured and held for ransom.

The fourth Lord Oliphant was a supporter of Bothwell and Mary Queen of Scots, and fought for the queen at Langside (1568). His son was involved in the Raid of Ruthven (1582), when King James VI was kidnapped in a complicated plot aimed against the Catholic Lennox party. Later banished, he may have ended up on the slave benches of a Turkish galley.

Thereafter the family declined, eventually losing all their lands. A cadet branch, the Oliphants of Gask, survived. They were notable Jacobites, and the house of Gask was plundered – without orders – by English soldiers after Culloden. Carolina Oliphant (later Lady Nairne) was named after the vanquished prince when she was born at Gask in 1766. She became a composer of verse and ballads, including the famous Jacobite songs, 'Charlie is my darling' and 'Will ye no come back again?'. Her comic ballads have been described as rivalling those of Burns.

CLAN ASSOCIATION

15 Davidson Crescent, Alford, AB33 8TP, Scotland

10 Glen Road, Cupshaw Lake, Ringwood, NJ 07456, USA

81 Halsey Road, Fulham, South Australia 504, Australia

RAMSAY

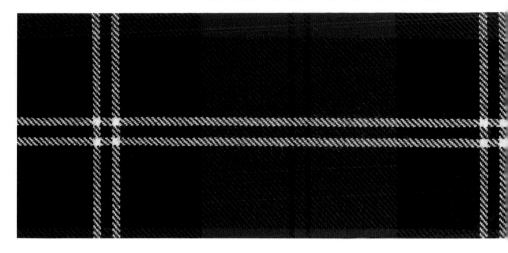

NAME AND PLACE

The Ramsays of Dalhousie were perhaps not related to all Ramsays in Scotland, and there is more than one explanation of the origin. It seems to be a place name, probably in East Lothian, but possibly Ramsay in the English Fens.

ORIGIN

The first known Ramsay in Scotland was Simon de Ramsay, possibly an Anglo-Norman who came north with David I and held lands in Lothian. Thereafter, various Ramsays appear in charters, and link Simon de Ramsay (alive in 1140) with William de Ramsay who held the lands of Dalhousie about 150 years later.

THE FAMILY

William de Ramsay swore fealty to Edward I in 1296, but later supported Bruce and signed the Declaration of Arbroath (1320). His son Alexander was active against the English, saving Dunbar Castle for its countess, when it was besieged in 1338. Legend ascribes to him other notable exploits against the English, but he incited the animosity of Sir William Douglas, the Knight of Liddesdale, who imprisoned him in Hermitage Castle, where he died in 1342.

The Dalhousie house prospered and founded branches, including Cockpen and Whitehill, and Balmain. George Ramsay was made Lord Ramsay of Melrose in 1618 but changed the title to Dalhousie. It was raised to an earldom in 1633. Since then many Ramsays have been notable soldiers and imperial officials, including the Marquess of Dalhousie, appointed governor-general of India in 1848 at the age of 34.

The most accomplished Ramsays, probably unconnected with Dalhousie, were the two Allan Ramsays, the poet (1686–1758) and his son (1713–84), one of Scotland's finest portrait painters.

FAMILY ASSOCIATION

Brechin Castle, Brechin
DD9 6SH, Scotland

Route 1, Box 232-A, Highlands,
NC 28741, USA

P O Box 60385, Arcadia, CA 91066-0385, USA

P O Box 22, Erskine, Alberta T0C 1G0, Canada

36 Patterson Street, Ainslie,
ACT 2602, Australia

ROBERTSON

In Gaelic the Robertsons are known as *Clann Donnchaidh* (the children of Duncan); this Duncan, *Donnchadh Reamhar* (the Stout), was the descendant of Conan (see below) and chief of the clan in the early 14th century. In 1451 the lands in Atholl were erected by royal charter into the barony of Struan for Duncan's grandson Robert, and the majority of the clan took then their name from him. Others took different names, such as Duncanson and MacConachie (see also Duncan). Since the 16th century the Chief of the Robertsons has been known as Struan Robertson.

ORIGIN

It is now accepted that the Robertsons are descended from the hereditary abbots of Dunkeld, the senior line of the kindred of St Columba and guardians of the saint's relics. Abbott Crinan of Dunkeld married a royal princess and their son was King Duncan, who was killed by MacBeth in 1040. From a younger son of King Duncan were descended the old earls of Atholl, and from Conan, son of Earl Henry of Atholl, the Robertsons derived their large territories in that magnificent region.

THE CLAN

Duncan Reamhar was a supporter of the Bruce who fought with his men at Bannockburn, and in later times Clan *Donnchaidh* were loyal adherents of the Stewart dynasty (the Robertson crest is a hand supporting a crown). Robert of Struan (then known as Robert Duncanson) received his barony as a belated reward for apprehending Sir Robert Graham, the murderer of King James I.

During the 16th century the Robertsons lost a large part of their lands to the Stewart earl of Atholl, though this did not affect their loyalty to the Stewart king of Scots. With other Atholl men they fought for Montrose in the civil war and were present at every engagement of that extraordinary campaign.

Alexander, seventeenth of Struan, had one of the most remarkable careers of any Jacobite chief. A poet of some renown, he was preparing to take holy orders when he succeeded to the chiefship about the time of the Revolution of 1688. He took up his sword on behalf of King James VII/II and fought under Bonnie Dundee at Killiecrankie. He was attainted and the estates forfeited, but pardoned after the

accession of Queen Anne. The Hanoverian succession and the ensuing Jacobite rising of 1715 had him reaching for his broadsword again. He was taken prisoner at Sheriffmuir, rescued, recaptured, again escaped, and got away to France, but he was back in plenty of time to rise again in 1745. After the Battle of Prestonpans he rode home in the carriage of the defeated English general Sir John Cope, but he was now in his mid-seventies and a little too old to fight even by Highland standards. At Culloden the clan was led by Robertson of Woodsheal.

What was left of the estates were forfeited but later briefly regained by Alexander's sister. Some territory in Rannoch remained to the Robertson chiefs – who for a time lived in Ruthven barracks, built to house troops to keep them in order – until the last was sold in the present century. In 1949 the chiefship passed to a resident of Jamaica, though his son remained to represent him in Scotland. The Clan *Donnchaidh* museum near Blair Atholl contains many relics of the clan including the magic stone, *Clach na Brataich*, which is said to have played a part in the fortunes of the clan since the time of Stout Duncan.

ABOVE *Loch Rannoch, in the beautiful Robertson country. The clan gradually lost their lands over the centuries, through dispossession and forfeiture (although they continued to live in the area), and the last remaining parts were finally sold off in the 20th century.*

CLAN ASSOCIATION

Clan Donnachaidh Centre, Bruar, Pitlochry PH18 5TW, Scotland

The Clan Society has numerous branches in the USA and Canada

P O Box 3012, Parramatta, NSW 2124, Australia

631 Huia Road, Parau, Auckland 7, New Zealand

ROSE

NAME AND PLACE

The evidence suggests that the ancestor of the Roses of Kilravock in the county of Nairn came from Normandy, where the territories of William the Conqueror's brother, Bishop Odo of Bayeux, included the district of Ros, near Caen.

ORIGIN

The Rose family can be traced back a very long way. Hugh, the first of that name in documentary records, was designated 'of Geddes' in about 1219, in a charter by Sir John Bisset of Lovat, a family with which the Roses were closely connected. The lands of Kilravock were acquired by Hugh's son and namesake on his marriage to a daughter of Sir Andrew de Bosco, whose wife was a Bisset. The connection of Roses, Boscos and Bissets tends to corroborate the theory that the family was of Norman origin.

THE CLAN

The Chief of Rose, known as the Baron of Kilravock from the 15th century and almost invariably named Hugh, remained in possession of Kilravock for over 600 years, succession proceeding in a direct line, father to son (or occasionally daughter). The castle of Kilravock was built by the seventh Rose of Kilravock in 1460. Much of the original building on the wooded banks of the River Nairn near Cawdor remains, and Sir Thomas Innes wrote that 'there is scarcely a family whose charter chest is more amply stored with documents, not only of private importance, but of great antiquarian interest.' The collection would be richer still had it not been for the destruction of family charters at Elgin when the Wolf of Badenoch set fire to the cathedral in 1390.

The history of the Roses of Kilravock proves that it was possible for Highland lairds to exist without constant involvement in bloody feuds and conflicts. When King James VI enquired in 1598 how the Black Baron, as the tenth Rose of Kilravock was called,

BELOW *Kilravock Castle, southwest of Nairn and only a mile or two from Cawdor, is still the home of this comparatively well-documented clan.*

managed to live among such violent neighbours, the baron replied that they were the best neighbours he could have since they made him say his prayers three times a day instead of only once.

Of course, trouble was not always avoided. The Black Baron's successor, for example, was thrown into prison for a time for failing to control some of his clansmen who were feuding with the Dunbars. Earlier, there was a tremendous feud with the Urquharts, and a great raid on the Mackenzies. Then there was the famous incident of the heiress of Cawdor, whose mother was a Rose and whose intended future husband was Kilravock's grandson, until she was abducted by the Campbells in distressing circumstances (see Campbell of Cawdor).

At times of national disturbance, fairly frequent it must be said, the Roses could not always remain on the sidelines even if they wished, and during the wars of independence they fought for Bruce. Moreover, no Rose appears on the famous Ragman's Roll of 1296, which lists those Scottish barons, the great majority of them (including Bruce), who swore fealty to Edward I of England.

In the early 18th century Kilravock opposed the 1707 union with England, but he was not a Jacobite. There were Roses on both sides in 1715 and 1745,

ABOVE *Bishop of Odo of Bayeux, who may have been the landlord of the ancestors of the Roses, wielding his club, in preference to a sword (since clergy were not supposed to shed blood), from the Bayeux Tapestry. Several knights of Ros came with him to England after his half-brother, William, defeated Harold at the Battle of Hastings.*

but the Baron of Kilravock, though he helped turn the Jacobites out of Inverness in 1715, otherwise concentrated on holding his own. Perhaps the most memorable illustration of the Roses' inclination to remain on friendly, or at least neutral, terms with mutually hostile forces occurred before Culloden, when Kilravock entertained the Jacobite prince and the Hanoverian duke on successive evenings. His sympathies were with the government, but Charles was better company.

In recent times the castle of Kilravock has been the scene of a great international reunion of the Roses.

FAMILY ASSOCIATION
1474 Montelegre Drive, San Jose, CA 95120, USA

ROSS

NAME AND PLACE

This clan's homeland was the peninsula
of Easter Ross north of the Cromarty
Firth, a spacious and fertile land giving
them room to expand without immediate
collision with hostile neighbours (an
uncommon benefit among Highland
clans). In Gaelic the Rosses are known as
Clann Aindreas, after the alleged
progenitor of the old Celtic earls of Ross
(and of the Mackenzies of Seaforth).

ORIGIN

The first of the earls of Ross was
Fearchar *Mac-an-t-Sagairt* (son of the
priest), founder of the clan whose
services to King Alexander II (he defeated
the king's enemies in Moray and
presented their heads in a bag) gained
him the earldom in 1226. As heir of the
hereditary abbots of Applecross in
Wester Ross Fearchar was already a
considerable landholder and a (possible)
descendant of the Irish King Niall of the
Nine Hostages (d. early 5th century).

THE CLAN

The early chiefs were thus the earls of
Ross, who wore in battle the sacred shirt
of St Duthac. The ruined sanctuary at
Tain where this garment was kept can
still be seen. It was there that Bruce's
queen sought refuge in 1306, only to be

BELOW *The church of St Duthus, at Tain
on the Dornoch Firth, Easter Ross, founded
in 1471. St Duthus, or Duthac, was a local
saint of the 11th century who is associated
with the ancestors of the earls of Ross. His
shrine is nearby and was visited by James
IV, among others. He was reputed to be one
of the most revered saints of Ross.*

hauled out and handed over, albeit
unwillingly, by William, third chief and
third earl, to the English, who exhibited
her in a cage. Subsequently the earl
rallied to Bruce, and his son, the fourth
earl, married Bruce's sister. The fourth
earl was killed at the battle of Halidon
Hill in 1333, despite St Duthac's shirt.

The fifth earl died in 1372 leaving no
direct male heir, and the earldom passed
to his daughter, resulting in the struggle
for the earldom between the lord of the
Isles and the Regent Albany culminating
in the grisly battle of 'Red' Harlaw in
1411 (see MacDonald of the Isles).

Meanwhile the chiefship passed to the
fifth earl's brother Hugh, who acquired
the lands of Balnagowan from his
brother-in-law King Robert II in 1374.
For over three centuries the Rosses of
Balnagowan remained chiefs of the clan.

News of the clan during most of that
time is rather hard to come by.
Occasional, mostly violent, incidents are
reported – the death of one chief in a
battle with the Mackays, the death of
another in a scuffle at Tain – but clearly
they prospered, since by the 17th century
the chief could raise 1,000 men. A 16th-
century chief, Alexander of Balnagowan,
was an exceedingly troublesome
character whose behaviour so alarmed
the many Ross chieftains that they issued
a remonstrance urging him to change his
ways. This had little effect, and the
chief's son was among those who were
commissioned to proceed against him
with fire and sword.

On the whole the clan played little
part in national affairs. Rosses fought in
the army that invaded England for
Charles II in 1651 only to be
resoundingly defeated by Cromwell at
Worcester. Later there was more trouble
with the Mackenzies, and David, the last
Balnagowan chief, who was another
bellicose character, was also threatened
with the withdrawal of support by his
kinsmen in 1676.

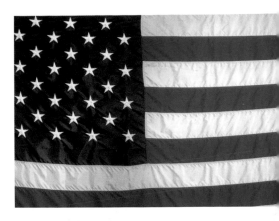

ABOVE *An early flag of the United States.
According to a doubtful tradition, a young
Philadelphia seamstress called Betsy Ross
(1752–1836) made the first 'stars and
stripes' for George Washington.*

After his death Balnagowan and the
still extensive Ross estates passed, more
or less legally, to another family named
Ross. They were unrelated Lowlanders
whose name derived from the Anglo-
Norman de Roos. The true heir in the
male line was Ross of Pitcalnie, a cadet
house, and in fact he and his successors
appear to have exercised the right of
chiefship *de facto*. In the present century
they became chiefs in name as well as
fact when the last of the usurping line of
Ross of Balnagowan died childless,
although the chiefship has since passed to
another branch, Ross of Shandwick, an
early cadet house descended from a
younger son of a 15th-century chief.

CLAN ASSOCIATION

5430 South 5th Street, Arlington,
VA 22204, USA

66 Crestwood Crescent, Winnipeg,
Manitoba, R2J 1H6, Canada

37 Boundary Road, Pennant Hills,
NSW 2120, Australia

RUTHVEN

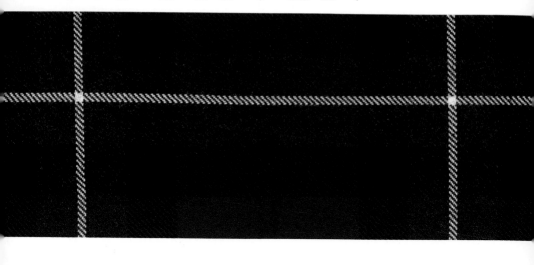

NAME AND PLACE

The Ruthvens may have been of Norse origin. They took their name from the lands of Ruthven in Rannoch, Perthshire, where the family was established in the Middle Ages.

ORIGIN

The progenitor of the Ruthvens is said to have been a Viking warrior who settled in Scotland. Little is known of the family until 1487, when Sir William Ruthven became a peer.

THE FAMILY

Ruthven is not a very common name today and in the early 17th century it was scarcely to be found at all – the result of government decree. The story of the Ruthvens in the preceding century is certainly a sensational one. Romantic novelists have had a fine time with it, their imagination fuelled by the obscurity of the facts.

The troubles started with Patrick, third Lord Ruthven, who was provost of Perth for many years. He was a leader of the gang of Protestant lords who at Holyrood Palace in 1566 murdered David Rizzio, a young Italian courtier of whom Mary Queen of Scots was extremely, though probably innocently, fond. The instigator was the egregious Lord Darnley, whom the queen had impetuously married. She was six months pregnant at the time, though the tradition that she was an eyewitness of the murder may be untrue.

Finding Darnley an unreliable protector, Ruthven fled to England and died there soon afterwards, but in spite of the hazard to which he had subjected the prenatal existence of King James VI, his son William, fourth Lord Ruthven, found favour with the young king and was created Earl of Gowrie in 1581. That did not last long. Three years later he was executed for treason, in effect for his part in the Raid of Ruthven in 1582, though he had previously been pardoned.

BELOW *The Murder of David Rizzio. Stories that the Queen was present, and that she was restrained by force from interfering, may be later embroideries, but it was a dastardly deed by any standards.*

In that notorious affair, he was a leader of the band of Presbyterian lords who, resentful of Catholic influence on the 16-year-old James VI, seized him and held him prisoner in Ruthven (later Huntingtower) Castle until he made his escape nearly a year later. It was a remarkable instance of the 'feckless, arrogant conceit' of the Scottish nobles of which the king later complained.

By this time, one might suppose, treason was in the blood, yet the extent of the treason of the third Earl of Gowrie in 1600 is not proven.

The official version of the Gowrie Conspiracy was this. The earl and his brother kidnapped the king in Gowrie House (not Huntingtower this time) in Perth, telling his courtiers that he had already left while he was in fact confined in an upper room. As the courtiers were hurriedly leaving to catch up with the king, James managed to attract their attention from the window of the room where he was held. They broke in at once and in the ensuing scuffle the Ruthven brothers were killed.

The only witness, apart from the king, had probably been 'bought', and it was suspected that this was actually an anti-Gowrie plot; that the king had in fact engineered the murder of Gowrie and his brother who, as fanatical Presbyterians with an unwholesome record of disloyalty, were undesirable subjects. However, the fury of James afterwards, abolishing the very name of Ruthven by act of parliament, seems unfeigned.

There were, of course, plenty of honourable Ruthvens, notably the Ruthvens of Freeland, descended from the second Lord Ruthven, who became the senior representatives of the name. Even the Gowrie earldom was revived in this century, for Sir Alexander Hore-Ruthven, governor-general of Australia, in 1945.

ABOVE *Huntingtower, formerly Ruthven, Castle near Perth, where the young James VI was held prisoner, is today open to the public.*

CLAN ASSOCIATION

Castlemartin, Kilcullen, Co. Kildare, Ireland

SCOTT

A Scott is a Scotsman in the way that an Inglis is an Englishman or a Wallace a Welshman. There is no known connection between the Scotts and the original Scots of Dalriada, nor between the majority of Scotts today and the famous Border clan.

ORIGIN

The Scotts have been traced back to Uchtred *filius Scoti* in the 12th century whose (assumed) son was Richard le Scot, father of the ancestor of the Scotts of Branxholm in the Borders.

THE CLAN

Richard le Scot acquired considerable estates in Lanarkshire, and they were hugely increased by his descendants, who were to be among the largest landowners in the kingdom. The most eventful period in the history of the 'saucy Scotts' – as wild and unruly on occasion as any other Border clan – was the century or so before the union of the monarchies of England and Scotland brought relative peace to the Borders in 1603.

Sir Walter Scott had a charter to the barony of Kirkud from King Robert II in 1389, and his son Robert acquired the lands of Branxholm.

The fortunes of the Scotts expanded after the eclipse of the mighty Douglases

in 1455. Branxholm was erected into a barony in 1488, although by that time the Scott chiefs had adopted the name 'of Buccleuch', in Edinburgh.

Scott of Buccleuch could raise 600 men in the 16th century, though no doubt he wished he could have raised more, for besides the frequent incursions of the English, who set fire to Branxholm Castle on at least two occasions, there was fierce rivalry with the Kerrs. Scott and Kerr sometimes split the ward of the Middle March between them, but Sir Walter of Buccleuch, who was sole warden, was killed by the jealous Kerrs in Edinburgh High Street in 1552. This was the man who had, it appears, once offered to turn the infant Mary Queen of Scots over to Henry VIII, a plan described by the Duke of Suffolk as 'not with the King's honour to be practised in such sort', although the English may have rejected the scheme merely out of scepticism about its likely success. Anyway, Sir Walter fought against them at Pinkie (1547).

His grandson and great-grandson, both also Sir Walter, were men of some distinction. The latter was a guerilla leader who raided Carlisle prison in 1596 to rescue an Armstrong chieftain. He became Lord Scott of Buccleuch in 1606 and later took some of his men to fight the Spaniards in the Netherlands. His son was made first Earl of Buccleuch in 1619.

The second Earl of Buccleuch died in 1651 leaving an only daughter, Anna. An eligible heiress, she was married to the Duke of Monmouth, an illegitimate son of Charles II, who took the name Scott and became also Duke of Buccleuch. She was made Duchess of Buccleuch in her own right and after her husband's rebellion and execution the title and lands remained intact through her.

The third Duke of Buccleuch married the Douglas heiress, thereby acquiring the huge estates of the duchy of Queensberry, including the Douglas seat at Drumlanrig, and becoming one of the richest men in Britain.

Cadet houses included Balweary, to which belonged Michael Scott, the wizard, known to 'loup on a muckle black horse that cam doon frae the cluds' and other equally remarkable feats. Another branch was the house of Harden, which produced not only the greatest of Scotts but surely one of the greatest Scots, Sir Walter of Abbotsford, who, through his novels, probably did more for his country's image and reputation than any single individual.

The Duke of Buccleuch has his seat at Branxholm in the Borders to this day.

ABOVE *Sir Walter Scott of Abbotsford (1771–1832). His erudite mind and extraordinary knowledge of Scottish rural customs and folkore resulted, more or less, in the invention of the historical novel. He virtually worked himself to death in an honourable effort to pay off the debts of a printing firm with which he was associated.*

CLAN ASSOCIATION
Bowhill, Selkirk TD7 5ET, Scotland

P O Box 13021, Austin TX
78711-3021, USA

SCOTT 248–249

SETON

NAME AND PLACE

The name is said to derive from the village of Sai in Normandy, although other explanations are offered, for instance that it means 'sea-town' and refers to Tranent, between Musselburgh and Haddington (and not much of a 'sea town' today), where the Setons held property at an early date.

ORIGIN

The Setons were not a clan, and there is little evidence of the different branches of the family acting in alliance, yet Seton is a famous name which became connected with several of the greatest Scottish families and was closely associated with the Stewart dynasty.

THE FAMILY

Alexander de Seton held lands in East Lothian in the mid-12th century. Several generations later Sir Alexander of Seton was a close adherent of Bruce. Sir Christopher Seton married Bruce's sister and was killed fighting the English.

The male line failed in the 14th century and the Seton heiress was abducted in 1347 by Alan of Winton, probably a cousin. Brought to justice, his fate was placed in the injured lady's hands: she had the choice of a wedding ring or the executioner's sword, and chose the ring. Alan of Winton later died on crusade, but their son William took the name of Seton and became a peer. From him descended many of the most notable Seton families. His second son married the Gordon heiress and their son became Earl of Huntly in 1449 (the first earl later settled the title on a younger son who took the Gordon name).

The Setons were great builders, responsible for several of the finest houses in Lothian. Sir George, great-great-grandson of Alan of Winton, built the Chapel of Seton in the mid-15th century. Another George, the fifth Lord Seton, was responsible for the

BELOW *The collegiate chapel of Seton, founded by Sir George Seton in the 15th century.*

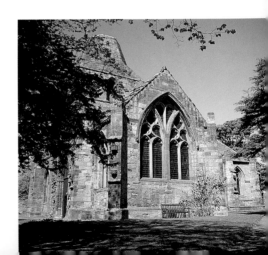

magnificent palace of Seton.

A frequent visitor there was Mary Queen of Scots, who regarded the builder of the palace as her 'truest friend'; his sister was one of the Queen's 'four Maries'. Seton helped the queen to escape from Loch Leven castle in 1568, and after her defeat at Langside he fled to Holland, where he drove a carrier's waggon and tried to enlist the support of the Duke of Alva for Mary.

Two of his sons, whether or not out of gratitude for their father's loyalty to his mother, were favoured by King James VI. The eldest son became Earl of Winton in 1600; a younger son, who was later Chancellor of Scotland, was created Lord Fyvie (1597) and Earl of Dunfermline (1605). He built much of the fine tower house of Fyvie in Aberdeenshire (some of the castle is older but one of the four turreted towers is named after him). The nearby classical garden of Pitmedden (now a National Trust for Scotland property) also dates from the 17th century. Lord Pitmedden (d. 1719), the famous judge, was a member of a cadet house of the Seton earls of Dunfermline, descended from a younger brother of the fourth and last earl, who held a subordinate command under Dundee at Killicrankie and was forfeited as a result.

Other branches of the family were active in the Jacobite rising of 1715, with generally unfortunate results. George, fifth Earl of Winton, was captured and sentenced to death, but escaped from the Tower of London. Several of his cousins were also attainted.

The Seton family has provided its own historians, the main – somewhat exhausting – work being George Seton's *A History of the Family of Seton during Eight Centuries* (1896).

ABOVE *Seaton House, from an old engraving, one of many fine buildings erected by members of the Seton family.*

SHAW

NAME AND PLACE

The Shaws, who were described as the
best fighters in Mar's forces during the
Jacobite rising of 1715, were a sept of the
Mackintoshes, and prominent members
of Clan Chattan, the confederation of the
Cat. The origin of their name is not
certain, but it is probably an
approximation of the Gaelic name
Sithech. The home of Clan Shaw was
Rothiemurchus.

ORIGIN

The question of the relationship between
Clan Shaw and the Lowland Shaws of –
mainly – Lanarkshire and Ayrshire has
also been much debated, the weight of
opinion maintaining that they were of
wholly different origins. Rothiemurchus
was part of the Mackintosh patrimony,
and according to legend it was bestowed
upon an ancestor of the clan for his
services at the famous (though
problematical) battle of the clans on the
North Inch of Perth in 1396.

THE CLAN

Grave doubts, however, have been
cast on the inscribed gravestone at
Rothiemurchus which purports to mark
the remains of Farquhar Shaw 'who
led ... this clan who defeated the 30
Davidsons of Invernahavon on the North

Insh at Perth in 1390'. The year is wrong and the inscription is relatively modern; no one can be sure what it said originally. There is record, moreover, of the Shaws receiving the lands of Rothiemurchus from the Bishop of Moray in 1226. Later, these lands were leased to the Comyns, who were reluctant to leave when the lease expired.

James Shaw of Rothiemurchus, son or grandson of Shaw *Corrfhiaclach* (Bucktooth) who is regarded as the first chief, was killed at the battle of Harlaw in 1411. His son Alasdair *Ciar* recovered Rothiemurchus, but in the 16th century the lands were lost after the young Shaw chief murdered his stepfather in a moment of rage. His lands were forfeited to the Crown and sold to the Laird of Grant, who bestowed them on his younger son Patrick. Despite efforts by Clan Chattan, ranging from gentle persuasion through legal writ to armed force, to regain them, Rothiemurchus has remained in Grant hands to this day.

The Shaws of Tordarroch descended from a younger brother of Alasdair *Ciar*, whose name was Adam or *Aodh* (Hugh), and were known as Clan Ay. This name is generally said to be derived from the founder, but Sir Iain Moncreiffe speculated that it is actually the genitive of Shaw, 'Clay Ay' meaning 'children of Shaw'. The significance of this is that it tends to confirm that after the collapse of the house of Rothiemurchus the Shaws of Tordarroch were widely recognised as chiefs of the name. They certainly signed the Clan Chattan bonds of union in the 17th century.

Tordarroch was held on a wadset (mortgage) from the Mackintosh, who reclaimed the property in the late 18th century, but it has since been regained by the chiefs of Clan Ay.

PLATE 2

ABOVE *A black wolf. The name Shaw may have derived from the Gaelic name for wolf, Sithech.*

CLAN ASSOCIATION

Newhall, Balblair, Conon Bridge
IV7 8LQ, Scotland

5643 East Angela Drive, Scottsdale,
AZ 85254, USA

SHAW 252–253

SINCLAIR

NAME AND PLACE

The name Sinclair (Saint-Clair) is of Norman origin. The main Sinclair homeland is remote Caithness.

ORIGIN

In the mid-12th century Henry de St Clair, perhaps the first of the name, held the lands of Herdmanston near Haddington, lands which remained in Sinclair hands for many centuries.

THE CLAN

His presumed descendant was Sir William Sinclair, a prominent figure in national affairs, guardian to the heir of King Alexander III, who gained the barony of Rosslyn, Lothian, in 1280. His son fought with Bruce at Bannockburn and his grandson, also Sir William, died fighting with Douglas in Spain against the Moors on their way to take Bruce's heart to the Holy Land.

The marriage of this crusader's son was to transport the Sinclairs to the far north, where some still remain, for his wife was the heiress of Orkney and Caithness. Their son Henry became in 1379 Earl (*jarl*) of Orkney, the premier title of the Norwegian nobility. Through his mother he was descended from the ancient Norse royal family whose rather unroyal nicknames (Halfdan the Stingy,

Eystein the Fart – in Sir Iain Moncreiffe's preferred translations) recede far into the mists of Scandinavian legend.

Viking blood seems to have had a powerful effect on the Sinclairs (unless one believes the Vikings were merely peace-loving farmers looking for a few spare fields to settle down). In 1395 the Sinclair Earl of Orkney went on the controversial voyage of the Zenos and may, like earlier Norsemen, have touched on North America. Zeno's account also tells us that he commanded a large fleet on behalf of the Earl of Orkney, the main business of which was piracy.

BELOW *Girnigoe Castle, a place still faintly redolent of unspeakable horrors. The Sinclair stronghold was built in the late 15th century, its walls rising sheer from the cliff and protected on the landward side by a deep, wide ditch. An adjoining building added about 1606 is often called Castle Sinclair, though it's really just an extension.*

The grandson of the Norwegian earl was the last of Orkney but the old family title of Earl of Caithness was restored to him in 1544. He was the builder of Rosslyn Chapel, a famous architectural gem. Its fine tracery is in marked contrast to the northern stronghold of the Sinclairs, the gaunt and impregnable Girnigo Castle, on a rocky promontory north of Wick overlooking Sinclair's Bay.

There was much in the history of the family that was appropriately grim for this setting, and violent deaths were not uncommon. The first Earl of Caithness's heir was retarded, so his second son received the old barony of Rosslyn and the third, William, became second Earl of Caithness. He was killed at Flodden, and the third earl died in a Sinclair civil war in the Orkneys. The fourth earl's eldest son, the Master (a common title for elder sons) of Caithness, was apparently more pacific than most of his line, and incurred his father's displeasure by making peace with the Murrays, parties to one of the Sinclairs' many feuds. For this he was thrown in a cell in Girnigo Castle and kept in chains until he died, seven years later, of deliberate ill treatment (to hasten his end, it is said, he was given salted meat and denied water). But the unfortunate Master had his moment of violence too. When, goaded by his younger brother, William of Mey, he managed to half-throttle his tormentor with the chains that held him. William died from his injuries and, having no legitimate children, the inheritance he had gloatingly anticipated passed to a third brother.

He did, however, have two illegitimate sons, from the younger of whom the Sinclairs of Ulbster descended. The outstanding member of this family (at any rate until Viscount Thurso, who served in Winston Churchill's war cabinet) was Sir John Sinclair of Ulbster (1754–1835), well known as an agricultural reformer, chiefly responsible

ABOVE *Roslin Chapel, in Midlothian, only two or three generations later than Girnigoe, is a very different building, renowned for its delicate decoration. The 'Prentice Pillar (above) was allegedly built by an apprentice whom his master subsequently killed out of jealousy.*

for the creation of the Board of Agriculture in 1793, and a considerable authority on Highland custom. His magnificent portrait by Raeburn is one of the splendours of the Scottish National Portrait Gallery.

In the north the Sinclairs came under pressure from various rivals, notably the Gordons, and eventually lost most of their lands. The title has passed through a large number of cadet houses, but there is still a Sinclair Earl of Caithness, who owned the long-ruined Castle of Girnigo until 1986.

CLAN ASSOCIATION

Churchill, Chipping Norton, Oxfordshire
OX7 5UX, England

124 24th Avenue East, Duluth,
MN 55812, USA

SINCLAIR 254–255

SKENE

The Skenes were an early sept of Clan *Donnchaidh*, most of whom later took the name Robertson. They appear to have adopted the name before they came owned the barony of Skene, west of Aberdeen. According to legend, the name comes from *sgian*, or 'skene', a knife.

ORIGIN

The inference is that the lands were named after them rather than vice-versa. Their origins are explained in a picturesque legend so familiar in variant forms in other families. It is the one about the young chief saving the king from a wild beast, a wolf on this occasion, which the progenitor of the Skenes fended off with an arm wrapped in his plaid and then stabbed with his knife. As a reward the king offered the brave lad as much territory as would be covered by a hawk in flight, and the obliging bird encompassed what became the barony of Skene.

More prosaically, the lands of Skene were erected into a barony by a charter of King Robert Bruce in 1318 for Robert, grandson of John de Skene whose name was among those swearing fealty to Edward I of England in 1296.

THE CLAN

In the course of the next century or two many Skenes crop up in the records, suggesting that the clan was prospering. A laird of Skene was killed at Harlaw (1411), fighting almost in his own territory. Another fell at Flodden (1513), but in 1546 the laird was excused attendance at Pinkie (1547) on the grounds of illness. In his place he sent his uncle, who did not survive the battle.

The lairds of Skene held on to their lands throughout the 17th and 18th centuries, and the last of the line, who was deaf and dumb as well as childless, died in 1827. The property was entailed to a nephew, the Earl of Fife, and the chiefship appears to have passed to a cadet branch settled in Austria.

Among notable Skenes was William Forbes Skene (1809–92), an authority on the history of Celtic Scotland. He belonged to the Skenes of Rubislaw, owners of the Rubislaw quarry which, besides Aberdeen granite, once yielded a type of non-gem beryl called Davidsonite.

CLAN ASSOCIATION

Pitlour, Strathmiglo
KY14 7RS, Scotland

433 2nd Avenue. Ripley,
WV 25271, USA

SMITH

NAME AND PLACE

In pre-industrial societies in many parts of the world, the trade of smith bestowed a certain status, higher than that of other crafts (Hephaestos was the only Greek god who did an honest day's work). Perhaps this explains why the name became so common – smiths being possibly more inclined to commemorate their trade than humbler craftsmen.

ORIGIN

Early Scottish examples included Alexander Smyth, who was the resident blacksmith at the abbey of Coupar-Angus in 1497 (where there was also a wheelwright called Wrycht, a mason called Mason and a porter called Porter), and James Smyth, smith to the Bishop of Dunkeld in 1506. In Latin charters the name sometimes appears as Ferro or Faber.

THE NAME

There was never such an association as a Clan Smith. Surnames based on a trade or craft are comparatively uncommon in Gaelic, which some have seen as evidence that Highlanders were not much inclined to industrial pursuits though other reasons, such as the predominance of patronymics until a very late date, seem more probable. The Gaelic name for smith, meaning not only a man who made ploughshares and horseshoes but also an armourer (certainly a vital craft among the clans) is *Gobha*, which is the origin of the names Gow and MacGowan (see Gow). However, even in the Gaelic-speaking Highlands the name appears to have been sometimes anglicised as Smith, and there are many Smiths in Lewis, where Gaelic is still generally spoken even now. A notable example is the bilingual poet and novelist, the late Iain Crichton Smith (*Iain Mac a'Ghobhainn*), who was born in Lewis.

The Gaelic *ceard*, which came to mean principally a tinker, originally also described a craftsman in metal, perhaps brass in particular. This is the origin of the name Caird, or Kerd (not to be confused with Cairns, which has a territorial origin). Some cairds took the name Tinker or Tinkler, and some, in the west, took the name Sinclair. Possibly others became Smiths.

CLAN ASSOCIATION

540 North May Street, Southern Pines, NC 28387, USA

STEWART

NAME AND PLACE

The Stewarts of course include the most notable, and last, royal Scottish dynasty. The name derives from the office of High Steward, or seneschal, held under David I by Walter fitzAlan.

ORIGIN

Sentiment ascribed a Celtic origin to the royal house of Stewart, but the Banquo of Shakespeare's *Macbeth*, the ghostly procession of whose heirs somewhat interrupts the action, was not a historical character – at least, there is no trace of him except in Holished's chronicle where Shakespeare found him. The ancestors of the Stewarts were, inescapably, of French origin, though probably Bretons rather than Normans, and conjecturally linked with the counts of Dol and Dinant. In that case, the Bretons being of Celtic origin, the Stewarts were of Celtic descent after all.

THE DYNASTY

The ancestor of the Stewarts came to England in the wake of the Norman conquest and acquired estates in Shropshire and Norfolk, among other places. A younger son, Walter fitzAlan, was among the entourage of King David I when he left the English court for his Scottish throne. He became High Steward (seneschal) of Scotland, the greatest office in the kingdom, which became hereditary in his family in the next reign and thus gave them their surname. From from the time of the French-raised Mary Queen of Scots it was often spelled Stuart, and that is the form generally adopted for the royal dynasty after the accession of James VI to the throne of England (as James I).

The sixth High Steward, Walter, married Bruce's daughter Marjorie and when David II died without children in 1371 their son, the first Stewart monarch, became king as Robert II.

The Stewarts were kings (and queen) of Scots for over three centuries and it is therefore difficult, though tempting, to generalise about them. To remain in possession of the Crown for so long was in itself success of a kind, and on the

BELOW *The gates of Traquair, which will stay shut until a Stewart is on the throne.*

whole the Stewart monarchs were both intelligent and ruthless, useful qualities in a sovereign, though also capable of pig-headedness and blindness.

To their feudal subjects – anyway, to those that mattered politically – the Stewarts were merely one of many noble houses who happened, more or less by lucky chance, to have gained the throne. To assert the authority of the Crown was the constant endeavour of the king, and to this end the Stewarts were prepared to employ almost any means. The experiences of the King James VI, treated as a pawn in the power struggles of aristocratic factions, resulted in his belief that monarchy in England, where the Crown had already emerged victorious from a similar contest with overmighty subjects, was a much more pleasant occupation that it was in his native land.

Perhaps the gravest criticism of the Stewart monarchy as a whole is that, far from uniting Highlands and Lowlands, it perpetuated and aggravated the division between the Gaelic-speaking north and the English-speaking south. Conciliation was tried occasionally, usually when force was impracticable, but the culmination of the Crown's efforts to bring the whole country under its authority was the deliberate, often brutal, suppression of Gaelic culture.

It is this that gives Jacobitism its bitter-sweet flavour. For the Stewart monarchy, historically no friend to the clans, turned to them in its hour of need when, largely through its own ineptitude, it had forfeited the loyalty of its English subjects, and it did not turn to them in vain. The final episode was the rising of 1745 and its aftermath, one of the saddest episodes in modern British history, which resulted not only in the final eclipse of the dynasty but also in the virtual extinction of the old clan system and the destruction of Highland society.

The last of the direct male line of the royal Stewarts was Henry, Cardinal Duke

ABOVE *James VI, who as James I took the Stewart dynasty to the English throne.*

of York, brother of Prince Charles, who lived until 1807 (Prince Charles died a sad drunk in 1788). Ironically but quite legitimately, representation of the royal Stewart line passed to the Hanoverian monarch George III, through his descent from James VI/I's daughter. The Cardinal acknowledged this by leaving the Scottish royal jewels that he possessed to George III and his descendants. One of the titles of the present Prince of Wales is Great Steward of Scotland.

Since 1807 the senior representatives of the male line have been the earls of Galloway, descended from the prolific Sir John Stewart of Bonkyl (see below).

The tartan known as the Royal Stewart appears to have little connection with the royal Stewarts.

CLAN ASSOCIATION

17 Dublin Street, Edinburgh
EH1 3PG, Scotland

111 Masonic Avenue, Monroe LA 71203
USA

STEWART OF ATHOLL

NAME AND PLACE: see Stewart

ORIGIN

The ramifications of the Stewarts were considerable, and at one time Stewarts have held no fewer than 17 earldoms, besides several dukedoms and many lesser titles. There is a saying that not all Stewarts are kin to the king; nevertheless, a great number of them were. Lines descending from Sir John Stewart of Bonkyl, a younger son of the fourth Steward (who was great-grandfather of King Robert II and married a granddaughter of the great Somerled of Argyll), were especially fruitful.

THE CLAN

The heavy Stewart settlement in Atholl dates from the time of Alexander Stewart, Earl of Buchan, second son of King Robert II and best known by his nickname, the Wolf of Badenoch (c. 1343–1405). The depredations of this man, ostensibly a pillar of official justice, were remarkable even by the standards of 14th-century Scotland. Having been censured by the Bishop of Moray for his treatment of his wife, he set fire to Forres and Elgin in revenge (1390). The Wolf's cubs were scarcely less savage than their sire: one of his illegitimate sons became Earl of Mar by the straightforward

BELOW *The last private army in Great Britain, the Atholl Highlanders, marching past Blair Castle, the old home of the Stewarts of Atholl, which now belongs to the Murrays.*

means of murdering the Douglas earl and forcing his widow to marry him.

On the death of the Wolf the earldom of Buchan passed to his brother Robert, Duke of Albany, from whose younger son James the Stewarts of Ardvorlich descended (Albany was also the direct male ancestor of the present Earl of Moray). Another illegitimate son of the Wolf of Badenoch, James, was the ancestor of the Stewarts of Garth, perhaps the most famous branch of the Atholl Stewarts, who included the 19th-century historian of the Highlands, General David Stewart of Garth. Other branches included the Steuarts (their preferred spelling) of Cardney as well as the Earls of Buchan.

After James I was murdered in 1437 his widow Joan Beaufort married another Stewart, Sir James, known as the Black Knight of Lorne, who was descended from another son of Sir John Stewart of Bonkyl. Their son Sir John Stewart of Balveny (d. 1512) was created Earl of Atholl by his half-brother, King James II (the title had been held previously by several Stewarts of the royal line, including the grandson of King Robert II, the Duke of Rothesay, who was starved to death in Falkland Castle by his overambitious uncle, Albany).

The most notable member of this line was the fourth earl (great-grandson of Sir John Stewart of Balveny), a leading Catholic noble in the reign of Mary Queen of Scots. After her defeat and flight he supported her restoration against the party of the young King James VI, and there was a strong suspicion that his death in 1578 was the result of poison.

After the death of the fifth earl in 1595 the earldom reverted to the Crown, but following the marriage of the heiress Lady Dorothea Stewart to the Murray Earl of Tullibardine, the title and about 200,000 acres of Atholl passed to that family (1629).

The Stewarts of Atholl were naturally zealous in the cause of the Stewart dynasty, and the leadership of their Murray overlords being doubtful in that cause they served under others. In Dundee's campaign against William III they were led by Stewart of Ballechin, whose family descended from an illegitimate son of King James II. There were said to be some 1,500 of them at that time.

STEWART OF APPIN

NAME AND PLACE: see Stewart

ORIGIN

Most of the main Stewart lines, including the Stewart earls of Atholl, descended from the fourth High Steward, whose younger son John married the heiress of Bonkyl, fought with Wallace, and produced seven sons. Three of these sons were the founders of noble families, the youngest of the three, Sir James Stewart of Pirston (Pearston) in Ayrshire, who died at Hallidon Hill in 1333, being the ancestor of the Stewarts of Appin. (The other two were Sir Alexander, whence the pre-Douglas earls of Angus, and Sir Alan of Dreghorn, whence the dukes of Lennox: see below.)

THE CLAN

The royal Stewarts could not be regarded as a clan in the usual sense of the word – the king was their 'chief' and the entire nation his 'clansmen' – but the Stewarts of Appin were effectively a West Highland clan in themselves.

A younger son of Sir James of Pierston had two sons, of Innermeath and of Durrisdeer, each of whom married an heiress of the MacDougall lords of Lorne. From Sir John of Innermeath (d. 1421) a number of famous Highland families descended, including the

BELOW *Castle Stalker perched on Cormorant's rock in Loch Linnhe. It was built by Duncan, second Stewart of Appin. Their war cry was Creag an Sgaibh – Cormorant's rock in Gaelic.*

Stewarts of Appin (and, from young younger sons, the earls of Atholl via the Black Knight of Lorne, and the Steuarts of Grandtully). The lordship of Lorne was held by the Stewarts for less than a century (1388–1470), afterwards passing to the Campbells.

Dugald, the great-grandson of Sir John of Innermeath, was the first Stewart of Appin, and his family held those lands for about 400 years. From his grandson Alan, third Stewart of Appin, numerous cadets stemmed – Achnacone (this family still holds land in Appin), Fasnacloich and Invernahyle. Another, later, cadet house of the Stewarts of Appin was Ardshiel, who provided their leader during Dundee's campaign in 1689 and again at the battle of Culloden (1746), the Appin chief being a minor on both occasions.

The Stewarts of Appin were at one with other branches of the family in loyalty to their royal kinsfolk, and a bond of association was signed by the Stewarts of Appin, Atholl and Balquhidder in 1645, following action with Montrose during the civil war.

The Appin regiment suffered heavy casualties at Culloden and their families suffered no less in the harrying of the clans which followed that defeat. The Appin Murder in this period has gained popular notoriety largely through the account of it in Robert Louis Stevenson's *Kidnapped*. Colin Campbell, whom Stevenson called the Red Fox of Glenure, a factor in charge of the forfeited estate of Ardshiel, was shot dead near Ballachulish in 1752. The suspected murderer, Allan Breck Stewart, escaped but James Stewart, brother of the chief, was arrested, charged with the murder in a Campbell court at Inveraray presided over by the Duke of Argyll himself, convicted and hanged.

Sir Alan Stewart of Dreghorn, son of Sir John of Bonkyl and brother of the ancestor of the Stewarts of Appin, was

the forefather of the dukes of Lennox and thus also an ancestor of the later Stewart kings. His descendant, Sir John Stewart of Darnley (d. 1429), who was also seigneur of Aubigny, married a daughter of Duncan, Earl of Lennox, and their grandson was to become the first Stewart Earl.

The second earl died at Flodden (1513) and his grandson, the fourth earl (d. 1571), having failed to acquire supreme power for himself by various machinations, secured the marriage of his son, usually known as Lord Darnley, to Mary Queen of Scots (Darnley's cousin). He thus became, eventually, grandfather of King James VI/I.

Darnley was soon disposed of, an explosion failing to conceal that he had been strangled before he was blown up, and the Earl of Lennox became one of the queen's chief opponents. He died in battle and was succeeded by his second son, the fifth earl, whose daughter Lady Arabella Stuart was the miserable lynchpin of numerous plots over the succession and died insane in the Tower of London in 1615.

Esmé Stewart, a glamourous, French-reared nephew of the fourth earl, won the affection of the young King James VI, who made him Duke of Lennox in 1581. His son, the second duke, became also Duke of Richmond and an Englishman.

'La Belle Stuart', who modelled for the figure of Britannia on the old penny coin, was the wife of the sixth Duke of Lennox, and herself a Stuart by birth. Whether she was also one of the mistresses of yet another Stuart, Charles II, has been disputed.

SUTHERLAND

NAME AND PLACE

Sutherland comes from the Norse *Sudrland*, which was how the Norsemen described the most southerly of their dominions, anomalous as it seems to persons resident in Britain. The Sutherland clan, unlike most clans, did not generally adopt the name of their chief in the days when surnames became common and many of them were in fact named Murray.

ORIGIN

The earldom of Sutherland, one of the oldest continuous earldoms in Britain, was created in the early 13th century for the lord of Sutherland, a descendant of William de Moravia (of Moray) who was also the ancestor of the Murrays.

THE CLAN

The second Earl of Sutherland fought for Bruce, and the fourth fell at Hallidon Hill fighting the English in 1333. The fifth earl continued the tradition, marrying a daughter of Bruce and providing a large company for the army which was defeated at the battle of Neville's Cross (1346). His son by the Bruce princess might have become heir to the throne, avoiding the Stewart succession, had he not died young. A son by the fifth earl's second wife became the next Earl of Sutherland, while another founded the notable cadet house of the Sutherlands of Forse. The fifth earl himself died in 1370, possibly a victim of the Mackays, who were at feud with the Sutherlands for centuries.

Robert, sixth earl, who married a daughter of the Wolf of Badenoch (son of King Robert II), was the builder of

BELOW *Dunrobin Castle, seat of the dukes of Sutherland, resembles a French château. One of the oldest continuously inhabited dwellings in Scotland, its present form dates mainly from the rebuilding of the 1850s.*

Dunrobin (Robin's castle), overlooking the sea near Golspie. Needless to say it had little in common with the present romantic – and huge – château (189 rooms), which is largely the work of Sir Charles Barry, architect of the Westminster Houses of Parliament in the 19th century (though Dunrobin was altered again early in the 20th century after a fire had destroyed part of it).

Both the eighth and ninth earls were afflicted with mental trouble. The latter's daughter Elizabeth was married to Adam Gordon of Aboyne, brother of the Earl of Huntly, and when the ninth Earl of Sutherland died Gordon took the earldom, an act with no justification which was resisted by Alexander Sutherland, half-brother of Elizabeth and the rightful heir. He had considerable local support and twice recaptured Dunrobin, but was killed in a skirmish, leaving the Gordons in possession.

Subsequent earls retained the name Gordon, presumably because the Earl of Huntly wished to retain them as a sept of his own clan. To protect themselves against Sutherland claimants, in 1601 the Gordons obtained a grant from James VI that if the direct line from Adam Gordon of Aboyne failed the earldom of Sutherland should pass to the Gordons of Huntly. The sixteenth earl took the name Sutherland at the end of the 17th century, but when his descendant died in 1766 leaving only a daughter, a great legal argument broke out over the succession. The Sutherlands lost again, and the title was bestowed on the late earl's daughter who became Countess of Sutherland in her own right (1771). She and her husband George Leveson-Gower, Marquess of Stafford, later became Duke and Duchess of Sutherland.

The duke and duchess are for ever associated with the notorious Sutherland Clearances of the late 18th century, which destroyed the ancient clan. It should be said that the duke's motives were charitable in origin. In forcing his tenants to move down to the coast where their poverty would be relieved by the booming kelp industry, he spent a good deal of his money (he could certainly afford it), since he was possibly the richest landowner in Europe. He was in a way the archetypal do-gooder, zealous in his pursuit of progress, oblivious to individual preference, and ignorant of local culture. The collapse of the kelp industry left his people in dire straits.

The third duke was a similar sort. He invested huge sums of money in the Highland Railway but insisted that it pursued a roundabout route which would not disturb the shooting.

With the death of the fifth duke in 1962 the ducal title passed to another family. His niece Elizabeth became countess of the old Scottish earldom and chief of the clan, not that, in Scotland, much was left of it.

Besides the Sutherlands of Forse, the Sutherlands of Duffus in Moray were a famous house. They were descended from the second son of the fourth earl and also had to withstand Gordon attempts at their deprivation. Kenneth, Lord Duffus, was 'out' in the Jacobite rising of 1715 (the earls of Sutherland supported the Hanoverians). His estates being forfeit, he fled abroad, served in the Russian navy and married into an aristocratic Swedish family. The estates were restored to his grandson, but the line became extinct in a later generation.

CLAN ASSOCIATION

Dunrobin Castle, Golspie
KW10 6SF, Scotland

3611 Kelway Avenue, Charlotte,
NC 28210, USA

23 Myall Road, Mount Colah,
NSW 2079, Australia

THOMSON (MACTHOMAS)

NAME AND PLACE

Thomson is a fairly common surname in Scotland, usually spelt without the P that is common in England. In the Gaelic-speaking Highlands the name is *Mac Thómais*. It was often anglicised as MacTavish, a relatively common name in Argyll where Clan Tavish was a minor sept of the Campbells, but the largest group was a sept of Clan Chattan in the central Highlands whose name was usually anglicised as MacThomas.

ORIGIN

The numerous variants of the name probably had no common origin.

THE CLAN

The MacTavishes of Argyll descended from an illegitimate son of the Lord of Lochow in the 13th century, and were possibly connected with the Border family of Thomson of that ilk. Some MacTavishes were also called Taweson. A sept of the MacFarlanes was also known as Thomason, or other variants; their ancestor was the son of a MacFarlane chief called Thomas.

However, the MacThomases of Clan Chattan, whose name had variations such as MacCombie, MacComa, etc, were believed to be descended from an illegitimate son of William, seventh Chief of Mackintosh. They settled mainly in Glenshee and Glenisla. A charter of 1571 confirmed John McComy-Muir (presumably *Mac Thomaidh Mór*) in the lands of Finzegand, Glenshee, but the MacThomases were named among the 'broken' clans in the late 16th century.

In the civil war the MacThomas chief was apparently a parliamentary agent, and in the 17th century MacThomases (or MacComies) conducted feuds with their Farquharson neighbours.

In the 18th century the name occurred in Lewis, home of the modern Gaelic poet *Ruaraidh MacThómais*, and other parts. In Shetland the usual form was the Scandinavian Thomasson.

Captain Patrick MacThomas was recognised by Lyon Court as Chief of Clan MacThomas of Glenshee in 1968.

CLAN ASSOCIATION

19 Warriston Avenue, Edinburgh
EH3 5ND, Scotland

3016 Manor Drive, Sebring,
FL 33872, USA

38 Scott Street, Kogarah,
NSW 2217, Australia

URQUHART

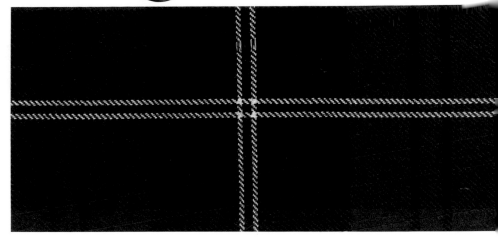

NAME AND PLACE

The name Urquhart is generally agreed to be of territorial origin. The Urquharts of Loch Ness, where Castle Urquhart enjoys a splendid situation on a promontory commanding the eastern end of the loch, probably derived their name from *Urchardau* meaning 'wood-side', but another likely derivation is from *urchar*, a cast or a shot. Professor Watson (in *The Celtic Place-Names of Scotland*) also suggested it may refer to 'a spur or offshoot of rising ground'.

ORIGINS

According to family tradition, the Urquharts, who at one time owned much of the Black Isle, were originally linked with Clan Forbes and the lords of Aird. In the 17th century Sir Thomas Urquhart traced his ancestry back to the third millennium BC, but history confirms no one earlier than the 14th century, when the Urquharts became hereditary sheriffs of Cromarty, as a result of marriage to a daughter of the Earl of Ross.

THE CLAN

The family prospered and established branches in Moray and Aberdeenshire. A 16th-century laird is said to have been the father of 25 sons, of whom seven were killed at the battle of Pinkie (1547).

ABOVE *Castle Urquhart, the guardian of Loch Ness, one of the largest castles in Scotland, but ruined 300 years ago. It fell into the hands of the Grants in the 16th century.*

His successor, Alexander Urquhart, seventh Sheriff of Cromarty, had two sons of whom the younger, John, was the founder of the house of Craigfintry. This was the tutor of Cromarty (an office which implies guardianship of both the person and the state of an under-age chief), who administered the lands with 'great dexterity in acquiring of many lands and possessions, with all men's applause' – well, perhaps not all.

The strain of eccentricity which reached full flower in Sir Thomas Urquhart of Cromarty in the 17th century was also apparent in his great-grandfather a century earlier. This man, also Sir Thomas, had himself hoisted to the battlements on a couch every evening in memory of Christ's Resurrection.

His grandson (1582–1642) was knighted by King James VI, whose scholarly if undisciplined interests he shared. He was not, according to his son, much of a businessman and proved a soft touch for 'many cunning sharks'.

His son, the famous Sir Thomas Urquhart (?1611–60), inherited his intellectual interests. He took part in the rising on behalf of Charles II in 1649 and was captured at Worcester. Unfortunately, he could not bear to be parted from his manuscripts and had taken them with him on campaign. Cromwell's soldiers, displaying the traditional contempt of the sword for the pen, used them as lavatory paper. Sir Thomas was imprisoned for two years in the Tower of London and it was probably then that he began the translation of Rabelais in which his literary fame chiefly resides.

Sir Thomas died in 1660, the joyous hilarity occasioned by news of the Restoration of the monarchy apparently inducing a fatal stroke, and the Cromarty estates passed to his cousin, John

ABOVE *The White Tower in the Tower of London. Sir Thomas Urquhart was held here for nine years after his capture at the Battle of Worcester. While there he translated the works of Rabelais, and apparently died of a fit of 'Rabelaisian' ironic laughter when hearing of the Restoration of King Charles II.*

Urquhart of Craigston, descended from the Tutor of Cromarty, who sold them. Another branch of the family regained them briefly in the 18th century. The attractive ruins of Castle Craig on the Cromarty Firth are today held by the Urquharts of Craigston. The chiefship was re-established recently in the person of an American citizen.

CLAN ASSOCIATION
Faliskeour, Balfron Station
G63 0QY, Scotland

56 Waldorf Drive, Akron,
OH 44313, USA

WALLACE

NAME AND PLACE

The name Wallace appears in old charters as Wallensis, meaning a Welshman, but in Scotland the name referred not to Wales but to the Ancient Britons' kingdom of Strathclyde.

ORIGIN

The first known Wallace was Richard Wallensis of Richardston (now Riccarton) in Ayrshire, formerly part of the kingdom of Strathclyde.

THE FAMILY

He was a vassal of Walter fitzAlan the Steward, ancestor of the Stewart dynasty. His grandson, Adam Wallace of Riccarton, had two sons, the younger of whom, Malcolm, received lands in Elderslie, Renfrewshire, where William Wallace, Scotland's national hero, was born in about 1275.

After a succession of generally strong and successful monarchs, Scotland was thrown into crisis by the early death of King Alexander III, leaving the infant daughter of the King of Norway as heir to the throne. The Maid of Norway's death soon afterwards meant that the royal line was at an end. There were many claimants, the strongest being Robert Bruce the elder and John Balliol, and the Scots took the decision,

ABOVE *The tower at Abbey Craig, north of Stirling, is a monument to Scotland's national hero, William Wallace.*

potentially hazardous but better than the certain alternative of civil war, to invite Edward I of England to adjudicate. He chose Balliol. That was the constitutionally correct choice, but it soon became clear that Edward, whose predecessors had claimed overlordship of the Scots with varying degrees of conviction, regarded himself as the true ruler. Even Balliol, expected to be compliant, could not stomach Edward's demands, but Edward was already poised to invade, and he made short work of Balliol and the divided Scots. Having conquered Scotland and despatched Balliol to the Tower, Edward regarded the whole episode as satisfactorily terminated.

About six months later, in the spring of 1297, there was a minor scuffle in the marketplace at Lanark between some English soldiers and the young William Wallace, who escaped aided by a young woman. The girl, possibly his wife, was later executed by the sheriff of Lanark. The same night Wallace killed the sheriff. He was automatically outlawed, but in a matter of weeks he was the leader of widespread national resistance to the English occupation. At Stirling Bridge Wallace and Sir Andrew Moray annihilated a large and well-equipped English army and freed most of Scotland.

However, in 1298 Wallace was heavily defeated by Edward I and for the next seven years he was on the run, limited to guerilla raids while the English soldiers ravaged the kingdom. In 1305 he was captured and after a trial in London executed with grotesque barbarity as a traitor, though as he said at his trial, he had never sworn fealty to Edward, not even, like most Scottish landholders, under duress at Berwick in 1296.

Not much is known for certain about Wallace. That he could achieve the

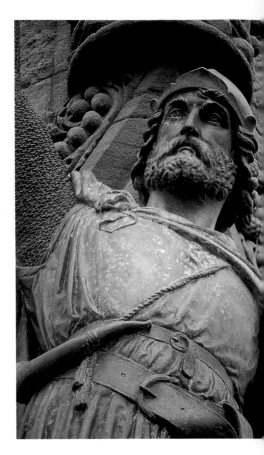

ABOVE *In this detail from the tower at Abbey Craig. Wallace himself is shown with sword upraised against the English. There is also a stained glass window depicting the hero.*

position he did, among the selfish, treacherous and quarrelsome Scottish barons, suggests a character of extraordinary force.

Wallace himself left no descendants, but a great many families of his name trace their descent from the Wallaces of Riccarton.

CLAN ASSOCIATION

1 Shearer Street, Kingston, Glasgow
G5 8TA, Scotland

2341 NE 48th Street, Lighthouse,
FL 33064-7925, USA

WEMYSS

NAME AND PLACE

The name is territorial. It is said to be a corruption of the Gaelic word for a cave, *uamh*, and there are indeed caves below what remains of the old castle at East Wemyss, known as MacDuff's Castle, which contain indecipherable drawings dating from Pictish times.

ORIGIN

The premier clan of medieval Scotland was Clan MacDuff, whose chiefs, descended from the royal line, were the earls of Fife. A younger son of Gillemichael, Earl of Fife in the first half of the 12th century, obtained the lands of Wemyss, which gave his descendants their surname, from his father.

THE FAMILY

In 1304 Sir Michael of Wemyss played host to Edward I of England but later joined Bruce's rebellion and incurred Edward's resentment, who sent orders 'to burn, destroy and strip' his lands. Later, the family established numerous branches and Wemyss of Wemyss eventually emerged as the senior line descended from the old MacDuff earls of Fife.

In the 17th century Sir John Wemyss became an earl. When his son died in 1679, he left only a daughter, Margaret, who married a kinsman, Sir James Wemyss of Caskyberry, later Lord Burntisland. Their son David, the fourth earl, married the eldest daughter of the Duke of Queensberry and their son, the fifth earl, was the first officially to be recognised as representative of the family of the MacDuff earls of Fife.

During the Forty-five the earl's eldest son Lord Elcho (a title first bestowed on the first Earl of Wemyss) raised a troop of cavalry for Prince Charles and was subsequently attainted. He died in exile, so the title went to his younger brother who had taken the name of Charteris (deriving from the French Chartres and pronounced Charters) on inheriting a fortune from his maternal grandfather, Colonel Francis Charteris, an unsavoury character who allegedly made most of his money by cheating at cards.

A third brother, James, inherited Wemyss, including the fine castle at West Wemyss which overlooks the Firth of Forth opposite Edinburgh.

The present chief, Wemyss of Wemyss, is descended from James, while the present Earl of Wemyss is descended from his elder brother.

ACKNOWLEDGMENTS

The publishers would like to thank the following sources for their permission to reproduce the photographs in this book.

ABBREVIATIONS
MEPL Mary Evans Picture Library
SMPC Still Moving Picture Company
SIF Scotland in Focus
CUKL Corbis UK Ltd
HGPC Hulton Getty Picture Collection

2 Left MEPL
2 Centre Left SMPC/David Robertson
2 Centre Right MEPL
2–3 Centre SMPC/Angus Johnstone
3 Right SIF/R. Matassa
3 Centre Left SIF/I. McLean
3 Centre Right SIF/D. Barnes
6 SMPC/Pinhole Productions
9 SMPC
10 SIF/J. Stephen
12 MEPL
14 Bottom Right SMPC/Bob West
15 MEPL
16 CUKL
17 Top Right MEPL/W. Smith
19 SIF/R. Weir
20 MEPL
22 SIF/A. G. Johnston
23 HGPC
24 SIF
25 HGPC
30 SMPC/Scottish Tourist Board(STB)
31 CUKL
32 SIF/J. MacPherson
33 SIF/R. Matassa
35 HGPC
36 SMPC/Pinhole Productions
38 SMPC/David Robertson
39 MEPL
42 SIF/R. Weir
43 MEPL
44 MEPL
45 SMPC/Doug Corrance
46 HGPC
47 SMPC/M. Brooke
48 SMPC/Donald Ford
49 National Monuments Record of Scotland
50 MEPL
53 HGPC/hulton
54 SMPC/Angus Johnston
55 SMPC/Doug Corrance
56 HGPC
57 MEPL
58 HGPC
59 HGPC
61 SMPC/STB
63 National Monuments Record of Scotland/Peter Reid
64 SMPC/Doug Corrance
66 MEPL
67 SMPC/Doug Corrance
68 SMPC/Pinhole Productions
69 MEPL

70 SIF/D. Houghton
71 SMPC/STB
74 SMPC/S. J. Whitehorne
76 Hulton Deutsch/Bettmann
77 National Museums of Scotland
78 SIF/M. Moar
79 MEPL
80 MEPL
81 HGPC
82 MEPL
83 SIF/R. Weir
84 HGPC
85 SMPC/STB
86 SMPC/Doug Corrance
88 HGPC
89 SMPC/STB
90 SIF/J. Weir
91 MEPL
93 MEPL
94 HGPC
96 MEPL
97 SIF/R. Weir
98 Scottish National Portrait Gallery/John Maxie Bain
99 SIF/D. Barnes
100 SIF/D. Barnes
101 HGPC
103 SIF/J. Smally
104 SIF/Willbir
105 HGPC
106 HGPC
107 SIF/C.K. Robeson
108 MEPL
109 SMPC/STB
110 SMPC/Doug Corrance
111 HGPC
112 SIF/R. Schofield
113 SIF/G. Satterley
115 SMPC/Paul Tomkins/STB
116 MEPL
117 SIF/C. K. Robeson
118 MEPL
119 SMPC/Angus G. Johnston
120 SIF/J. Smalley
121 HGPC
122 SMPC/Derek Laird
124 SIF/J. Guidi
125 MEPL
127 SMPC/Angus G. Johnston
128 SMPC/STB
129 MEPL
132 National Monuments Record of Scotland
134 Bridgeman Art Library, London/New York/City of Edinburgh Museums and Art Galleries
135 SMPC/STB

136 SIF/R. Weir
137 SIF/Dorthy Burrows
138 SMPC/M. Brooke
139 SIF/J. MacPherson
141 MEPL
143 SMPC/Stephen Kearney
144 SIF/G. Williams
146 SMPC/David Robertson
147 SMPC/Angus Johnston
148 SIF/R. Matassa
149 Bridgeman Art Library, London/New York/National Gallery of Scotland
150 HGPC
152 SIF/R. Matassa
154 SIF/R. Matassa
155 Hulton Deutsch/Bettmann
156 SIF/D. Kerr
158 SMPC/Doug Corrance
159 SIF/Matt Miller
161 SMPC/S. J. Taylor
163 SIF/D. Barnes
164 SIF/R. Weir
165 SIF/G. Williams
166 SIF/R. Weir
167 Bridgeman Art Library, London/New York/Scottish National Portrait Gallery, Edinburgh
168 MEPL
169 SMPC/David Robertson
170 SIF/J. Byers
171 British Broadcasting Corporation
172 SIF/B. Williams
175 MEPL
177 CUKL/Alissa Crandall
178 SMPC/STB
179 MEPL
180 SMPC/Harvey Wood
182 SMPC/Angus G. Johnston
184 SIF
187 MEPL
188 SMPC/Doug Corrance
189 SMPC/Scottish Tourist Board
190 SMPC/Niall Benvie
191 MEPL
192 SIF/R. Matassa
196 SIF/I. McLean
197 HGPC
199 Bridgeman Art Library, London/New York/United Distillers and Vintners
201 SIF/R. Weir
202 SIF/J. MacPherson

204 SMPC/M. Scott
205 SMPC/Gilbert Summe
206 CUKL/Steve Austin
208 MEPL
209 SMPC/Marcus Brooke
210 SIF/Wilbir
211 HGPC
212 SMPC/Doug Corrance
213 SIF/R. Matassa
214 MEPL
217 MEPL/J. Godfrey
218 CUKL/Steve Austin
220 SMPC/Robert Lees
222 SMPC/Ken Paterson
223 Bridgeman Art Library London/New York/Scottish National Portrait Gallery
225 Bridgeman Art Library London/New York/Junior Infrantrymen's Battalion, Shroncliffe, Kent
227 SIF/J. Weir
228 SIF/G. Dey
229 National Museums of Scotland
230 SMPC/Harvey Wood
232 SMPC/David Robertson
233 SIF/R. Matassa
236 MEPL
241 SMPC/Robert Lees
242 SIF/R. Weir
243 Bridgeman Art Library London/New York/Musee de Tapestry, Bayeux, France
244 National Monuments Record of Scotland
245 CUKL/Joseph Sohm
246 MEPL
247 SMPC/Ken Paterson
249 HGPC
250 SMPC/STB
251 MEPL
253 MEPL
254 SIF/A. Gordon
255 SMPC/STB
258 SMPC/STB
259 MEPL
260 HGPC/John Pratt
262 SMPC/David Robertson
264 SIF/J. Weir
267 SIF/David Tarn
268 MEPL
269 SMPC/David Robertson
270 SMPC/David Robertson